Strategies for teaching children mathematics

Strategies for teaching children mathematics

Ralph T. Heimer
Cecil R. Trueblood
The Pennsylvania State University

Addison-Wesley Publishing Company

Reading, Massachusetts • Menlo Park, California
London • Amsterdam • Don Mills, Ontario • Sydney

Second printing, May 1978

Copyright © 1977 by Addison-Wesley Publishing Company, Inc. Philippines copyright
1977 by Addison-Wesley Publishing Company, Inc.

ISBN 0-201-02882-4
EFGHIJKLMN-MA-8987654321

Preface

There have been many recent advances in educational thought and practice which have special pedagogical significance, and this book represents an attempt to incorporate some of the more important developments into a pragmatic approach to the problems of teaching mathematics to young children. In short, the authors have attempted to construct a text that is in line with contemporary thrusts in teaching and in teacher education.

The special features and characteristics which the authors have tried to build into the book include the following:

1. Every chapter contains a list of teacher competencies to be acquired. Collectively, these competencies reveal the book's major foci and directions. The book, therefore, should fit well into CBTE programs.

2. Each chapter is accompanied by an *Exercise Set* which has been carefully constructed to correspond to the list of teacher competencies which has been specified. Overall, therefore, the Exercise Sets constitute a set of tasks aimed at assisting the prospective or practicing teacher attain the stated competencies.

3. An extensive *bibliography* is provided with each chapter for the purpose of permitting the reader to gain easy access to the published professional literature on the subject. This feature should enhance the potential of the book for independent study, and also allow for exploration of those ideas which have not been treated extensively or explicitly in the text.

4. The focus of many of the chapters has centered around the construction and analysis of *flowcharts* which prescribe the sequences in which interrelated concepts should be taught. These flowcharts are merely reflections of *learning hierarchies* which have been developed, and their usefulness in the formation of strategies for the assessment of children's learning states *(diagnosis)* and related tactics is given great emphasis.

5. The subject of *conservation* (according to Piaget) and its import as a condition of learning is given careful attention as a pragmatic issue that is of concern to the practicing teacher.

6. Great value is placed on the concept of *student involvement* and the use of *laboratory* settings for learning. Accordingly, all those chapters that deal with the teaching of specific classes of mathematical concepts and skills contain ideas for creating laboratory learning experiences, activities, and games. Moreover, these ideas are keyed to the flowcharts, and hence are fairly comprehensive in their coverage of important concepts.

7. Each of the chapters that deal with specific mathematical concepts and skills is organized into two sections, one entitled *theory*, the other *practice*. In the theory sections, the mathematical ideas of concern are described and

ways of thinking about them are presented. Also, the flowcharts for teaching are developed and discussed, as are other pedagogical issues of special interest. The practice sections, on the other hand, deal exclusively with ideas for formulating appropriate types of learning experiences. This type of chapter design, including the bibliography, was created to permit the text to serve as a useful handbook of information and ideas about crucial topics and how to teach them.

In summary, the authors wish to acknowledge the patience and assistance of the many undergraduates who worked with preliminary forms of the manuscript, and the graduate teaching assistants who used them as a text. Special thanks also is given to Ms. Ann Russell and Mr. Fawzy Ibrahim who conducted the initial compilation of the bibliographies, and finally Ms. Carol Reish who typed the manuscript.

University Park, Pennsylvania   R. T. H.
October 1976   C. R. T.

Contents

1
Planning for instruction

Synopsis and objectives   2
A child's cognitive development: a baseline for learning   3
Setting goals for learning: some general considerations   6
The need for precise instructional objectives   7
Preparing statements of objectives   8
Classifying objectives in the cognitive realm   9
Mathematical structure and its import for the design of learning
hierarchies   13
Assessment of knowledge states: a critical factor in judging readiness   15
Summary   16

2
The design of instructional strategies

Synopsis and objectives   22
The child as a learner: implications for teaching   23
The development of diagnostic/prescriptive teaching strategies   27
Tactics for assuring retention of learning   27
Coping with the problem of reading   28
Designing laboratory learning environments   29
The issue of verbal problem solving   30
The issue of learning by discovery   33
The function of games as a teaching strategy   34
A checklist for making preliminary judgments about the adequacy
of an instructional system   40
A perspective about teaching   41
A note about the design of the remaining chapters   41

3
Teaching the basic concepts of number and numeration

Synopsis and objectives   52

Theory
The cardinal numbers, 0–9   53

The concept of counting   57
Place value and the decimal system of numeration   58
Nondecimal systems of numeration   60
The system of integers   62

Practice

Activities for student involvement
  Sets; set membership   63
  Set equivalence and nonequivalence   64
  Cardinal numbers, 0–9   65
  Counting   66
  Place value and the decimal numeration system   67
  Nondecimal numeration systems   68
  The integers   70

4

Teaching addition of cardinal numbers

Synopsis and objectives   76

Theory

A definition for addition   79
The basic addition facts   81
The addition algorithm: cases not involving regrouping   83
The addition algorithm: cases involving regrouping   86
The addition algorithm: other problem types   88
Addition involving negative integers   88

Practice

Activities for student involvement
  Phase I: the meaning of addition   91
  Phase II: basic addition facts   94
  Phases III and IV: the addition algorithm for cases
  involving and not involving regrouping   98
  Addition of integers   109

5

Teaching subtraction of cardinal numbers

Synopsis and objectives   120

Theory

Subtraction as the inverse of addition   121
The "take-away" interpretation of subtraction   122
Flowcharts for teaching subtraction   122

The basic subtraction facts   123
A translation of the Phase III addition flowchart into a flowchart
for teaching subtraction   124
Algorithm development   124

Practice

Activities for student involvement
    Phase I: the meaning of subtraction   126
    Phase II: the basic subtraction facts   128
    Phase III: the subtraction algorithms for involving and not
    involving regrouping   131

6

Teaching multiplication of cardinal numbers

Synopsis and objectives   146

Theory

Basic concepts   149
The basic multiplication facts   151
The multiplication algorithm:
    Problem type 1   153
    Problem type 2   154
    Problem type 3   157
    Problem type 4   159
    Other problem types   161
Multiplication in cases where one or both factors are negative   162

Practice

Activities for student involvement
    Phase I: the meaning of multiplication   163
    Phase II: basic multiplication facts   166
    Phases III and IV: product of a one-digit number and a two-digit
    number, with and without regrouping   172
    Phase V: product of a pair of two-digit numbers with and without
    regrouping   176

7

Teaching division of cardinal numbers

Synopsis and objectives   188

Theory

Division as the inverse of multiplication   191
Division as set partitioning   192
Division as repeated subtraction   193

Flowcharts for teaching division   194
The basic division facts   194
A translation of the (Phase III) multiplication flowchart into a
flowchart for teaching division   195
Algorithm development   196
A note on the rules for division when either the dividend or
divisor is negative   198

Practice
Activities for student involvement
   Phase I: the meaning of division   199
   Phase II: the basic division facts   202
   Phases III and IV: division of a two-digit number by a one-digit
   number, with and without regrouping   207
   Phase V: multi-digit division with and without regrouping   210

8

Teaching rational number concepts

Synopsis and objectives   220

Theory
Some basic concepts   223
A flowchart for teaching rational number concepts and uses   223
The meaning of a proper fraction   224
The concept of equivalence of fractions   225
Ordering fractional numbers   226
Improper fractions and mixed numerals   228
Addition of fractional numbers   229
Properties of addition of fractional numbers   232
Subtraction of fractional numbers   233
Multiplication of fractional numbers   234
Division of fractional numbers   238
Decimal numerals; some basic concepts   239
Computation with decimals   241

Practice
Activities for student involvement
   Meaning of a proper fraction   242
   The concept of equivalence   243
   Comparing fractional numbers   244
   Multiplication and division of fractional numbers   246
   Decimals: concepts and operations   247

9

Teaching the basic concepts of informal geometry

Synopsis and objectives   256

Theory
The first considerations for teaching   257
The initial Euclidian concept   258
The concepts of perpendicularity and parallelism   260
The study of circles   260
The study of polygons   261
Three-dimensional figures   263
Geometric constructions   266
The coordinate plane   268

Practice
Activities for student involvement
    Some elementary topological notions   271
    Some Euclidian notions   273
    The coordinate plane   276

IO

Teaching measurement concepts and skills

Synopsis and objectives   284

Theory
Some basic considerations   285
A general hierarchy for teaching measurement competencies   285
Basic concepts of linear measurement   286
A flowchart for teaching linear measurement concepts and skills   287
Basic concepts of area measurement   288
Basic concepts of the measurement of volume and quantity   291
Basic concepts of teaching measurement of weight   294
The metric system: some basic concepts   295
Area and volume measurement in the metric system   296
The measurement of weight (mass) in the metric system   297

Practice
Activities for student involvement
    Comparison of lengths of objects   298
    Measurement of objects   299

Comparison of areas of regions   304
Area measurement   305
Area measurement by use of formulas   306
Comparison of volumes of objects   308
Volume measurement   310

Index   317

Planning for instruction

Synopsis and objectives

Chapter 1 provides you with an opportunity to explore the factors and considerations that should be taken into account in planning an effective elementary school mathematics program. The approach that we have taken places strong emphasis upon the need for gathering information about a child's level of cognitive development and prior knowledge of mathematics as crucial factors in setting goals for learning.

As you study Chapter 1, keep in mind that an extensive bibliography is provided so that you may explore the various ideas presented in greater depth—according to your own personal interests and propensities. It is also important to note that the various themes introduced keep recurring throughout the text, so you will have opportunities later to apply the ideas you learn to the teaching of specific mathematical concepts. A careful study of Chapter 1 should enable you to

1. name the four stages of mental growth through which Piaget claims every child progresses;

2. explain and briefly illustrate Piaget's general strategy for determining whether a child is at the concrete operational stage of development for a concept;

3. explain the educational implications of knowing that a child has not yet reached the concrete operational stage of development for a particular concept;

4. describe the significance of the child's stage of cognitive development upon the selection of learning goals for the child;

5. describe the major factors and forces which must be taken into account in formulating goals for the learning of mathematics;

6. write instructional objectives with familiar content that precisely describe observable (learner) behaviors and the conditions under which the behaviors are to be seen;

7. name in order the six levels of cognition that are described in Handbook I, *Taxonomy of Educational Objectives,* by Bloom *et al.,* and briefly describe the nature of each level;

8. name and briefly describe the five cognitive levels of mathematical thinking specified by the School Mathematics Study Group;

9. describe the general characteristics of a behavioral (or learning) hierarchy, and how one is formed;

10. explain the general role of learning hierarchies in the development of *systems* of instructional objectives.

Planning for instruction

A CHILD'S COGNITIVE DEVELOPMENT: A BASELINE FOR LEARNING

In recent years, the research of Jean Piaget has been very much in the forefront of educational thought. His theory of intellectual development has particularly important implications for teaching and learning; thus the basic principles of it and their consequences should be well known to every teacher.

Piaget claims that as children interact with their social and physical environment their mental growth progresses through four qualitatively distinct stages: (1) *sensory-motor,* (2) *preoperational,* (3) *concrete operational,* and (4) *formal operations.* Piaget's research reveals that while the ordering of these stages is constant, the rate of progress at which a child moves through the stages is different for each individual. Generally speaking, however, a child is in the sensory-motor stage from birth to about 2 years, in the preoperational stage from 2 years to about 7 years, in the concrete operational stage from about 7 years to 12 years, and in the formal operations stage thereafter. The following table provides a brief description of the basic characteristics of, and distinctions among, these stages of development.

Stage of development	Approximate duration	Fundamental characteristics
Sensory-motor	0–2 years	Preverbal, presymbolic stage. Children progress from spontaneous movements and reflexes to acquired habits and then to acts of intelligence.
Preoperational	2–7 years	Children develop the ability to use words to represent things and begin to manipulate symbols or representations of their physical world. There is, however, no reversible thought process that will allow for logical thought.
Concrete operational	7–12 years	Children develop logical thought that is based in part on physical manipulation of objects. Their thought processes are reversible.
Formal operations	12–	Children learn to reason in a hypothetic-deductive manner using symbols or ideas. Their thought processes are no longer tied to physical manipulation of objects.

It is clear that children are in, or near, the concrete operational stage of cognitive development during most of the time that they are in elementary school. Consequently, the characteristics of a child at this stage of development and the corresponding implications for teaching are especially important to the elementary teacher. We shall elaborate upon them in the following paragraphs. The reader who is interested in studying about the other substages, as well as exploring the concrete operational stage in greater detail, should examine reference [29].

Piaget has studied the concrete operational stage using the concept of *conservation* as a standard for characterizing this stage of mental development. The following example should help illuminate the general concept of conservation and how it is used to determine whether a child is functioning at the concrete operational level.

Suppose we show a child two identical glasses which contain the same amount of water, and the child acknowledges the fact that the amount of water in the two glasses is the same. Then suppose the water in one of the glasses is poured into a shorter glass with a larger diameter and the child is asked to compare the amount of water in the two glasses.

Initial
condition

Altered
condition

If the child recognizes that the amount of water in the two glasses is still the same in spite of what his perception suggests, he is reasoning logically and would be classified as a *conserver* for this concept. On the other hand, if the child's thinking is dominated by his perception (one looks like more), he/she is not reasoning logically and would thus be classified as a *nonconserver* for this concept.

It should be pointed out that associated with the ability to exhibit conservation is the ability to demonstrate *reversibility* of thinking. In the case of the above example, for instance, a conserver very likely would demonstrate that the amount of water remained unchanged by reversing the process and pouring the water back into its original glass.

It should also be noted that the term *concrete operational* suggests that the child's thinking is "operational" only in the presence of actions on concrete representations of associated ideas. The implication is that teachers must plan learning experiences that require actions upon objects in the child's environment—particularly for initial concept development.

Of course, if a child is a nonconserver of a particular concept, the teacher should not attempt to teach that concept to the child at that time. Suppose,

Here the teacher checks to see if the child can conserve area.

for example, that a child cannot conserve volume; the implication is that the child cannot think of volume as an invariant, stable quantity. That means the child cannot adequately conceptualize the notion of volume at that particular stage in his or her development.

This brings us to another point regarding Piaget's research, namely, that it probably is not possible to "hurry up" the cognitive developmental processes. Instead, it is believed that movement from one stage of cognition to another is largely based upon maturational factors over which we do not have a substantial amount of control. In this connection, Piaget has stated [8]:

This question [of accelerating learning] never fails to amuse students and faculty in Geneva, for they regard it as typically American. Tell an American that a child develops certain ways of thinking at seven, and he immediately sets about to try to develop those same ways of thinking at six or even five years of age. Investigators in countries other than America have tried to accelerate the development of logical thinking, and we have available today a considerable body of research on what works and what doesn't work. Most of the research has not worked.

Piaget, in his study of the concrete operational stage, has examined the issue of conservation over a wide range of concepts, including those of *number, distance, length, area, time,* and *volume.* These matters will be discussed in greater detail at the appropriate points in Chapters 3 through 10.

Piaget's research in showing how children develop their conceptions of number, time, and space provides useful information that should be taken into consideration when planning mathematical learning experiences for children in elementary school programs. His theory of mental development, however, has many subtleties and complexities. No abbreviated version can do it justice. Suffice it to say that information about the child's stage of cognitive development serves as basic data for judging the readiness of a child for engaging in various intellectual pursuits. The bibliography for this chapter includes several titles that the interested reader may consult for further study of this topic.

SETTING GOALS FOR LEARNING: SOME GENERAL CONSIDERATIONS

Every elementary school teacher should become familiar with the nature and content of elementary school mathematics programs. In doing so, it is natural to consider how a school mathematics curriculum is formulated. Why, for example, are certain topics included and others neglected? What is the rationale or basis for selection? By whom are the choices made?

These questions are significant in view of the recent "curriculum revolution" in school mathematics. As a result of this revolution, substantial changes have taken place both in the content of school mathematics and the methods of teaching it. A combination of factors and forces are responsible for the changes. Included are the needs of society, the views of professional mathematicians and mathematics educators, and the perceptions of teachers themselves.

Society has a way of influencing curriculum by placing a premium upon certain competencies. The net effect of this influence is to bring pressure upon schools to design their courses of study so that people will attain these competencies. Educators traditionally have looked to the professionals in mathematics for guidance regarding the central ideas in mathematics and the form that the school program should take in order to assure proper treatment of these ideas. An examination of the history of mathematics education in the United States reveals a long list of committees, groups, projects, and so on, who were assigned responsibilities of this sort. But teachers themselves, we believe, undoubtedly constitute the most potent force in curriculum determination.

The processes that lead to the establishment of a particular curriculum in a particular school at a given point in time, therefore, are complex and difficult to trace, let alone control. It is difficult for even the most experienced teachers to appreciate the significance of the role they play in setting goals for the mathematics education of their students. They must, however, take responsibility in trying to understand proposals for curricular changes, and in giving careful attention to curricular recommendations made by professional groups.

We believe, though, that concern for the child must be at the center of all curricular decisions. We know that every child passes through a sequence of stages of cognitive development and that these stages largely depend upon maturational factors and are nonmanipulatable. This knowledge is important in making decisions about the sort of intellectual tasks a child can grapple with on a meaningful basis. A child's stage of cognitive development establishes an uncompromisable baseline for setting goals for meaningful learning.

THE NEED FOR PRECISE INSTRUCTIONAL OBJECTIVES

There seems to be little argument about the desirability of establishing goals for school mathematics. These goals should form a basis for making determinations about the content of the program. Unfortunately, however, statements of goals for mathematics education have often taken the form of platitudes that have not been very helpful for planning or guiding instruction. This problem has been widely discussed in the literature of the past two decades, and there appears to be a growing feeling that many of the ills of education can be attributed, at least in part, to a widespread lack of a clear conception of what we want children to learn.

Interestingly, the original impetus for framing instructional objectives in clear and unambiguous terms probably was the result of efforts to improve achievement testing. Along these lines, years ago, Tyler [39] wrote:

Two problems are usually involved in formulating the objectives of a particular course. One is to get a list which includes all of the important objectives to be reached. The other is to state the objectives in such clear and definite terms that they can serve as guides in the making of examination questions. Many statements of objectives are so vague and nebulous that, although they may sound well, they prove to be glittering generalities which are of little value as guides in teaching and useless in making examinations.

In the intervening years, teachers, researchers, and curriculum specialists have had time to reflect about objectives, and there now seems to be wide support of them for purposes of *guiding* and *evaluating* instruction. The Advisory Committee of the School Mathematics Study Group, for example, has released the following statement on objectives in mathematics education [34].

As mentioned in the introduction, the importance of the objectives of mathematics education has recently been substantially enhanced. The SMSG Advisory Board hopes that those stating objectives and also those who use statements of objectives will keep the following principles in mind.

I. Statements of objectives should be hortatory. They should be taken seriously by teachers, curriculum workers, and textbook writers as important and realistic guidelines. They should *not* be expressions of wishful thinking.

II. On the other hand, statements of objectives should be taken as floors, not ceilings. If a teacher or a school can go beyond stated objectives, so much the better.

III. If the statement of a particular objective is to be taken seriously, then the purpose of the objective has to be made clear. Further, a serious, relevant objective must be so clearly characterized as such as to be easily distinguishable from a personal whim.

IV. If statements of objectives are to be taken seriously, then the objectives must be clearly verifiable and feasible. It is not enough to know that an objective has not been shown to be infeasible. Before it should be advocated, it should have been positively shown to be feasible (and verifiable).

V. To be consonant with the above, we believe that all statements of mathematics educational objectives should be put in terms of student behavior. [The one exception is that we advocate a particular pedagogical objective:

Teach understanding of a mathematical process before developing skill in the process.

We believe there is enough empirical evidence in favor of this to make it a realistic objective.]

VI. Also, to be in conformance with point IV, we advocate at present no affective objectives. There is no evidence available to show that attitudes toward mathematics can be manipulated, so such objectives are not, at present, feasible.

VII. None of the above should be taken as suggesting that we ignore goals which are, at the moment, not feasible or not verifiable. Indeed, such goals indicate the most important areas in which to concentrate our future research efforts.*

These principles appear to have a *prima facie* quality of soundness, and thus are adopted here as forming the backdrop for all further discussion of objectives and their implications for mathematics education.

PREPARING STATEMENTS OF OBJECTIVES

When formulating statements of objectives, it is important to use verbs which suggest observable and unambiguous behaviors. A list of some of these verbs is given on the next page.

---

* School Mathematics Study Group, *Newsletter 38*, Palo Alto, Calif.: Stanford University, August 1972, pp. 17–18. Reprinted by permission.

solve	generalize	apply
identify	write	extrapolate
distinguish	graph	convert
order	express	state
describe	translate	generate
evaluate	prove	classify
analyze	demonstrate	find
define	construct	simplify
compute	name	factor

Many ideas have been put forward for ways of stating objectives. For practical purposes, an informal style similar to the one used in stating the objectives for the various chapters of this book is usually preferred. On the other hand, greater precision can be obtained by stating objectives in two parts: (1) *given conditions* and (2) *required performance*, and adding a statement which describes the basis for deciding whether or not the objective has been achieved. Two examples are given below. Study them carefully.

Example 1:   The student can name the cardinal number of any set of nine or fewer elements.

Given	Required performance	Mastery criterion
A set containing nine or fewer elements.	Name the cardinal number of the set.	Eighteen (or more) out of twenty instances.

Example 2:   The student can determine the sum of any pair of two digit numbers where regrouping is not required.

Given	Required performance	Mastery criterion
Two 2-digit numbers where no regrouping is necessary to find the sum.	Compute the sum.	Nine (or ten) out of ten instances.

A note is in order regarding the criteria that have been stated. It is important to recognize that establishment of criteria is a judgmental matter; we don't wish to be too lenient, but neither do we wish to be too stringent. It is necessary to find some "middle ground" which may be best arrived at by experience.

CLASSIFYING OBJECTIVES IN THE COGNITIVE DOMAIN

One of the difficult problems of preparing objectives for a program of instruction is to be reasonably certain that the totality of objectives which are formulated adequately reflects the overall goals of the program. One significant and well-known effort to provide a framework to assist teachers in the formulation of *comprehensive* sets of instructional objectives is the *Taxonomy of Educational Objectives Handbook I* by Bloom and others [3]. This Taxonomy affords a set of categories for classifying educational goals according to notions about depth of cognition.

An outline of the six major categories, and their primary subcategories is given below. Each successive major category is understood to (1) represent a more complex level of thinking than that represented by the preceding categories, and (2) be, stepwise, more inclusive than the preceding category (e.g., an *analysis* behavior may rest in part upon knowledge, comprehension, or application behaviors).

1.00 Knowledge

   1.10 Knowledge of specifics.
   1.20 Knowledge of ways and means of dealing with specifics.
   1.30 Knowledge of the universals and abstractions in a field.

2.00 Comprehension

   2.10 Translation.
   2.20 Interpretation.
   2.30 Extrapolation.

3.00 Application

4.00 Analysis

   4.10 Analysis of elements.
   4.20 Analysis of relationships.
   4.30 Analysis of organizational principles.

5.00 Synthesis

   5.10 Production of a unique communication.
   5.20 Production of a plan or proposed set of operations.
   5.30 Derivation of a set of abstract relations.

6.00 Evaluation

   6.10 Judgments in terms of internal evidence.
   6.20 Judgments in terms of external criteria.

The authors of the Taxonomy, in stating a rationale for its development, have listed the following potential values of it:

1. It should provide teachers with a range of *possible* educational goals for outcomes in the cognitive area, and thus assist them in avoiding the inadvertent exclusion of wanted objectives.

2. It should help enable teachers to gain a perspective on the emphasis given to certain behaviors by a particular set of educational plans.

3. It should help teachers specify precise instructional objectives, which in

turn makes the task of planning learning experiences and the preparation of evaluation devices easier.*

It should be noted that the School Mathematics Study Group has employed a scheme for categorizing objectives which they evolved from the foregoing Taxonomy. They state [34]:

When a student adds two three-digit numbers he is working at a different cognitive level (or is using a different cognitive process) than when he selects from a set of geometric shapes those which are not convex. When he locates the maximum values, over an interval, of a particular polynomial function, he is working at still another level.

There are many schemes for the categorization of cognitive levels. However, most of them have evolved from the Taxonomy defined by Bloom (1956). The categorization scheme which will be used in this report is essentially the one used in the NLSMA study. This scheme also evolved from the Bloom Taxonomy and, as in the Taxonomy, each category is more complex than the previous one. In some cases, the categories can even be considered as hierarchical. That is, a lower category may be a necessary prerequisite for a higher category. The five categories which we find most appropriate for precollege mathematics education are *Knowledge of Facts, Computation, Comprehension, Application, and Analysis.* A more precise definition of each cognitive level category is as follows.

Knowledge of Facts. Objectives which require the recall of specifics such as terminology, symbols, or conventions; emphasis is on recall, not upon synthesis, generalization, or translation of the recalled information.

Computation. Objectives which require straightforward manipulation of problem elements according to rules the subjects presumably have learned; emphasis is upon performing operations, not upon deciding which operations are appropriate.

Comprehension. Objectives which require either recall of concepts and generalizations or transformation of problem elements from one mode to another; emphasis is upon demonstrating understanding of concepts and their relationships, not upon using concepts to produce a solution.

Application. Objectives which require (1) recall of relevant knowledge, (2) selection of appropriate operations, and (3) performance of the operation. Objectives are of a routine nature requiring the subject to use concepts in a specific context and in a way he has presumably practiced.

Analysis. Objectives which require a nonroutine application of concepts. Under this heading come problem formulation and mathematical modeling.†

Later, in the same document, they state:

It is relatively easy to construct tests which measure student achievement at the cognitive levels of Facts and Computation. However, it does not seem to be

---

* B. S. Bloom *et al., Taxonomy of Educational Objectives, Handbook 1: Cognitive Domain.* New York: McKay, 1956, pp. 1–2.
† School Mathematics Study Group, op. cit., pp. 6–7. Reprinted by permission.

widely appreciated that it is also possible to measure student achievement at the higher cognitive levels. For a full discussion of this, see Chapter 3 of Romberg and Wilson (1969). Here, however, are two sample test items, suitable for junior high school students, to illustrate each of the last three cognitive levels. Choose the correct answer.

Comprehension

1. The product of 356 and 7 is equal to
    a) $(300 \times 7) + (50 \times 7) + (6 \times 7)$
    b) $356 + 7$
    c) $(300 + 50) + (6 \times 7)$
    d) $(3 \times 7) + (5 \times 7) + (6 \times 7)$
    e) $300 \times 50 \times 6 \times 7$

2. This drawing suggests a rational number. Choose the fraction on the right which names the same rational number.

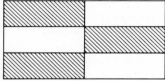

    a) 1/2   d) 3/4
    b) 2/3   e) None of these
    c) 1/3

Application

1. A family spent an average of $46 per month on food for a 2-month period. If food cost $39 one of those months, how much was spent on food the other month?

    a) $32   b) $42.50
    c) $49.50   d) $53
    e) $60

2. What is the *area* of the shaded portion in the figure square shown below?

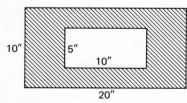

    a) 25 square inches
    b) 30 square inches
    c) 50 square inches
    d) 100 square inches
    e) 150 square inches

Analysis

1. A chess club ran a weekly tournament in which every member played every other member just once. When *one more* member was admitted,

it was found necessary to play *eight* more games per tournament. Now how many members are there in the club?

a) 20   b) 16

c) 12   d) 9

e) 8

2. In a certain classroom, the teacher notes that when the attendance is 92% there are exactly seven empty seats, but when the attendance is 88% there are eight empty seats. What is the total number of empty seats when the attendance is 100%?

a) five   b) four

c) three   d) two

e) none*

The major advantages of the SMSG classification scheme over the Taxonomy are that the categories are more closely aligned with desired mathematical learning and there are fewer categories to deal with. It should be noted, however, that regardless of the scheme that is employed, the classification of objectives on a cognitive scale is a function of the learner—his age, prior learning history, and so on. For example, a particular objective for one learner might, by virtue of his previous experience, be classified as analysis while the same objective for another learner with a different background might be classified as application.

MATHEMATICAL STRUCTURE AND ITS IMPORT FOR THE DESIGN OF LEARNING HIERARCHIES

Mathematics as a subject is a highly organized and carefully structured system of interrelated ideas. It is not surprising to find, therefore, that an examination of the growth of a mathematical concept often reveals a foundation of subconcepts that is hierarchical in nature.

This situation is a mixed blessing for the teacher of mathematics, for while it proves helpful in some respects, it poses problems in others. The virtue of the structure rests in the fact that mathematical ideas *are* interrelated, a quality which should help make the subject easier to understand and remember provided it is taught meaningfully. Yet this same feature is the cause of serious teaching/learning problems which occur when one or more of the links in the structure are missing.

The possibility of missing links is an important consideration for teachers to take into account; it has been the impetus for considerable study and writing on the topic of *learning hierarchies*. The procedure for constructing a learning hierarchy is to start with an objective—where it is assumed that the statement of the objective includes a description of the task the learner must be able to perform in order to demonstrate achievement of the objective. This task

---

* *Ibid.*, pp. 8–9. Reprinted by permission.

is considered a *terminal* behavior and is placed at the apex of a pyramid of behaviors, where the behaviors on any given level are assumed to be sub-ordinate to those listed above it. These subordinate behaviors are arrived at by making what Gagne has called a *task analysis*. This is done by starting with the terminal behavior and asking: "What must the learner be able to do before

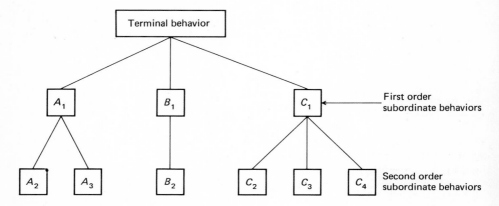

Fig. 1.1 A schema showing the basic characteristics of a behavioral hierarchy.

he can exhibit this behavior?" The answer normally reveals a collection of first-order subordinate tasks that the learner must be able to perform in order to be able to perform the terminal task. The process is repeated, over and over, until the behaviors being identified are either known, or assumed, to be part of the learner's repertoire of competencies. A schemata of the form that a be-havioral hierarchy may take is shown in Fig. 1.1.

Presumably, the practice of constructing learning hierarchies enables a teacher to avoid leaving *logical* gaps in the development of learning sequences.

A sample hierarchy for the concept of addition of cardinal numbers is shown in Fig. 1.2.

Observe that the chart suggests that before you can meaningfully learn the concept of addition of cardinal numbers (0, 1, 2, 3, . . .), you must have pre-viously learned at least the rudimentary concepts of number, disjoint sets, and set union; before you can meaningfully learn the concepts of disjoint sets and set union, you must have previously learned about sets and the concept of set membership; and so on.

A detailed discussion of this hierarchy and its components is given in Chapter 4, but it is important at this point to recognize how learning hierar-chies look and to be aware of their significance in building effective learning sequences for children. The main idea to remember is simply this: *a child can meaningfully learn a concept only when the supporting subconcepts are a part of the child's knowledge.* Accordingly, the teacher should know the learning hierarchies for those concepts they wish to teach. Many basic learning hierar-chies are provided in this text in a reflective form called *flowcharts for teaching.*

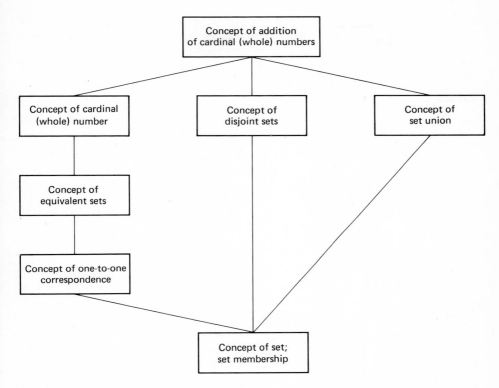

Figure 1.2

For example, the reader may wish to examine the comprehensive flowcharts for teaching addition and multiplication in Chapters 4 and 6, respectively.

Finally it should be noted that learning hierarchies play a crucial role in the construction of *systems* of objectives for learning, for once an objective is selected all of its prerequisites must also be included as part of the child's learning program. Continued discussions of how to take learning hierarchies into account in teaching are provided throughout the text.

ASSESSMENT OF KNOWLEDGE STATES: A CRITICAL FACTOR IN JUDGING READINESS

It was pointed out earlier that a child's level of cognitive development is a mark of readiness for learning. This means that the teacher must formulate goals for learning that are in tune with the child's cognitive status. In order to do so, of course, this information must be at the disposal of the teacher.

The teacher must also have available data that shows the child's level of achievement in the various learning hierarchies embraced by the program. As standard procedure, the teacher should have available a comprehensive *profile* _of achievement_ for each child. A child's stages of development and prior achievement should be the basis for selecting learning tasks that are within his/her grasp. To fail to take such data into account is to invite learning failure and the multitude of undesirable consequences associated with it.

SUMMARY

The construction of an adequate base for teaching may be summarized as follows:

1. The mathematics curriculum must be well-defined. That is to say that the mathematical ideas that are embraced by the curriculum, as well as their logical interrelationships, must be a matter of record. The actual competencies that it is hoped that children will acquire should be specified in behavioral terms.

2. The designation of learning tasks should always be in harmony with the child's developmental stages. Consequently, the teacher should have the appropriate developmental assessment instruments available for use as necessary.

3. Learning tasks should be prescribed only after the prerequisite competencies have been acquired. This means that teachers must have the instruments for producing and maintaining comprehensive and detailed profiles of achievement. In this way learning tasks can be selected that are in keeping with the child's previous record of accomplishment.

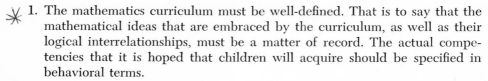

Exercise set

1. In order to determine whether a child can conserve quantity, a task like that described on page 4 is structured. Try this experiment with at least two children, one in the 6–7 years age range and one in the 8–9 age range. Do not prompt the child. Write down the questions you ask and the child's answers to them. Discuss the implications of your findings.

2. Write the specified number of criterion (test) items for the objectives indicated below. Also, in each case, describe the special considerations that you think should be taken into account in constructing the items (e.g., variety, etc.).

    a) Example 1, page 9; 10 items

    b) Example 2, page 9; 5 items

3. Select a contemporary set of elementary school mathematics textbooks and write an objective in the "Given–Required Performance–Criterion–Sample Test Item" format in each of the following content areas.

a) addition   b) subtraction
c) multiplication   d) division
e) fractions   f) measurement
g) geometry   h) sets

4. For each of the following pairs of objectives, choose the one that you think calls for the highest level of cognitive achievement, and give a brief explanation for your choice.

   a) The child can count aloud from one to fifty.

      The child can demonstrate how to use sets of blocks to find the sum of two numbers, m and n, where both m and n are less than or equal to 5.

   b) The child can identify all of the rectangles in a mixed set of plane geometric figures.

      The child can state the definition of a prime number.

5. In the Avital-Shettleworth monograph [2] it is stated: ". . . it is extremely important to bear in mind that the classification of educational objectives according to the Taxonomy is always determined by the relation between what the student is expected to do and what he has been exposed to." Discuss that issue in light of your responses to question 4.

6. Sudy the five categories of cognition specified by the School Mathematics Study Group and try to construct an objective which fulfills the conditions of each level. In each case, use mathematical content of your own choice.

7. What implications, if any, would the idea of classifying instructional objectives according to levels of cognition have for a teacher who is concerned about "teaching for understanding"? Discuss.

8. Construct a learning hierarchy for the following objective which you consider to be complete through at least the second order of subcompetencies. You may wish to examine the comprehensive flowchart for teaching addition given in Chapter 4.

   Terminal behavior.   The child can demonstrate how to find the sum of a two-digit number and a one-digit number using multibase arithmetic blocks (or a comparable type of embodiment).

9. Discuss why it is necessary to maintain a profile of prior achievement for each child.

10. Look at the flowchart for teaching the concept of number at the beginning of Chapter 3. Why has the decision point regarding conservation of number been included in the flowchart?

11. Choose a mathematical concept and describe how teaching that concept might differ for children in the concrete operations and formal operations stages of development.

12. A mnemonic device was developed by Paulson [25] to aid in the recall of the "ABCD's" of writing adequate instructional objectives. The letters in

the mnemonic require specification of the Audience, Behavior, Conditions, and Degree of attainment. Use this idea to write several instructional objectives for students at different grade levels for a specific concept of your choice.

READINGS FOR ADDITIONAL STUDY

For each of the following topics, read one of the articles listed in the bibliography and write a one- or two-page report that consists of (1) a brief *summary* of the article, and (2) your *reaction* to the positions which have been taken.

13. Piaget's Developmental Theory and its implications for teaching.

14. Instructional/learning objectives.

Bibliography

1. American Educational Research Association. *Instructional Objectives.* Monograph 3. Chicago: Rand NcNally, 1969.

2. Avital, S. M., and S. J. Shettleworth. *Objectives for Mathematics Learning: Some Ideas for the Teacher.* Bulletin No. 3. Toronto: The Ontario Institute for Studies in Education, 1968.

3. Bloom, B. S., M. D. Engelhart, E. J. Furst, W. H. Hill, and D. R. Krathwohl, *Taxonomy of Educational Objectives, Handbook 1: Cognitive Domain.* New York: McKay, 1956.

4. Brock, Robert V. "Measuring arithmetic objectives." *The Arithmetic Teacher* **12** (November 1965): 537–42.

5. Burns, R. W. "The theory of expressing objectives." *Educational Technology* **VII** (October 1967): 1–3.

6. Callahan, L. G., and V. J. Glennon. *Elementary School Mathematics: A Guide to Current Research.* Washington, D.C.: Association for Curriculum Development, 1975.

7. Canfield, A. A. "A rationale for performance objectives." *Audio-visual Instruction* **13** (February 1968): 127–29.

8. Copeland, Richard W. *How Children Learn Mathematics: Teaching Implications of Piaget's Research.* New York: Macmillan, 1974.

9. Farnham-Diggory, S. "On readiness and remedy in mathematics instruction." *The Arithmetic Teacher* **15** (November 1968): 614–22.

10. Fogelman, K. R. *Piagetian Tests for the Primary School.* London: The National Foundation for Educational Research, 1970.

11. Gagne, R. M. *The Conditions of Learning*. New York: Holt, Rinehart and Winston, 1965, Chapter 9.

12. Gagne, R. M. "The analysis of instructional objectives for the design of instruction." *Teaching Machines and Programed Learning*. Edited by R. Glaser. Washington, D.C.: National Education Association, 1965.

13. Gagne, R. M. "Curriculum research and the promotion of learning." *Perspectives of Curriculum Evaluation*. AERA Monograph 1. Chicago: Rand McNally, 1967.

14. Gagne, R. M., "Learning hierarchies," *Educational Psychologist* **6** No. 1 (1968): 3–6.

15. Inhelder, B., and J. Piaget. *The Growth of Logical Thinking from Childhood to Adolescence*. New York: Basic Books, 1958.

16. Inskeep, James E., Jr. "Building a case for the application of Piaget's theory and research in the classroom." *The Arithmetic Teacher* **19** (April 1972): 255–60.

17. Krathwohl, D. R., B. S. Bloom, and B. B. Masia. *Taxonomy of Educational Objectives, Handbook II: Affective Domain*. New York: McKay, 1956.

18. Krathwohl, D. R. "Stating objectives appropriately for programs, for curriculum, and for instructional materials development." *Journal of Teacher Education* **16** (1965): 83–92.

19. Mager, R. F. *Preparing Instructional Objectives*. Palo Alto: Pearon Publishers, 1962.

20. National Council of Teachers of Mathematics. *Historical Topics for the Mathematics Classroom, Thirty-first Yearbook*. Washington, D.C.: The Council, 1969.

21. National Council of Teachers of Mathematics. *A History of Mathematics Education in the United States and Canada, Thirty-second Yearbook*. Washington, D.C.: The Council, 1970.

22. Nichols, Eugene D. "Are behavioral objectives the answer?" *The Arithmetic Teacher* **19** (October 1972): 419, 474–76.

23. O'Brien, Thomas C., and B. J. Shapiro. "Problem solving and the development of cognitive structure." *The Arithmetic Teacher* **16** (January 1969): 11–15.

24. Overholt, Elbert D. "A Piagetian conservation concept." *The Arithmetic Teacher* **12** (May 1965): 317–26.

25. Paulson, Casper F. "Specifying Behavioral Objectives." National Research Training Institute Manual for Participants in Research Development (CORD) Projects. Monmouth: Teaching Research Division, Oregon State System of Higher Education, August 1967.

26. Piaget, Jean. "How Children Form Mathematical Concepts." *Scientific American* (November 1953).

27. Piaget, Jean. *Science of Education and the Psychology of the Child*. New York: Orion Press, 1970.

28. Piaget, Jean. *The Child's Conception of Number*. New York: Humanities Press, 1952.

29. Piaget, J., and B. Inhelder. *The Psychology of the Child*. New York: Basic Books, 1969.

30. Popham, W. J. "Objectives and instruction." *Instructional Objectives*. AERA Monograph 3. Chicago: Rand McNally, 1969, 32–64.

31. Rosskopf, Myron F. "Piagetian research and the school mathematics program." *The Arithmetic Teacher* **19** (April 1972): 309–14.

32. Sandel, D. H. "Teach so your goals are showing!" *The Arithmetic Teacher* **15** (April 1968): 320–23.

33. Sawada, Daiyo. "Piaget and pedagogy: fundamental relationships." *The Arithmetic Teacher* **19** (April 1972): 293–98.

34. School Mathematics Study Group, *Newsletter 38.* Palo Alto, Calif.: Stanford University, August 1972.

35. Smith, L. T., and G. G. Bitter. "Cultural considerations in mathematics education in Arizona." *The Arithmetic Teacher* **21** (February 1974): 86–89.

36. Strauss, Sidney. "Learning theories of Gagne and Piaget: implication for curriculum development." *Teacher College Record* (September 1972): 81–102.

37. Sullivan, H. J. "Objectives, evaluation, and improved learner achievement." *Instructional Objectives*. AERA Monograph 3, Chicago: Rand McNally, 1969, 65–99.

38. Trueblood, Cecil R. "A model for using diagnosis in individualizing mathematics instruction in the elementary school classroom." *The Arithmetic Teacher* **18** (November 1971): 505–11.

39. Tyler, R. W. *Basic Principles of Curriculum and Instruction*. Chicago: University of Chicago Press, 1950.

40. Tyler, R. W. "Some persistent questions on the defining of objectives." *Defining Educational Objectives*. Edited by C. M. Lindvall. Pittsburgh: University of Pittsburgh Press, 1964.

41. Wadsworth, Barry J. *Piaget's Theory of Cognitive Development*. New York: David McKay, 1971.

42. Walbesser, H. H. "Curriculum evaluation by means of behavioral objectives." *Journal of Research in Science Teaching* **1** (1963): 296–301.

43. Walbesser, H. H. "Behavioral objectives, a cause celèbre," *The Arithmetic Teacher* **19** (October 1972): 418, 436–40.

44. Weaver, J. F. "Some concerns about the application of Piaget's theory and research to mathematical learning and instruction." *The Arithmetic Teacher* **19** (April 1972): 263–70.

The design of instructional strategies

2

Synopsis and objectives

Chapter 2 provides you with a framework for viewing the factors involved in developing effective learning environments for young children. Twelve instructional principles are stated that have implications for the design of teaching strategies, and the basic concepts opened up by each of them is discussed individually in more detail. Finally, the principles are recast in the form of a *checklist* which can help you assess the adequacy of a child's learning environment.

In your study, keep in mind that a comprehensive bibliography is provided to enable you to explore in greater depth the various topics presented. You will have an opportunity later to expand your knowledge of these topics as they will be referred to in the teaching of specific mathematical concepts taken up in subsequent chapters.

A careful study of Chapter 2 should enable you to

1. explain the instructional implications of knowing that a child is at the concrete operational stage of cognitive development for a particular concept;

2. describe the role of relevance in forming instructional strategies;

3. explain the role of perceptual variation in forming instructional strategies;

4. describe the function of learning hierarchies in developing diagnostic approaches to teaching;

5. explain the relationships among student readiness conditions, desired learning outcomes and the selection of teaching actions;

6. specify how the tactics of "teaching for discovery" or "teaching problem solving" relate to the goals of higher-order cognitive attainment;

7. explain the role of feedback in the design of an instructional system that is nonadaptive;

8. describe the consequences of an instructional system that is nonadaptive;

9. discuss the meaning and significance of motivation in the formation of learning environments;

10. explain the necessity for designing instructional systems that will help children retain important learned concepts and skills;

11. describe how a child's reading level affects the determination of teaching strategies;

12. explain the nature of, and rationale for, the laboratory teaching approach at the elementary school level;

13. describe the role of games in the learning environment for children.

The design of instructional strategies

THE CHILD AS A LEARNER: IMPLICATIONS FOR TEACHING

In the final analysis, it is the job of the teacher to manipulate the learning environment to provide the best opportunity for the child to grow in desirable ways. Thus the teacher is constantly confronted with the task of choosing the *means* for attaining some specified set of *ends*.

How are these choices to be made? They are influenced by desired outcomes and by the ability and circumstances of the learner. Teaching should occur in the presence of a claim of the following sort:

> *Under circumstances* C, *if teaching action* A *is taken, learning outcome* L *will occur,*

but unfortunately, educational theory has not yet advanced to the point where very many substantiated statements of this type are to be found. Instead, teachers must formulate their own instructional claims based on the best information they can assemble, be willing to test them in their day-to-day classroom activities, and accept the need to modify them as circumstances warrant.

The following general principles are offered as potentially useful guides to the teacher in making selections of teaching actions. It should be noted that the principles are interrelated and, as a system, are mutually supportive.

Principle 1
The learning tasks that are selected for children should be consistent with their stages of cognitive development.

This means that the teacher should not impose learning tasks for which there is no hope of success. For example, if a child cannot conserve *area*, then at that point in time the teacher should not attempt to teach area concepts to that particular child.

Principle 2
Elementary age school children are, in the main, at the preoperational and concrete operational stages of cognitive development and therefore are heavily dependent upon the use of their physical environment for concept formation.

The primary implication of Principle 2 is that initial learning experiences for elementary age children should be based upon observation and real-world representations of mathematical ideas. It follows that a high premium should be placed upon the use of *laboratory* approaches for learning.

Principle 3
A child's learning potential is enhanced if the learning tasks are perceived by the child as being meaningful and relevant.

Principle 3 is closely related to Principle 2. Care should be taken to construct learning experiences for children which have obvious relationships to the real world as the child sees it. It is not necessary, indeed is probably counter-productive, to use contrived settings for mathematical learning rather than concrete, meaningful learning experiences.

> **Principle 4**
> *The learning of mathematical concepts is enhanced when the ideas are embodied in a variety of ways. Moreover, the preferred order of concept representation in learning sequences is from* concrete *to* semiconcrete *to* abstract.

Principle 4 says that, where possible, children should have an opportunity to examine mathematical ideas from a variety of perspectives. Learning experiences should start with concrete, real-world forms of an idea and move toward more abstract representations.

> **Principle 5**
> *The learning tasks that are selected for children should be consistent with their level of previous achievement.*

Principle 5 implies that a child's potential for learning a particular concept may be impeded if one or more of the learnings on which it is based are not already part of the child's knowledge repertoire. Again, this situation points up the necessity for teachers to know the hierarchical relationships among concepts. It also means that teachers must keep track of individual student achievement.

> **Principle 6**
> *Purposeful and productive teaching can occur only in the presence of clearly defined goals.*

Principle 6 says that the teacher should have an understanding of the goals of the mathematics program, and also should be clear about the purposes of each teaching action.

> **Principle 7**
> *When teachers formulate the goals for mathematical learning, they must be certain to include aims which stress the development of the higher-order cognitive processes.*

Principle 7 helps bring into focus a number of contemporary educational aims such as *discovery learning* and *problem solving*. Children should *learn how to learn,* and the instructional strategies for accomplishing such ends would seem to call for the construction of learning activities which afford the child an opportunity to explore, to formulate and evaluate hypotheses, to study patterns, and to examine and discuss their successful attacks on problems.

Principle 8
The learning of mathematical concepts is enhanced if the learning environ-ment is both adaptive and responsive.

For a learning environment to be *adaptive* and *responsive,* it must provide students with constant *feedback* about the appropriateness of their moves; moreover, if a student fails to progress toward desired goals, the learning system is not functioning properly and must be adjusted to the individual's needs; otherwise student learning problems will arise.

Principle 9
Teachers should construct a learning environment which permits students to develop an acceptable self-image.

Elementary age school children are gregarious and in a highly formative stage of social development. Children need to feel socially acceptable, to enjoy successful learning experiences, to have fruitful interactions with their peers, and in general to develop a wholesome attitude about themselves. Teachers should try to create learning environments which are free of trauma, frustration, and failure. Compulsory schooling is based on the idea that every child can succeed, but patterns of schooling have not always been consistent with this belief.

Principle 10
A child's potential for learning is facilitated when care is taken to develop and maintain a high level of motivation.

Principle 10 is important for the practicing teacher to note. There are many well-known devices for developing and maintaining motivation: establishing meaningful and constructive *incentives,* capitalizing on a child's natural *curios-ity,* allowing a child to express his or her own *interests* where appropriate, and in general giving the child an opportunity to exercise some *independence* in the choice of day-to-day goals.

Principle 11
The learning of mathematical concepts is aided by use of teaching methods that ensure the retention of basic concepts and skills.

There are many mathematical concepts and skills that children probably should remember because of their usefulness either in the development of other important mathematical ideas or in other aspects of the child's life. But in order to achieve this goal, *forgetting* is a potent force which must be taken into account. Teachers must plan *drill and practice* activities for the concepts and skills they want the students to remember. Such activities needn't be boring or tedious; they can and should be interesting and exciting.

Drill and practice activities are being conducted in a supportive and stimulating environment.

Principle 12
The teacher should make sure that the level of reading skills required by the learning tasks that are assigned is within the span of the child's independent reading level.

Perhaps one of the most overlooked sources of learning difficulties is associated with reading ability. Teachers must be certain that the written communications which are included in the child's learning environment are in concert with the child's reading competence.

In the statements of the foregoing principles, several terms were employed that need to be elaborated upon. These and related ideas are taken up in the following sections.

THE DEVELOPMENT OF
DIAGNOSTIC/PRESCRIPTIVE TEACHING STRATEGIES

In Webster's New Collegiate Dictionary (1973), the term *diagnosis* is defined as an "investigation or analysis of the cause or nature of a condition, situation, or problem." As implied by this definition, a common context in which diagnosis is practiced is in the case of specific learning problems. We must, of course, determine the cause of a learning problem before we can devise ways of correcting it.

The process of diagnosis, as suggested above, is part of a much larger need of the teacher to acquire essential data and background information about each student. At a general level of diagnostic analysis, there are at least three basic considerations that the teacher should take into account before assigning a learning task to a child:

1. Is the child's stage of cognitive development appropriate for the task?
2. Has the child developed the prerequisite competencies associated with the task?
3. Is the task agreeable to the child?

It follows that in a carefully designed instructional program, periodic efforts should be made to obtain information about the cognitive development of each child so as to avoid making gross errors in the assignment of learning tasks. For the same reason, teachers need to develop means for obtaining and keeping track of student achievement data. And, finally, teachers should try to determine special student interests and propensities. The teacher who has attended to these matters then has a sound platform upon which to *prescribe* learning tasks that have a high probability for success.

When all of the above steps have been taken, however, and learning problems still occur, a more specific level of analysis is required. When such an event takes place, the teacher must function in a manner akin to a detective and look for clues which suggest the source of the difficulty. Possibly the child has forgotten something that forms one of the enabling links to learning the new concept; or perhaps the child did not understand the communications which were provided; or perhaps some necessary prerequisite learning was inadvertently overlooked by the teacher. There are a myriad of other possibilities. In any event, the intended outcome of such a diagnosis again is the formulation of a prescription; a new approach or a technical adjustment designed to correct the learning problem. Such is the nature of diagnostic/prescriptive teaching.

TACTICS FOR ASSURING RETENTION OF LEARNING

There is a large body of research literature which deals with the phenomenon of *forgetting*, but we cannot deal with it here in any detail. Suffice it to say that while some types of behaviors are more quickly forgotten than others, in the absence of *use* nearly every type of learned behavior is quickly forgotten. Teachers must, therefore, carefully devise and implement plans for helping children retain the learnings that are important to their further intellectual growth or to their ability to function in the world in which they live.

These are two good principles to follow in devising drill and practice:

1. Develop a *comprehensive* plan which *guarantees* the involvement of the child in drill and practice at specified points in the learning process.

2. Take care that drill and practice exercises are meaningful and interesting. This can be accomplished through the use of *games* and other *fun activities*.

Numerous practical ideas for classroom drill and practice activities may be found in the literature of the field. The interested reader will find many references to this topic in the chapter bibliographies in this book.

COPING WITH THE PROBLEMS OF READING

Reading mathematical material presents children with a variety of special problems which, if not given specific attention, will seriously impede their potential for learning. Several of the more important ones are discussed here.

To begin with, mathematics has its own technical vocabulary. Success in mathematics learning requires that students have a clear understanding of the technical symbols and words used to express mathematical concepts. Therefore, teachers should provide direct instruction on words and phrases that have meaning specific to mathematics—for example, words such as *numerator* and *denominator*. There are other words— such as *power* and *product*—that involve learning a mathematical interpretation that differs from the words' common everyday meaning. Word games and crossword puzzles are examples of the types of learning activities that can be used to help students develop their mathematical vocabulary.

A second issue arises from the fact that in the study of mathematics students must learn to attach meaning to abbreviated *symbols* (for example, $+, -, \times, \div$) and learn to extract meanings from *formulas, graphs,* and *diagrams*. In the case of symbol and formula learning, tactics similar to those employed for vocabulary acquisition are appropriate. Learning to interpret graphs and diagrams is probably best taught by providing the students with examples displaying data and information that have some personal meaning for them. Children also can be taught to construct their own graphs and diagrams.

A third issue that merits consideration is that the reading of mathematical material frequently requires a student to be able to recall a good deal of previously learned concepts and skills. If a student cannot remember the needed information, he will not be able to comprehend the new material. Students should be given guidance, therefore, in discerning what is worth remembering for a short period of time and the basic and often-needed information and ideas that should be committed to memory.

A fourth consideration that should be taken into account pertains to the matter of *reading rate*. Many students try to read mathematical discourse at the rate of speed that they read less difficult material. Unfortunately, many teachers encourage this procedure by placing a premium on speed reading.

They erroneously believe that "good" readers are fast readers. The *best* readers are those who can adjust their reading rate according to the difficulty of the material and their purpose for reading. This means that successful reading of mathematical material often requires careful reading and rereading in order to understand and interpret the technical words and phrases and the relationships among the concepts to which they refer.

DESIGNING LABORATORY LEARNING ENVIRONMENTS

The word *laboratory* is defined by Webster's New Collegiate Dictionary (1973) as "a place equipped for experimental study in a science or for testing and analysis; a place providing opportunity for experimentation, observation, or practice in a field of study." In general, this definition provides an apt description of the nature and function of a mathematics laboratory. The laboratory learning approach emphasizes the concept of *learning by doing*, of actual manipulation of apparatus. This "hands-on" experience with physical-world objects serves a basic need in the child's concept development. The presence of concrete learning experiences helps to bring meaning to the symbolic representations necessary to embody mathematical concepts. The following diagram suggests the desired learning sequence.

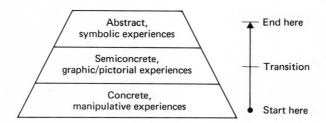

As indicated by the diagram, the teacher should arrange first to have the child engage in concrete, manipulative types of learning experiences; then move the child to a semiconcrete learning environment; and finally introduce the abstract forms of the ideas to be learned. Thus when a child is working with mathematical symbols, the symbols have concrete referents in the child's experience. Such is the basis for meaningful learning.

A laboratory learning environment has at least two other virtues which are important to recognize:

1. It permits exploratory types of learning activities and hypothesis formulation and testing.

2. It allows students to examine patterns and relationships, and thus gain a broader view of mathematics and its significance in the world in which we live.

Properly used, then, laboratory learning settings can offer students the opportunity to develop heuristic approaches to problem solving; in general to engage in creative activities of a high order. It is through such mechanisms that the teacher can help promote the attainment of highly sought-after competencies. It follows that laboratory learning experiences should be commonplace in the classroom—in individual and in small and large group patterns of instruction. For such use, the teacher must have access to a wide range of learning aids.

Some comments regarding the organization and supervision of laboratory learning activities also are in order. It is desirable to teach students to assume responsibility for their behavior as well as responsibility for the selection and care of the materials (aids) with which they will work. Most behavior problems in laboratory settings result from students not knowing what to do or what procedures to follow. One method that has become very popular for guiding student involvement in laboratory learning activities has been to use what have become known as *task cards*. While many different forms of task cards have been developed, the features found on most of them include a reference to some learning objective, a list of materials or apparatus that will be needed, and a set of directions (tasks) to be followed. The task may call for individual efforts, or the combined efforts of a group of children.

It is a good idea to index the cards according to the competencies with which they are intended to deal. A task card file can be organized around the scheme shown below.

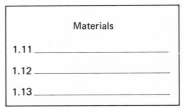

Front of task card   Back of task card

Note the numbering system relates the problem to an objective and the materials required to work on the assigned task. Material so organized can be placed in boxes and labeled according to the concept to be developed. These are sometimes referred to as *single-concept kits*. Other types of activities, such as games and cassette tapes designed to teach vocabulary, skills, and so forth, can be boxed and labeled in a similar fashion.

The teacher also should write down procedures for the students to check out the task cards and concept kits and to record the work as they complete it. In the primary grades this will probably require the help of the teacher or a teacher aide.

THE ISSUE OF VERBAL PROBLEM SOLVING

There are many reasons why verbal problem solving is considered an important part of the elementary school mathematics curriculum. Chief among these reasons is that verbal problems can provide a realistic and motivational context in which specific problem-solving skills can be taught. They also allow students to apply mathematics to many practical everyday problem situations, such as balancing a checkbook, unit pricing at the store, and evaluating advertisement claims.

At least 250 studies have been conducted on a variety of issues related to teaching verbal problem solving. These studies indicate that there are a variety of factors which influence problem difficulty. One is the factor of *reading level* where problems are expressed in written form. This circumstance should not lead to the conclusion that teaching problem solving should be delayed until children can read, however, because there are other ways for framing problems, such as in pictorial or graphic form, as illustrated below.

Another practical procedure is to express problem situations orally; for example, many teachers record verbal problems on cassette tapes for student use. Also, for students whose reading skills are slow in developing, teachers have used short *miniproblem* statements like the one below to help students develop their reading vocabulary.

6 dogs.

2 run away.

How many left?

Some of the other significant factors which affect a child's ability to solve verbal problems are as follows:

1. Knowledge of technical vocabulary.
2. Computational ability.
3. Amount of irrelevant information.
4. Ability to recognize the relationships among given data.
5. Ability to assess the reasonableness of proposed answers.

6. Ability to select the correct mathematical operation(s).

7. Ability to supply missing information.

8. Ability to translate a problem into a number sentence.

What are some practical ways of teaching the problem-solving skills that will help students learn to deal with the factors just described? Consider the following techniques and suggestions.

1. *Technical vocabulary.* Have students practice restating problems in their own words. This technique will help the teacher and the pupil gain insight into which technical terms are presenting difficulties. By keeping track of the difficult vocabulary words, the teacher can begin to use crossword puzzles, special games, and other activities to teach specific word meanings and thus increase the child's functional vocabulary.

2. *Computation.* Have students solve mathematical sentences such as

$$13¢ + 10¢ = 23¢$$

and then ask them to make up their own verbal problems which could be solved using that special mathematical sentence.

3. *Irrelevant data.* Create problems that provide too much data. Have the students describe what data are (a) required and (b) not required to solve the problem. It is also useful to supply problems that *cannot* be solved by using the information given in the problem.

4. *Recognizing relationships among data.* Provide students with problems and ask them to describe relationships among data that are presented.

5. *Estimating the reasonableness of answers.* Provide students with problem statements and a set of possible answers only one of which is reasonable. Then have students see if they can find and defend that answer.

6. *Selecting the correct mathematical operation.* Present students with problems that do not contain any specific numbers, and ask them what operation(s) must be performed to find the answer. For example, consider the problem:

Jack wants to buy a pencil, an eraser, and a notebook for use in school. How can he find out if he has enough money to purchase all of the items?

7. *Supplying missing information.* Present problems like the following example.

Mrs. James paid $1.70 for two dozen grade A large eggs. How much money would she have saved if she had bought grade A medium eggs?

Then ask the students what information they need before they can answer the question.

8. *Translating problem into a number sentence.* Present problems like the one below and ask the students to restate them in their own words.

Jill wants to buy four pieces of bubble gum that cost 5¢ each. How much money does she need?

Place student restatements, like the ones below, on the board. Then ask the students to see if they can write their statements in number sentence form. For example:

The question asks me to find out how much four nickels equal. So, $4 \times 5\cancel{c}$ = ☐ $\cancel{c}$. It asks me to figure out what four 5's equal. So,

$$5 + 5 + 5 + 5 = \boxed{}.$$

THE ISSUE OF LEARNING BY DISCOVERY – *later*

In recent years, much discussion and writing has been devoted to the issue of designing instructional strategies so as to enable children to *discover* mathematical properties and relationships—as opposed to the didactical practice of simply relating such information to the child. The proponents for the use of

Understanding reached through exploration and guided discovery results in meaningful learning.

such tactics claim that children who "discover" a new (for them) mathematical idea learn more than the idea itself; they learn something about how to learn; they learn the *heuristics* of how to solve a problem. To put it another way, they learn the *processes* of *analysis, synthesis,* and *evaluation,* the higher order cognitive skills discussed in Chapter 1. Thus it is clear that the major intent of the incorporation of the "learning by discovery" movement is to provide children with an opportunity to acquire competencies which will be invaluable to them as tools for lifelong learning.

There have been many attempts to define the conditions under which a teaching strategy would fall in the discovery category, and though they vary significantly, the one element which most of them seem to share is the emphasis upon *induction* and the attendant skills of formulating potentially fruitful hypotheses, of testing hypotheses; in short, of searching and exploring. In terms of the "instructional claim," when teachers select a "discovery method," they have chosen a teaching action (A) which they believe may result not only in having the child acquire some defined competence (L), but which also may help the child develop powerful ways of thinking—those evasive, but eminently important goals of education.

THE FUNCTION OF GAMES AS A TEACHING STRATEGY

It is a well-known fact that under certain circumstances teachers can use mathematical games to good advantage in the classroom. Games can be used not only to introduce interest and excitement into the child's learning program, but also to help the child attain a wide range of competencies—from basic intellectual skills to problem solving. A list of good reasons for the occasional use of "game strategies" in the classroom would include the following:

1. If appropriately designed, games can be used successfully with children who have special types of learning problems, such as some form of language deficiency (reading or verbal skills).
2. Games can be used to help students who exhibit discipline problems which are the result of being bored with the regular classroom routine.
3. Games fit well into the classroom where the laboratory or learning center approach is used. This feature is made possible when the game is made to operate independent of direct teacher control.
4. Games provide students with an opportunity to exert control and influence over their social environment by enabling them to switch from being passive consumers of information to being active decision makers.
5. Games can promote desirable social interactions among children by encouraging cooperation and discussion with each other.
6. Games can provide teachers with diagnostic information which they can use to help individual children correct misconceptions or to fill gaps in their learning structure.
7. Games can be used to integrate mathematics with other subjects, and they also can be geared to conform to the particular interests of students.

A good set of procedures for teachers to follow in designing games for use in their own classrooms has been developed by Trueblood and Szabo [83].* According to their plan, there are seven steps which should be taken.

I. *Establish specific outcomes.*

Describe what you expect the students to learn or how you expect them to benefit as a result of playing the game. The idea is that the game should have some well-defined educational purpose.

II. *Make simple materials.*

Develop the materials necesssary to play the game.

III. *Write simple rules and procedures.*

Formulate the rules and procedures which the children must know in order to play the game.

IV. *Make provisions for immediate feedback.*

Decide how you want students to obtain knowledge of results.

V. *Build in some suspense.*

Create some way for chance to enter into the playing of the game.

VI. *Create the materials so as to allow variation.*

Determine the features of the game that can be easily changed to vary the focus or rules of the game, and construct the materials so as to permit such changes.

VII. *Evaluate the game.*

Find out what the students think of the game and attempt to determine whether the game was successful in meeting its purpose.

An example of how to follow the foregoing procedures in the construction of a game is described below.

I. Desired outcomes.

- Given a set of common objects, the students can estimate the objects' weight correct to the nearest kilogram. (Observation and estimation)

- Given an equal-arm balance, the students can determine and record the weights of common objects correct to the nearest kilogram. (Measurement)

- Given an object's estimated and observed weight correct to the nearest kilogram, the students can compute the error in estimation. (Computation and number relationships)

---

* Cecil R. Trublood and Michael Szabo, "Procedures for designing your own metric games for pupil involvement," *The Arithmetic Teacher* **21** (May 1974): 404–408. © 1974 by the National Council of Teachers of Mathematics. Reprinted by permission. The material on the next six pages is taken from this source.

II.   Make simple materials.

The following materials were constructed or assembled to help students attain the objectives previously stated in an interesting and challenging manner.

- Sets of 3-by-5 cards with tasks given on the front and correct answers and points to be scored on the back (see Fig. 2.1).
- A cardboard track (see Fig. 2.2) made from oak tag. Shuffle the E's (estimate cards), M's (measurement cards), and the D's (difference cards) and place them on the gameboard in the places indicated.

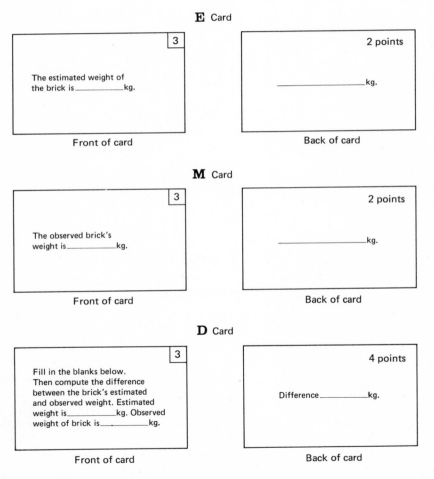

Figure 2.1

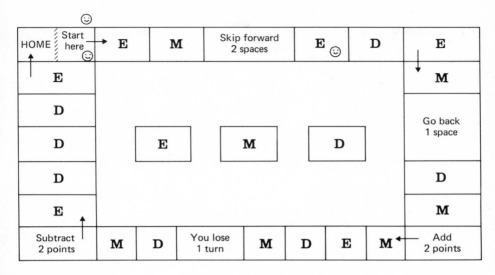

Figure 2.2

- An equal-arm balance that can weigh objects up to at least 7 kilograms.
- A pair of dice and one different-colored button per player.
- A set of common objects that weigh less than 7 kilograms and more than 1 kilogram.
- Student record card (see Fig. 2.3).

Student's name_____ Date_____		
Card number	Answer given	Number of points
E_3	2 kg	2
E_2	1 kg	1

Figure 2.3

III. Write simple rules and procedures.

The rules and procedures are crucial to making a game self-instructional. In the following set of directions note how a student leader and an answer card deck serve to ease the answer processing needed to keep the game moving smoothly from one player to another. It is essential to keep the rules simple and straightforward so that play moves quickly from one student to another.

* Number of players, two to six.
* The student leader or teacher aide begins by rolling the dice.

The highest roll goes first. All players start with their buttons in the "Start here" block. The first player rolls one die and moves his button the number of spaces indicated on the die. If he lands on a space containing an E, M, or D, he must choose the top card in the appropriate deck located in the center of the playing board or track and perform the task that is indicated. The player then records the card number, his answer, and the points awarded by the student leader on his record card. The student leader checks each player's answer and awards the appropriate number of points by reading the back side on the task card. He then places that card on the bottom of the appropriate deck and play moves to the left of the first player. The player who reaches "Home" square with the highest number of points is the winner. At the end of the play each player turns in his score to the student leader who gives them to the teacher.

IV. Provide immediate feedback.

By placing the answer on the back of the task card and appointing a student leader, the teacher who developed this game built into it an important characteristic: immediate knowledge of the results of each player's performance. In most cases this feedback feature can be built into a game by using the back of the task cards, by creating an answer deck, or by using a student leader whose level of performance would permit him to judge the adequacy of other students' performances in a reliable manner. Feedback is one of the key features of an instructional game because it has motivational as well as instructional impact.

V.   Build in some suspense.

Experience has shown that games enjoyed by students contain some element of risk or chance. In this particular game a player gets a task card based upon the roll of the die. He also has the possibility of being skipped forward or skipped back spaces, or of losing his turn. Skipping back builds in the possibility of getting additional opportunities to score points; this feature helps low-scoring students catch up. Skipping forward cuts the number of opportunities a high-scoring player has to accumulate points. The possibility of adding or subtracting points also helps create some suspense. These suspense-creating features help make the game what the students call "a fun game."

VI. Create the materials to allow variation.

A game that has the potential for variation with minor modifications of the rules or materials has at least two advantages. First, it allows a new game to be created without a large investment of time on the part of

Math games motivate and help children to learn.

the teacher. Second, it keeps the game from becoming stale because the students know all the answers. For instance, the sample game can be quickly changed by making new task cards that require that students estimate and measure the area of common surfaces found in the classroom such as a desk or table top. By combining the two decks, mixed practice could be provided.

VII.   Evaluate the game.

Try the game and variations with a small group of students and observe their actions. Use the first-round record cards as a pretest. Keep the succeeding record cards for each student in correct order. By comparing the last-round record cards with the first-round record cards for a specific student, you can keep track of the progress this particular student is making. Filing the cards by student names will provide a longitudinal record of a student's progress for a given skill as well as diagnostic information for future instruction.

Finally, decide whether the students enjoy the game. The best way is to use a self-report form containing several single questions like the following, which can be answered in an interview or in writing:

- Would you recommend the game to someone else in the class? ___ Yes ___ No
- Which face indicates how you felt when you were playing the game?

- What part of the game did you like the best?
- How would you improve the game?

VIII.   Have students record diagnostic information.

The student record card is an important feature of the game. The cards help the teacher to judge when the difficulty of the task card should be altered and which players should play together in a game, and to designate student leaders for succeeding games. The card also provides the player with a record that shows his scores and motivates him to improve.

This evaluative feature can be built into most games by using an individual record card, by having the student leader pile cards yielding right answers in one pile and cards with wrong answers in another pile, or by having the student leader record the results of each play on a class record sheet.

A CHECKLIST FOR MAKING PRELIMINARY JUDGMENTS ABOUT THE ADEQUACY OF AN INSTRUCTIONAL SYSTEM

For designing learning environments, a checklist should be useful as a first-level tool for judging the adequacy of the planned instructional system.

INSTRUCTIONAL SYSTEM CHECKLIST	*Yes*	*No*
1. Have you selected instructional objectives that are in agreement with your students' records of previous achievement?	___	___
2. Have you sequenced the objectives in conformance with carefully developed learning hierarchies, such as those provided in this book?	___	___

	Yes	No

3. Do the learning experiences you have planned provide for concrete, semiconcrete, and symbolic activities appropriate to your students' prior learning history and their developmental stages? ____ ____

4. Does each instructional activity provide students with feedback about the correctness of their performances? ____ ____

5. Will the learning experiences you have organized appeal to your students' expressed and diagnosed needs and interests? ____ ____

6. Have you provided follow-up activities that will permit your students to practice the skills or review the concepts they have learned? ____ ____

7. Have you checked to see that the instructional activities use a reading vocabulary within the range of your students' independent reading levels? ____ ____

8. Do the records you or your students keep relative to their learning histories provide an adequate basis for evaluation and prescription? ____ ____

9. Have you made provision to find out whether the students enjoy the learning activities you have provided? ____ ____

10. Have you planned how to observe the way in which students follow the rules and guidelines for behavior in the classroom or mathematics laboratory? ____ ____

A PERSPECTIVE ABOUT TEACHING

In the remaining chapters an effort is made to translate the ideas which have been presented in these first chapters into precise and coherent strategies for teaching those mathematical concepts which are common to most elementary school mathematics programs. Before embarking upon this adventure, however, it may be fruitful to mention the pedagogical foundations of our course of study; to consider them from a comprehensive perspective.

Perhaps the most important idea to recognize is that the pedagogical platform we have built constitutes an *eclectic* approach; it was our intent to try to meld ideas from the *developmental, humanistic,* and *behavioristic* movements into a sound and consistent structure which has pragmatic import for teaching. We feel there must be good in all of these philosophical positions, and so you will observe the influence of all of them as you examine the arguments and positions we have taken.

A NOTE ABOUT THE DESIGN OF THE REMAINING CHAPTERS

As indicated in the previous section, the remaining chapters are intended to provide specific suggestions for teaching particular mathematical concepts.

The approaches that are employed are consistent with the considerations and ideas expressed in Chapters 1 and 2. Cognitive stages of development are taken into account where appropriate; great emphasis is placed on the development of learning hierarchies which are translated into what the authors refer to as *flowcharts for teaching;* the laboratory approach is treated extensively in every chapter as are the uses of games and activities as important strategies for promoting child involvement in the learning process. As you study the following chapters, therefore, you should look back and reflect upon our instructional principles to see how they may be interpreted as *directives for practice.*

You will observe that each chapter is set up in two parts, the first dealing with *theory* and the second dealing with specific ideas for classroom *learning activities* (practice) which have particular relevance to the topics under consideration. In the theory sections, there is a brief summary of the essence of the mathematical ideas to be taught, together with an analysis of their logical prerequisites. These analyses set forth fundamental learning hierarchies which, as mentioned earlier, take the form of flowcharts for teaching. These flowcharts are intended to aid the teacher in conceptualizing the interrelationships of large blocks of the curriculum, and hence serve as a basis for diagnostic/prescriptive teaching. The theory sections also include analyses of methods for teaching specific mathematical concepts.

The sample activities are organized according to the content and sequence notions presented in the theory sections. The sample activities are organized so that a teacher can choose appropriate activities to teach particular mathematical ideas; the mathematical content to be learned can be related to what the children already know and to their perceptions of how these concepts are embodied in real-life situations. The developmental nature of learning mathematics is stressed; furthermore we have attempted to show how mathematics content should be taught through active child involvement in meaningful concrete, semiconcrete and abstract activities. Both teacher-directed and student-directed activities are provided.

Each instructional activity is described in terms of the materials to be used and the type of activity in which the students should be engaged. Consequently for those teachers who are so inclined, performance or behavioral objectives can be quickly formulated. The titles for the activities were derived by identifying the concept to be taught and the instructional materials and/or manipulatives to be used by the students. This should help the teacher begin the construction of an activity file organized around mathematical topics and associated teaching materials.

Exercise set

1. Explain why a child's stage of cognitive development is a factor which should be taken into account in teaching. Include in your discussion some reference to how stages of cognitive development figure in the formulation of specific instructional objectives.

2. Describe the rationale for employing the laboratory approach for teaching mathematical concepts in the elementary grades.

3. List as many reasons as you can why a teacher should try to relate the learning of mathematical concepts to the physical world of the child.

4. The notion of *perceptual variation* suggests that a child is apt to acquire a much more comprehensive and powerful grasp of a concept under conditions where the child has seen and experienced the concept represented in many ways. Describe how this idea relates to Principle 4.

5. Some learning theorists argue that most learning failures can be explained by the learning hierarchy phenomenon. This idea was taken into account by Principle 5. Discuss this issue in the light of your own personal experience in studying/learning mathematics.

6. In Chapter 1, it was reported that the Advisory Committee of the School Mathematics Study Group has suggested that ". . . statements of objectives should be taken as floors, not ceilings. If a teacher or a school can go beyond stated objectives, so much the better." Discuss the relationships among this idea, the statement of Principle 7, and the use of so-called "discovery" teaching strategies.

7. Most teachers embrace the idea of "learning by doing." How does this notion relate to Principle 10?

8. Principle 8 suggests that teachers should design learning environments for children which are responsive and adaptive. Discuss these requirements in light of your own knowledge of classroom learning environments. Are these requirements difficult to fulfill?

9. Several of the instructional principles which have been stated have direct implications for Principle 9. Trace as many of these connections as you can.

10. In what ways and for what purposes do you think that games can be employed as a useful strategy in teaching mathematics?

11. Describe the function and importance of drill and practice in a contemporary elementary school mathematics program.

12. Discuss the practice of diagnostic/prescriptive teaching in terms of the twelve instructional principles which have been stated.

READINGS FOR ADDITIONAL STUDY

For each of the following topics, read one of the articles listed in the bibliography and write a one- or two-page reaction report which consists of (1) a brief *summary* of the article, and (2) your *reaction* to the positions which have been taken.

13. Laboratory approach
14. Discovery teaching/learning
15. Verbal problem solving
16. Games/activities
17. Reading level
18. Retention of learning
19. Modes of representation of concepts (concrete, semiconcrete, abstract)
20. Interest/motivation
21. Stages of cognitive development à la Piaget
22. Learning hierarchies (e.g., see reference [26])
23. Teaching students with special education needs

Bibliography

1. Adler, Irving. "Mental growth and the art of teaching." *The Arithmetic Teacher* **13** (November 1966): 576–84.

2. Alexander, Vincent E. "The relationship of selected factors to the ability to solve problems in arithmetic." *Dissertation Abstracts* **202:221.**

3. Atta, Frank V. "Calculators in the classroom." *The Arithmetic Teacher* **14** (December 1967): 650–51.

4. Atta, Frank V. "Doubt in discovery teaching." *The Arithmetic Teacher* **15** (April 1968): 343–380.

5. Barney, Leroy. "Problems associated with the reading of arithmetic." *The Arithmetic Teacher* **19** (February 1972): 131–33.

6. Barson, Alan. "The mathematics laboratory for the elementary and middle school." *The Arithmetic Teacher* **18** (December 1971): 565–67.

7. Beuthel, Donald G. and Phyllis I. Meyer. "A regular classroom plus a mathematics laboratory." *The Arithmetic Teacher* **19** (November 1972): 527–30.

8. Biggs, Edith E. "Mathematics laboratories and teachers centres—the mathematics revolution in Britain." *The Arithmetic Teacher* **15** (May 1968): 400–408.

9. Biggs, Edith E., and Maurice L. Hartung. "The role of experience in the learning of mathematics?" *The Arithmetic Teacher* **18** (May 1971): 278–95.

10. Bitter, Gary G., and Jerald L. Mikesell. "Materials, competence, and confidence: products of a district mathematics laboratory." *The Arithmetic Teacher* **22** (February 1975): 114–16.

11. Bruni, James V., and Helene Silverman. "Making and using attribute materials." *The Arithmetic Teacher* **22** (February 1975): 88–95.

12. Bruni, James V., and Helene Silverman. "Making and using board games." *The Arithmetic Teacher* **22** (March 1975): 172–79.

13. Chandler, Arnold M. "Mathematics and low achiever." *The Arithmetic Teacher* **17** (March 1970): 196–98.

14. Clark, John R. "The informal-intuitive versus the formal-deductive approach to learning." *The Arithmetic Teacher* **12** (January 1965): 99.

15. Cohen, Louis S., and David C. Johnson. "Some thoughts about problem solving." *The Arithmetic Teacher* **14** (April 1967): 261–62.

16. Cohen, Louis S. "Open sentences—the most useful tool in problem solving." *The Arithmetic Teacher* **14** (April 1967): 263–67.

17. Coltharp, Forrest L. "Mathematical aspects of the attribute games." *The Arithmetic Teacher* **21** (March 1974): 246–51.

18. Corle, Clyde G. "In answer to your questions—Why do children have difficulty with verbal problems?" *The Arithmetic Teacher* **12** (January 1965): 13, 18, 23.

19. Crouse, Richard, and Elizabeth Rinehart. "Creative drill with pictures." *The Arithmetic Teacher* **20** (April 1973): 300–302.

20. Davidson, Patricia S., and Arlene W. Fair. "A mathematics laboratory—from dream to reality." *The Arithmetic Teacher* **17** (February 1970): 105–10.

21. Deans, Edwina. "Games for the early grades." *The Arithmetic Teacher* **13** (February 1966): 140–41.

22. Eisenberg, Theodore A., and John G. Beynen. "Mathematics through visual problems." *The Arithmetic Teacher* **20** (February 1973): 85–90.

23. Ewbank, William A. "The mathematics laboratory: what? why? when? how?" *The Arithmetic Teacher* **18** (December 1971): 559–64.

24. Englehardt, Max D. "The relative contributions of certain factors to individual differences in problem-solving ability. *Journal of Experimental Education* **1** (September 1932): 19–27.

25. Fennema, Elizabeth. "Manipulatives in the classroom." *The Arithmetic Teacher* **20** (May 1973): 350–52.

26. Gagne, Robert M. "Learning and proficiency in mathematics." *The Mathematics Teacher* **56** (December 1963): 620–26.

27. Galton, Grace K. "Individualized instruction: speaking from reality." *The Arithmetic Teacher* **19** (January 1972): 23–25.

28. Gessel, Robert C., Carolyn Johnson, Marty Boren, and Charles Smith. "Rainy-day games." *The Arithmetic Teacher* **19** (April 1972): 303–305.

29. Gibb, E. G. "Through the years: individualizing instruction in mathematics." *The Arithmetic Teacher* 17 (May 1970): 396–402.

30. Gibb, E. G., and Alberta M. Castaneda. "Experiences for young children." *Mathematics Learning in Early Childhood.* NCTM, 1975.

31. Golden, Sarah R. "Fostering enthusiasm through child-created games." *The Arithmetic Teacher* 17 (February 1970): 111–15.

32. Gorman, Charles J. "A critical analysis of research on written problems in elementary school mathematics." *Dissertation Abstract* 28:4818A–19A; No. 12, 1968.

33. Green, Roberta. "A color-coded method of teaching basic arithmetic concepts and procedures." *The Arithmetic Teacher* 17 (March 1970): 231–33.

34. Hampton, Homer F. "The concentration game." *The Arithmetic Teacher* 19 (January 1972): 65–67.

35. Hater, Mary Ann, Robert B. Kane, and Mary Ann Byrne. "Building reading skills in the mathematics class." *The Arithmetic Teacher* 21 (December 1974): 662–68.

36. Hawthorne, Frank S. "Hand-held calculators: help or hindrance?" *The Arithmetic Teacher* 20 (December 1973): 671–72.

37. Henderson, Kenneth B., and James H. Rollins. "A comparison of three stratagems for teaching mathematical concepts and generalizations by guided discovery." *The Arithmetic Teacher* 14 (November 1967): 583–88.

38. Henney, Maribeth. "Improving mathematics verbal problem-solving ability through reading instruction." *The Arithmetic Teacher* 18 (April 1971): 223.

39. Hess, Adrien L. "Discovering discovery." *The Arithmetic Teacher* 15 (April 1968): 324–27.

40. Hess, Marvel. "Second-grade children solve problems." *The Arithmetic Teacher* 13 (April 1966): 317–18.

41. Homan, Doris R. "The child with a learning disability in arithmetic." *The Arithmetic Teacher* 17 (March 1970): 199–203.

42. Immerzeel, George, and Don Wiederanders. "Ideas: Student-oriented problem-solving experiences." *The Arithmetic Teacher* 20 (December 1973): 663–70.

43. Immerzeel, George, and Don Wiederanders. "Ideas: Experiences in problem solving." *The Arithmetic Teacher* 21 (March 1974): 209–16.

44. Jacobs, Israel. "If the hands can do it the head can follow." *The Arithmetic Teacher* 19 (November 1972): 571–77.

45. Jencks, Stanley M., and Donald M. Peck. "Symbolism and the world of objects." *The Arithmetic Teacher* 22 (May 1975): 370–71.

46. Jones, Phillip S. "Discovery teaching—from Socrates to modernity." *The Arithmetic Teacher* 17 (October 1970): 503–10.

47. Kaplan, Jerome D. "An example of a mathematics instructional program for disadvantaged children." *The Arithmetic Teacher* 17 (April 1970): 332–34.

48. Kerr, Donald R., Jr. "Mathematics games in the classroom." *The Arithmetic Teacher* **21** (March 1974): 172–75.

49. Kersh, Bert Y. "Learning by discovery: instructional strategies." *The Arithmetic Teacher* **12** (October 1965): 414–17.

50. Kevra, Barbara, Rita Brey, and Barbara Schimmel. "Success for slower learners, or Rx: relax . . . and play." *The Arithmetic Teacher* **19** (May 1972): 335–43.

51. Kopp, Audrey, and Robert Hamada. "Fun can be mathematics." *The Arithmetic Teacher* **16** (November 1969): 575–77.

52. Lankford, Francis G. "What can a teacher learn about a pupil's thinking through oral interview?" *The Arithmetic Teacher* **21** (January 1974): 26–32.

53. Liedtke, W., and L. D. Nelson. "Activities in mathematics for preschool children." *The Arithmetic Teacher* **20** (November 1973): 536–41.

54. Liedtke, W. "Experiences with blocks in kindergarten." *The Arithmetic Teacher* **22** (May 1975): 406–12.

55. Lundberg, Kristina. "Kindergarten mathematics laboratory—nineteenth-century fashion." *The Arithmetic Teacher* **17** (May 1970): 372–86.

56. Lyda, W. J., and Frances M. Duncan. "Quantitative vocabulary and problem solving." *The Arithmetic Teacher* **14** (April 1967): 289–91.

57. Maroun, Sister M., S.S.J. "Discover and learn." *The Arithmetic Teacher* **14** (December 1967): 677–78.

58. Masse, Marie. "Drill some fun into your mathematics class." *The Arithmetic Teacher* **21** (May 1974): 422–24.

59. Mathison, Sally. "Solving story problems and liking it." *The Arithmetic Teacher* **16** (November 1969): 577–79.

60. Matthews, Geoffrey, and Julia Comber. "Mathematics laboratories." *The Arithmetic Teacher* **18** (December 1971): 547–50.

61. May, Lola. "Individualized instruction in a learning laboratory setting." *The Arithmetic Teacher* **13** (February 1966): 110–12.

62. Orans, Sylvia. "Go shopping! Problem-Solving activities for the primary grades with provisions for individualization." *The Arithmetic Teacher* **17** (November 1970): 621–23.

63. Patterson, W. H., Jr. "Making drill more interesting." *The Arithmetic Teacher* **21** (February 1974): 126–28.

64. Post, Thomas R. "A model for the construction and sequencing of laboratory activities." *The Arithmetic Teacher* **21** (November 1974): 617–22.

65. Pottenger, Mary Jo, and Leonard Leth. "Problem solving." *The Arithmetic Teacher* **16** (January 1969): 21–24.

66. Ranucci, Ernest R. "Discovery in mathematics." *The Arithmetic Teacher* **12** (January 1965): 14–18.

67. Richardson, Lloyd I. "The role of strategies for teaching pupils to solve verbal problems." *The Arithmetic Teacher* **22** (May 1975): 414–21.

68. Riedesel, C. A. "Problem solving: Some suggestions from research." *The Arithmetic Teacher* **16** (January 1969): 54–58.

69. Rupkey, J. B. "Inductive teaching vs. deductive teaching." *The Arithmetic Teacher* **13** (March 1966): 218–20.

70. Salzer, Richard T. "Discovering what 'discovery' means." *The Arithmetic Teacher* **13** (December 1966): 656–57.

71. Schaefer, Anne W., and Albert H. Mauthe. "Problem solving with enthusiasm— the mathematics laboratory." *The Arithmetic Teacher* **17** (January 1970): 7–14.

72. Schnell, Jacqueline H., and Lane K. Klein. "Development of a mathematics laboratory." *The Arithmetic Teacher* **21** (October 1974): 492–96.

73. Shuster, A. H., and Fred L. Pigge. "Retention efficiency of meaningful teaching." *The Arithmetic Teacher* **12** (January 1965): 24–31.

74. Smith, Lewis B. "A discovery lesson in elementary mathematics." *The Arithmetic Teacher* **18** (February 1971): 73–76.

75. Smith, Rosalind B. "Teaching mathematics to children through cooking." *The Arithmetic Teacher* **21** (October 1974): 480–84.

76. Steffe, Leslie P. "The relationship of conservation of numerousness to problem-solving abilities of first-grade children." *The Arithmetic Teacher* **15** (January 1968): 47–52.

77. Swadener, Marc. " 'Activity board'—the board of many uses." *The Arithmetic Teacher* **19** (February 1972): 141–44.

78. Taylor, George R., and Susan T. Watkins. "Active games: an approach to teaching mathematical skills to the educable mentally retarded." *The Arithmetic Teacher* **21** (December 1974): 674–78.

79. Trafton, Paul R. "Individualized instruction: Developing broadened perspectives." *The Arithmetic Teacher* **19** (January 1972): 7–12.

80. Troutman, Andria P. "Strategies for teaching elementary school mathematics." *The Arithmetic Teacher* **20** (October 1973): 425–36.

81. Trueblood, Cecil R. "Promoting problem-solving skills through nonverbal problems." *The Arithmetic Teacher* **16** (January 1969): 7–9.

82. Trueblood, Cecil R. "A model for using diagnosis in individualizing mathematics instruction in the elementary school classroom." *The Arithmetic Teacher* **18** (November 1971): 505–11.

83. Trueblood, Cecil R., and Michael Szabo. "Procedures for designing your own metric games for pupil involvement." *The Arithmetic Teacher* **21** (May 1974): 404–408.

84. Vance, James H., and Thomas E. Kieren. "Laboratory settings in mathematics: What does research say to the teacher?" *The Arithmetic Teacher* **18** (December 1971): 585–89.

85. Weaver, J., F. "Applications and problem solving." *The Arithmetic Teacher* **12** (October 1965): 412–13.

86. West, Tommie A. "Diagnosing pupil errors: looking for patterns." *The Arithmetic Teacher* **18** (November 1971): 467–69.

87. White, Philip, Bonnie Brownstein, and Victor Wagner. "Initiating task card activities with teachers." *The Arithmetic Teacher* **22** (April 1975): 274–76.

88. Wilderman, Ann M., and Stephen Krulik. "On beyond the mathematics laboratory." *The Arithmetic Teacher* **20** (November 1973): 543–44.

89. Wilkinson, Jack D. "Teacher-directed evaluation of mathematics laboratories." *The Arithmetic Teacher* **21** (January 1974): 19–24.

90. Wilson, John W. "The role of structure in verbal problem solving." *The Arithmetic Teacher* **14** (October 1967): 486–97.

91. Young, Carolyn. "Team learning." *The Arithmetic Teacher* **19** (December 1972): 630–34.

92. Zweng, Marilyn J. "A reaction to 'the role of structure in verbal problem solving'." *The Arithmetic Teacher* **15** (March 1968): 251–53.

Teaching the basic concepts of number and numeration

Synopsis and objectives

Chapter 3 gives you a comprehensive framework for teaching the basic concepts of *number* and *numeration*. The chapter is organized in two sections, one dealing with **theory** and the other with **practice**. The theory section is organized around a flowchart which shows the order in which the important concepts should be taught as well as the key developmental factors that need to be taken into account as conditions for learning. The practice section contains various ideas for classroom activities that are keyed to the concepts discussed in the theory section.

In your study of Chapter 3, you may want to use the bibliography and explore the ideas and activities in greater detail. A careful study of Chapter 3 should enable you to

1. use sets of objects to illustrate the meaning of the terms *one-to-one (1–1) correspondence, equivalent sets,* and *nonequivalent sets;*

2. use sets of objects to illustrate the meaning of the idea of (cardinal) number;

3. use sets of objects to demonstrate the meaning of *greater than* and *less than,* with reference to the cardinal numbers;

4. explain and demonstrate the foundations of the procedure of counting;

5. develop and illustrate meaningful interpretations of the *empty* set;

6. use concrete teaching/learning aids such as an abacus or multibase blocks to demonstrate place value systems of numeration;

7. demonstrate how to use concrete teaching/learning aids to translate nondecimal numerals to decimal numerals, and conversely;

8. explain the necessity for a child to be a number conserver as a condition for the study of number ideas;

9. demonstrate how to use concrete teaching/learning aids to extend the cardinal number system to the system of integers;

10. develop games/activities for child involvement which will assist them in attaining specific number/numeration concepts.

Teaching the basic concepts of number and numeration

Theory

THE CARDINAL NUMBERS, 0–9

A flowchart for teaching the basic ideas about cardinal numbers is given in Fig. 3.1.

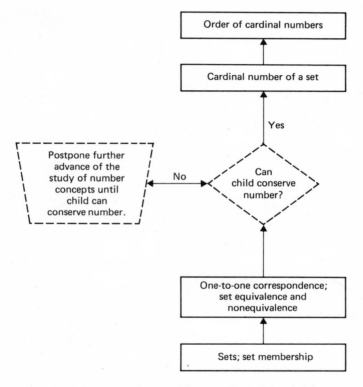

Fig. 3.1 A flowchart for teaching the basic ideas about cardinal numbers.

As suggested by the flowchart, the notion of a cardinal (whole) number is constructed upon very basic ideas about sets. For most children, the fundamental notion of set and set membership are quite natural, being a part of their everyday world. Most children are accustomed to such expressions as "a set of dishes," "a set of checkers," and so on, and they are able to make elementary determinations of set membership. Nevertheless, because of the importance of these ideas in the development of the idea of cardinal number, the teacher should take steps to guarantee that each child has a good grasp of the notions of set and set membership.

The next concepts that the child should acquire deal with being able to determine whether the elements of two sets can be placed in a *one-to-one correspondence*. If they can, the two sets are said to be *matching*, or *equivalent*, sets. Otherwise, they are nonmatching, or nonequivalent sets. The fundamental ideas may be illustrated in the following way.

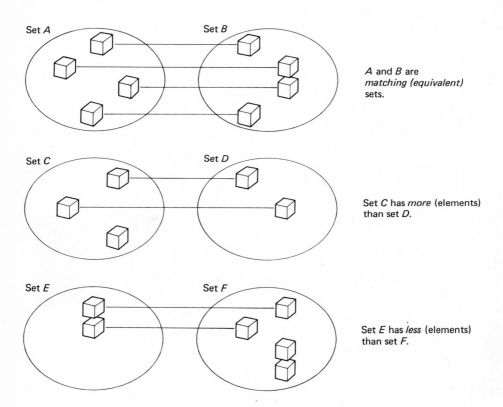

A and *B* are matching (equivalent) sets.

Set *C* has *more* (elements) than set *D*.

Set *E* has *less* (elements) than set *F*.

To be more specific, you want the child to learn how to determine whether a given set has *more, less,* or as many elements as another set. The point is that the "more than," "less than," and "as many as" relations are *prenumber* ideas, and should be treated accordingly.

At this stage of teaching you also should examine whether the child can conserve number. In order to make such a determination, Piaget has developed a procedure in which two equivalent sets of objects are displayed in a pattern like that shown at the top of the next page. The child is then asked to tell if each set has as many elements as the other.

If it is agreed this is so, the elements in one of the sets are spread apart, as shown below, and the child again is asked if each of the sets has as many elements as the other.

If the child responds that one of the sets now has more, or less, than the other, the child is not a number conserver in the Piagetian sense. What this means is that the child is not able to perceive the "more than," "less than," and "as many as" relations as stable, invariant quantities, and thus he or she is

This teacher checks to see if the child can conserve number.

not ready to learn about numbers. The flowchart given in Fig. 3.1 takes this consideration into account. The flowchart also suggests that if the child is a number conserver, then presumably the child is ready to learn about the concept of cardinal number.

Basically, the cardinal number idea is an idea associated with sets. Every set has a number property, and two sets have the same number property if and only if they are equivalent. Consider, for example, the set shown here.

We say this set has the number property 1. Every set that is equivalent to it also has the number property 1.

In the following diagram, sample sets having the number properties 0–9 are displayed. For instance, the set of apples, and every set which is equivalent to it, has the number property 4. Note that the chart also reveals the fact that 2 is one more than 1, 3 is one more than 2, and so on. Finally, observe that 0 is the number property of the *empty* set.

0	
1	▢
2	◐ ◐
3·	⌇ ⌇ ⌇
4	🍎 🍎 🍎 🍎
5	人 人 人 人 人
6	⌂ ⌂ ⌂ ⌂ ⌂ ⌂
7	◉ ◉ ◉ ◉ ◉ ◉ ◉
8	🌲 🌲 🌲 🌲 🌲 🌲 🌲 🌲
9	★ ★ ★ ★ ★ ★ ★ ★ ★

These observations form the basis for teaching the preliminary ideas about the "less than" and "greater than" number relations. The general line of reasoning can be illustrated in the following way.

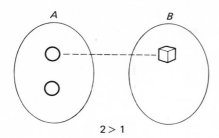

Since set A has more elements than set B, 2 is greater than 1.

$2 > 1$

By designing teaching strategies along these lines, the child should learn all the basic order relationships:

$$0 < 1 < 2 < \cdots < 8 < 9$$

or equivalently that

$$9 > 8 > \cdots > 1 > 0.$$

THE CONCEPT OF COUNTING

As many primary-level teachers know, it is not unusual for children to begin their schooling with some very rudimentary behaviors associated with counting. Often these counting behaviors are simply a manifestation of the rote learning of a set of number names. One typical example of this is where a child attempts to count the members of some set, and recites the number names in an improper order (one, two, four, seven, five, . . .).

Another example is where the child recites the number names in the correct order, but does not construct a one-to-one match-up between the objects being counted and the number names being recited. Here the result is that the number reported is most likely incorrect.

As suggested by the previous example, the process of counting rests heavily upon the concept of 1–1 correspondence; to illustrate, we have the following example.

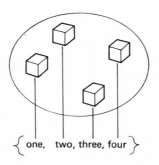

$\{$ one,   two, three, four $\}$

Observe that each of the number names is associated with one and only one of the elements of the set to be counted. Observe also that the number property of the set {one, two, three, four} is 4. That is

$$n \text{ \{one, two, three, } four\text{\}} = 4.\text{*}$$

Thus, since the set of objects to be counted and the set of number names are equivalent, and since the number property of the set of number names is 4, it follows that the number property of the set of objects is also 4. This idea is generalizable, of course, and forms the basis for the process of meaningful counting.

PLACE VALUE AND THE DECIMAL SYSTEM OF NUMERATION

The decimal system of numeration is a *place value* system based on the *powers of ten.* The scheme is illustrated below.

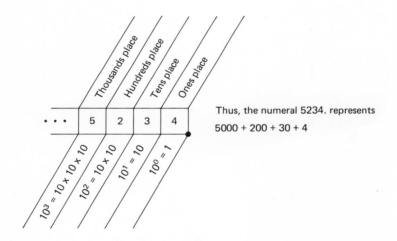

Thus, the numeral 5234. represents

5000 + 200 + 30 + 4

Therefore, in order for the child to advance beyond a working knowledge of the whole numbers 0–9, the basic notions of place value must be learned.

To expand the number system to include numbers greater than 9, the teacher should devise activities where the children are given a set of ten or more objects and are asked to write the numeral which tells how many objects are in the set. A sample problem might be constructed as follows.

---

* The notation n {   }, where a lower case "n" is written in front of a set which has been represented in roster form, is customarily used to denote the number property of the set.

Problem

Here is a set of rods. Write the numeral which tells how many rods are in the set.

Solution

You can make one set of ten rods, and there are two more. So there are 12 rods in the set.

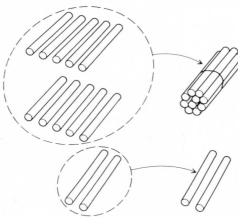

The opposite task which consists of displaying a numeral and asking the child to build a set with the specified number of elements is also valuable in helping the child develop his or her understanding of the decimal system of numeration. There are other devices and aids which have special virtue in this respect, namely, the *abacus, multibase blocks,* and *Cuisenaire rods.* Here are examples of how they can be used.

Abacus

Sample task: What number is shown on the abacus?

Sample task:
Show the number 42 on the abacus.

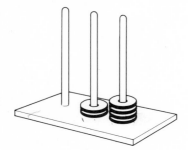

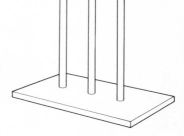

Multibase blocks

Sample task: What number is shown by the blocks?

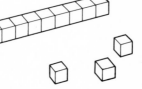

Sample task: Use the blocks to show the number 46.

Cuisenaire rods

Sample task: What number is shown by the Cuisenaire rods?

Sample task: Use the Cuisenaire rods to show the number 12.

Activities like this can help the child learn the basic ideas about order of the cardinal numbers.

NONDECIMAL SYSTEMS OF NUMERATION

The decimal system of numeration is now used throughout the world, but it is generally acknowledged that the use of ten as a base is attributable to the fact that human beings have ten fingers. Indeed, had human beings developed with four fingers on each hand, it is probable that we would have a base eight numeration system.

In any event, it has become fairly popular to include some study of nondecimal systems of numeration in contemporary elementary school mathematics programs. The reasons cited are that a study of nondecimal systems should (1) help the child develop a better understanding of the principle of place value and its role in the design of the decimal system; (2) explode the myth that ten is the "best" base for a system of numeration; and (3) provide the child with the intellectual grounding necessary to understand the binary system and its role in the design and operation of computers. As you should note, nondecimal systems are constructed in the same manner as the decimal system; the only basic difference is in the choice of a base number. For example, consider the place value schemes for base two and base five.

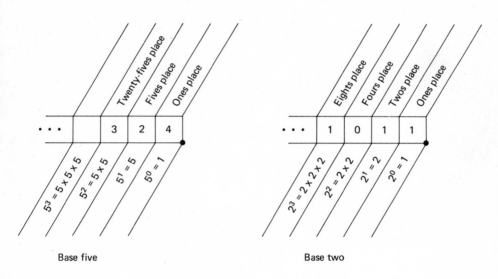

Base five   Base two

So, for example,

$$324_{\text{five}} = 3 \times 5^2 + 2 \times 5^1 + 4 \times 5^0$$
$$= 3 \times 25 + 2 \times 5 + 4 \times 1$$
$$= \quad 75 \quad + \quad 10 \quad + \quad 4$$
$$= 89_{\text{ten}}$$

Similarly,

$$1011_{\text{two}} = 1 \times 2^3 + 0 \times 2^2 + 1 \times 2^1 + 1 \times 2^0$$
$$= 1 \times 8 + 0 \times 4 + 1 \times 2 + 1 \times 1$$
$$= \quad 8 \quad + \quad 0 \quad + \quad 2 \quad + \quad 1$$
$$= 11_{\text{ten}}$$

Both the abacus and multibase blocks, mentioned earlier as useful devices for teaching the basic concepts about the decimal system of numeration, are constructive aids for learning about nondecimal systems of numeration.

In the case of the abacus, all that is necessary to make it useful as a teaching aid is to relabel the place values of the various positions on the abacus. For example, 213_{five} would be shown on an abacus in the following way.

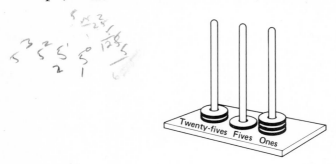

Multibase blocks are perhaps even more helpful as a learning aid, as shown by the example below which illustrates the block representation of 24_{five}.

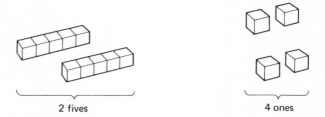

2 fives   4 ones

Observe that such a representation is easily convertible to base ten. That is,

$$24_{\text{five}} = 14_{\text{ten}}$$

THE SYSTEM OF INTEGERS

In real life we many times have a need for *negative numbers*. With this in mind many elementary school programs include learning objectives involving their interpretations and uses.

The *number line* can be used to good advantage as an aid in extending the set of cardinal numbers, $\{0, 1, 2, \ldots\}$, so as to form the set of *integers*,

$$\{\ldots, -3, -2, -1, 0, 1, 2, 3, \ldots\}.$$

One of the key ideas for the child to learn is that every integer is the *additive inverse* or *opposite* of exactly one integer. For example, $^{-}1$ and 1 are opposites in the sense that their sum is zero. Similarly, ⁻2 and 2 are opposites since ⁻2 + 2 = 0, and so on. Note also that zero is its own opposite.

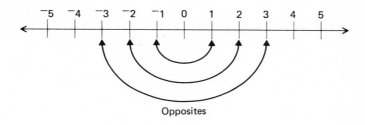

Opposites

Once the child understands negative numbers he is ready to add, subtract, multiply, and divide in cases where negative numbers are involved. These processes are taken up in the chapters which deal with the teaching of the fundamental operations.

Practice

In this section you will find ideas for classroom use which were designed for helping children learn the specific concepts and skills discussed in the preceding **theory** section. As you study and try out these activities in your classroom, keep in mind that they are merely samples of the types of learning experiences for children that you may find helpful. Feel free to modify them as conditions warrant. Also see if you can use some of them as models for the design of other activities for learning.

ACTIVITIES FOR STUDENT INVOLVEMENT: SETS; SET MEMBERSHIP

As suggested by the flowchart given in Fig. 3.1, the concept of number grows out of the ability to deal with the notions of set and set membership. The child must be able to classify objects into sets and come to understand the set inclusion relation. You can help children develop this ability by asking them to sort objects on the basis of *size, color, shape,* and other physical characteristics. The following activities are presented with such thoughts in mind.

Sample activity 1 (Beads and string)
Supply each student with a tray of various colored beads that differ in size and pieces of string of various lengths. Have the students do the following activities:

1. String beads by color groups and identify sets and subsets.
2. String beads by size groups and identify sets and subsets.
3. Make sets from a listing of characteristics of set membership (e.g., large, red beads).

Sample activity 2 (Dot cards)

Make sets of flash cards like the ones below using 3″ x 5″ cards and colored pen-cils. Then have the children describe the sets (and their subsets) that are shown on the cards.

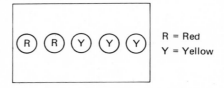

R = Red
Y = Yellow

Sample activity 3 (Cuisenaire rods)

Provide each student with a box of Cuisenaire rods. Have the students group the rods into sets by color or length.

SET EQUIVALENCE AND NONEQUIVALENCE

If you employ activities in your classroom like those described below, you will provide chidren with an opportunity to sharpen their concepts of the "more than," "less than," and "as many as" relations, and at the same time help them develop the vocabulary associated with these ideas.

Sample activity 1 (Open-ended abacus)

Provide the children with an abacus like the one below and a tray of colored beads. Have them do the following activities:

1. String more beads beside the (teacher's) sample.
2. String as many yellow beads as your partner has green beads.
3. String less beads beside the (teacher's) sample.

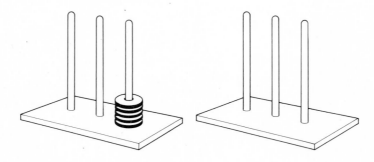

Sample activity 2 (Flash cards)

Make a set of flash cards like the one shown below. Have the student compare the sets on each card and describe which relationship holds: first set is *equivalent* to second set; first set has *more than* second set; first set has *less than* second set.

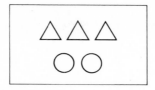

Encourage students to draw copies of the sets and set up 1–1 correspondences to determine their answers.

ACTIVITIES FOR STUDENT INVOLVEMENT: CARDINAL NUMBERS 0–9

Students should have a variety of learning experiences involving the identification of the cardinal number property of a set as well as the converse task of constructing a set which has a specified number property. The following activities should give you some ideas about how to build such learning experiences.

Sample activity 1 (Team play)

Prepare two sets of cards, one corresponding to each of these samples.

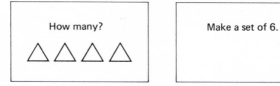

Mix the two sets of cards together and shuffle them well. Then form two teams of students and give each team half of the deck. Each member of each team takes a card from the team deck and tries to answer it. Each correct answer gives the team one point. The team with the most points at the end of play wins.

Sample activity 2 (Card puzzle)

Make matching puzzle cards for the numbers 0–9 by using 3″ × 5″ cards like the one shown here.

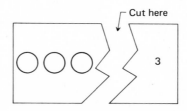

Organize the students into small groups and mix the puzzle pieces. Then have the students match the cards correctly and put the puzzles in numerical order as shown below.

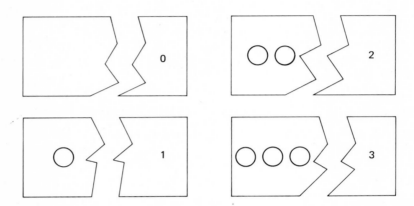

ACTIVITIES FOR STUDENT INVOLVEMENT: COUNTING

The focus of counting activities is to assure the development of *rational* counters, so you should take care to put counting activities in meaningful settings. This is particularly important in instances where the child is a *rote* counter.

Sample activity 1 (Songs)

Many songs can be used or adapted to teach counting, songs that range from jumprope chants that children create themselves to well-known songs. Among the latter are "This Old Man . . ." and "Inchworm."

Sample activity 2 (Bulletin boards)

Students need practical experiences which show why they need to know how to count. A calendar on the bulletin board like the one here requires the student to put up numbered tags for each day of the month. The teacher can ask students to refer to the board by questions like:

1. How many days have passed since Joe's birthday?
2. How many days are there until Thanksgiving vacation?

Sun.	Mon.	Tues.	Wed.	Thurs.	Fri.	Sat.
		1	2	3	4	5

NOVEMBER

ACTIVITIES FOR STUDENT INVOLVEMENT:
PLACE VALUE AND THE DECIMAL NUMERATION SYSTEM

The initial activities you choose to help children learn place value concepts should make use of concrete learning aids such as those described in the theory section with an abacus, blocks, or Cuisenaire rods. Afterwards you can move on to the use of semiconcrete and abstract exercises. The key idea to teach students is that the place in which a digit is written (or shown) determines whether it represents ones, tens, hundreds, and so on. This is a prerequisite for the study of operations with whole numbers.

Sample activity 1 (Pocket chart)
Make a pocket chart and paper strips like the ones below. Then provide the class with examples using the pocket chart and have them write the correct numeral.

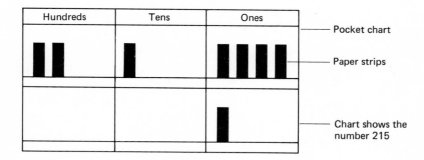

As a preliminary activity, the students may be asked to write expanded numerals for the examples. In the case of the given example, for instance, the students would construct the expanded numeral

$$200 + 10 + 5.$$

Sample activity 2 (Number tables)
Prepare number tables like the one below. Then have the students perform tasks like the following:

1. Compare the digits in the one's place in each column. How do they differ?

2. Find the largest two-place numeral.

3. Find the number that is one less than 50.

1	2	3	4	5	6	7	8	9	10
11	12	13	14	15	16	17	18	19	20
21	22	23	24	25	26	27	28	29	30
31	32	33	34	35	36	37	38	39	40
41	42	43	44	45	46	47	48	49	50
51	52	53	54	55	56	57	58	59	60
61	62	63	64	65	66	67	68	69	70
71	72	73	74	75	76	77	78	79	80
81	82	83	84	85	86	87	88	89	90
91	92	93	94	95	96	97	98	99	100

Sample activity 3 (Periods chart)

Provide students with a pocket chart like the one below. Write a numeral on the board, have students place its digits in the proper places in the pocket chart, and then have them read the numeral correctly. Emphasize the proper use of the period names.

Periods	4th			3rd			2nd			1st		
Names	Billions			Millions			Thousands			Ones		
Place names within periods	Hundreds	Tens	Ones	Hundreds	Tens	Ones	Hundreds	Tens	Ones	Hundreds	Tens	Ones
Numeral	2	4	3	7	3	4	3	1	4	6	0	1

ACTIVITIES FOR STUDENT INVOLVEMENT: NONDECIMAL NUMERATION SYSTEMS

As you examine the following ideas for activities aimed at helping children learn the basic concepts about nondecimal systems of numeration, remember that the abacus and multibase arithmetic blocks are also powerful teaching tools, and that activities involving their use are easy to construct.

Sample activity 1 (Tally marks)

Present students with a numeral in a nondecimal base such as 143 base five. Have them use tally marks to represent counting done in that base and the meaning of the place values.

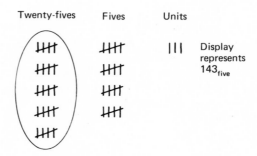

Sample activity 2 (Board display and Place value chart)

Construct a display using tally marks as shown in the following example. Have the students translate the display into the correct numeral.

Sixteens	Fours	Ones
$\vert\vert$	$\vert\vert\vert$	$\vert$

The desired numeral is 231_{four}.

Sample activity 3 (Dot drawings)

Have the students use dot drawings to convert from one base to another. See the following example.

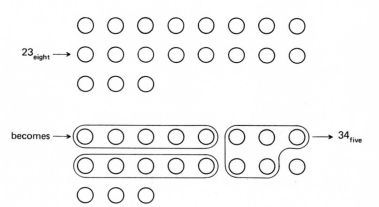

Sample activity 4 (Bulletin board calendar)

Make a bulletin board calendar for one month using some nondecimal base. See the base six example below. Then ask the students to make the displays for the remaining 11 months of the year. Ask them to use the calendars and write the dates for birthdays, holidays, and other important days. You can also ask them to find how many days come between certain specified dates.

June

S	M	T	W	T	F	S
1	2	3	4	5	10	11
12	13	14	15	20	21	22
23	24	25	30	31	32	33
34	35	40	41	42	43	44
45	50					

ACTIVITIES FOR CHILD INVOLVEMENT: THE INTEGERS

Sample activity 1 (Temperature comparisons)

The students can compare differences between extreme temperatures of various locations in the United States. This information can be secured from the yearly almanacs.

The students can also keep track of daily temperatures in their locality using a Celsius thermometer. Their readings can be compared with those provided on the daily weather reports on radio or TV.

Sample activity 2 (Elevation comparisons)

The students can compare the difference between locales which are above and below sea level. New Orleans and Death Valley, for example, are below sea level. Current undersea oceanographic projects also provide a source of data for such a study.

Exercise set

1. Describe how to construct a concrete approach for teaching the following concepts.
   a) Sets/sets membership.
   b) Set equivalence and nonequivalence—including the more than/fewer than relations.

2. Describe how to construct a concrete approach for teaching the following concepts.
   a) Number concepts, 1–9.
   b) Number zero.
   c) Greater than/less than number relations.

3. Describe a plan for teaching the number concepts, 10–18, which makes use of
   a) popsicle sticks,
   b) multibase blocks,
   c) an abacus.

4. Construct a plan for an activity designed to teach children how to write the numerals 0–9. The generally accepted patterns for writing these numerals are shown at the top of the next page.

5. Describe how a number line might be used to help children learn both (a) counting skills and (b) basic concepts of order.

```
    0   1   2   3   4   5   6   7
←───•───•───•───•───•───•───•───•───→
```

6. The positions of objects in a linear sequence may be specified by *ordinal* numbers; namely, *first, second, third,* and so on. Design a game or activity whose purpose is to help children learn the ordinal number concepts.

7. A "hundred chart" is constructed in the following way.

1	2	3	4	5	6	7	8	9	10
11	12	13	14	15	16	17	18	19	20
21	22	23	24	25	26	27	28	29	30
31	32	33	34	35	36	37	38	39	40
41	42	43	44	45	46	47	48	49	50
51	52	53	54	55	56	57	58	59	60
61	62	63	64	65	66	67	68	69	70
71	72	73	74	75	76	77	78	79	80
81	82	83	84	85	86	87	88	89	90
91	92	93	94	95	96	97	98	99	100

The hundred chart can be used to teach counting skills, concepts of place value, and many other ideas. Describe how it could be used to help children learn how to

a) count by tens,

b) learn the basic concepts of place value,

c) learn the number names from 10–100.

8. Describe how to use multibase blocks to teach children how to compare numbers that are larger than ten.

9. Prepare a list of examples that indicate where the idea of a set is used in everyday life.

10. How should sets be used to actively involve children in number relations?

11. Describe how our money system can be used to teach the meaning of the base ten place values.

12. What priority should be given to verbal problem-solving activities in the primary grades? Use the following to structure your answer—types of problem situations, use of pictures and orally presented problem situations, and the level of mathematical content.

13. Write a set of learning objectives for each of the following topics that may be suitable for most children at the primary level.

   a) Sets/set membership.
   b) Set equivalence/nonequivalence.
   c) Cardinal number concepts.
   d) Ordinal number concepts.
   e) Order (number comparison).
   f) Place value/decimal system of numeration.
   g) Counting.

READINGS FOR ADDITIONAL STUDY

For each of the following topics, read one of the articles listed in the bibliography and write a one- or two-page reaction report which consists of (1) a brief *summary* of the article, and (2) your *reaction* to the positions which have been taken.

14. Sets/set membership.
15. Set equivalence/nonequivalence.
16. Cardinal number concepts.
17. Ordinal number concepts.
18. Order (number comparison).
19. Place value/decimal system of numeration.
20. Counting.
21. The integers (signed numbers).

Bibliography

1. Ashlock, Robert B., and Tommie A. West. "Physical Representations for Signed-Number Operations." *The Arithmetic Teacher* **14** (November 1967): 549–53.

2. Enstrom, E. A. and Doris C. Enstrom. "Numerals still count." *The Arithmetic Teacher* **13** (February 1966): 131–34.

3. Blomgren, Gwen P. "What's in the box?—subsets!" *The Arithmetic Teacher* **17** (March 1970): 242.

4. Brace, Alec, and L. D. Nelson. "The preschool child's concept of number." *The Arithmetic Teacher* **12** (February 1965): 126–133.

5. Breithaupt, Keith A. "The key to Roman numerals." *The Arithmetic Teacher* **15** (April 1968): 374.

6. Bruni, James V., and Helene Silverman. "Developing the Concept of Grouping." *The Arithmetic Teacher* **21** (October 1974): 474–79.

7. Burns, Marilyn. "IDEAS." *The Arithmetic Teacher* **22** (October 1975): 477–84.

8. Calvo, Robert C. "Placo—a number-place game." *The Arithmetic Teacher* **15** (May 1968): 465–66.

9. Carman, Robert A., and Marilyn J. Carman. "Number Patterns." *The Arithmetic Teacher* **17** (October 1970): 637–39.

10. Cochran, Beryl S. "Children Use Signed Numbers." *The Arithmetic Teacher* **13** (November 1966): 587–88.

11. Cohen, Louis S. "A Rationale in Working With Signed Numbers." *The Arithmetic Teacher* **12** (November 1965): 563–67.

12. Coxfind, Arthur E. "Piaget, Number and Measurement." *The Arithmetic Teacher* **10** (November 1963): 419–27.

13. Cruikshank, Douglas C. "Sorting, Classifying, and Logic." *The Arithmetic Teacher* **21** (November 1974): 588–98.

14. Geddes, Dorothy, and Sally I. Lipsey. "Sets—natural, necessary, (k)nowable?" *The Arithmetic Teacher* **15** (April 1968): 337–40.

15. Goodrich, Merton T. "Concrete Interpretations of Directed Numbers." *School Science and Mathematics* **34** (June 1934): 623–35.

16. Hess, Adrien L. "A critical review of the Hindu-Arabic numeration system." *The Arithmetic Teacher* **17** (October 1970):493–97.

17. Hollis, Loye Y. "Multiplication of Integers." *The Arithmetic Teacher* **14** (November 1967): 555–56.

18. Jeffers, Verne G. "A New Look for the Hundreds Chart." *The Arithmetic Teacher* **21** (March 1974): 203–208.

19. Keller, Robert W. "A discovery approach with ancient numeration systems." *The Arithmetic Teacher* **19** (November 1972): 543–44.

20. Lerner, Norbert, and M. A. Sobel. "Sets and Elementary School Mathematics." *The Arithmetic Teacher* **5** (November 1958): 239–46.

21. Muente, Grace. "Where do I start teaching numerals?" *The Arithmetic Teacher* **14** (November 1967): 575–76.

22. Niman, John. "A game introduction to the binary numeration system." *The Arithmetic Teacher* **18** (December 1971): 600–601.

23. Payne, Joseph N., and Edward C. Rathmell. "Number and numeration." *Mathematics Learning in Early Childhood*, NCTM, 1975.

24. Peterson, Wayne. "Numeration—a fresh look." *The Arithmetic Teacher* **12** (May 1965): 335–38.

25. Rahmlow, Harold F. "Understanding different number bases." *The Arithmetic Teacher* **12** (May 1965): 339–40.

26. Rinker, Ethel. "Eight-ring circus: A variation in the teaching of counting and place value." *The Arithmetic Teacher* **19** (March 1972): 209–16.

27. Rudnick, Jesse A. "Numeration systems and their classroom roles." *The Arithmetic Teacher* **15** (February 1968): 138–47.

28. Sanders, Walter J. "Cardinal numbers and sets." *The Arithmetic Teacher* **13** (January 1966): 26–29.

29. Schoen, Harold L. "Some difficulty in the language of sets." *The Arithmetic Teacher* **21** (March 1974): 236–37.

30. Smith, Karl J. "Inventing a numeration system." *The Arithmetic Teacher* **20** (November 1973): 550–53.

31. Smith, Lewis B. "Venn diagrams strengthen children's mathematical understanding." *The Arithmetic Teacher* **13** (February 1966): 92–99.

32. Smith, Robert F. "Diagnosis of pupil performance on place-value tasks." *The Arithmetic Teacher* **20** (May 1973): 403–408.

33. Steinberg, Zina. "Will the set of children`...`?" *The Arithmetic Teacher* **18** (February 1971): 105–108.

34. Vaughan, Herbert E. "What sets are not." *The Arithmetic Teacher* **17** (January 1970): 55–60.

35. Ziesche, Shirley S. "Understanding place value." *The Arithmetic Teacher* **17** (December 1970): 683–84.

Teaching addition of cardinal numbers

4

Synopsis and objectives

Chapter 4 includes the basic theoretical and practical information you need to teach the concepts and principles of the operation of addition. The **theory** section is organized around a series of flowcharts showing the order in which the addition concepts and computational skills should be learned. The **practice** section contains a variety of instructional activities for classroom use that are classified according to *modes of representation* (concrete, semiconcrete, or abstract). These activities also are keyed to the flowcharts.

In planning your study of Chapter 4, you will want to use the bibliography that is provided to explore some of the ideas which are discussed in greater detail or to expand upon the given list of classroom activities for child involvement. You may want to begin the construction of a card file of activities organized according to addition concepts and types of child involvement.

As a result of a careful study of Chapter 4 you should be able to

1. state the definition of addition of whole numbers, and illustrate it;

2. define and illustrate the meaning of the terms *addend* and *sum*;

3. construct the addition number sentence corresponding to a specific set union sentence or illustration, and conversely;

4. construct and illustrate a (Phase I) flowchart for teaching the meaning of addition which reveals the crucial subordinate behaviors;

5. classify a sum, $x + y$, as belonging or not belonging to the set of basic addition facts;

6. demonstrate how to use the associative property of addition to determine the basic addition facts where the sums are greater than ten;

7. construct and illustrate a (Phase II) flowchart for teaching addition which has the basic addition facts as a terminal learning outcome, and which reveals the crucial subordinate competencies;

8. state and provide illustrations of the commutative and associative properties of addition;

9. state the closure property of addition of whole numbers;

10. state which whole number is an additive identity and illustrate the additive identity property by means of an example;

11. construct and illustrate a (Phase III) flowchart for teaching addition for cases not involving regrouping (terminal behavior: find the sum of a pair of two-digit numbers; entry behavior: knowledge of the basic addition facts);

12. construct and illustrate a (Phase IV) flowchart for teaching addition for cases involving regrouping;

13. illustrate, by means of examples, the various formats which are popularly used as intermediate steps leading to the standard form of the addition algorithm;

14. construct sample problems for each component of the comprehensive flowchart for teaching addition;

15. order a collection of different types of addition problems into a sequence which represents an acceptable teaching arrangement;

16. describe how to use the flowcharts for teaching addition as an aid in the diagnosis of learning states;

17. generalize the addition algorithm to cases not discussed specifically;

18.–20. formulate concrete, semiconcrete, and abstract mode activities for pupil involvement which will facilitate the learning of the meaning of addition, the basic addition facts, and the basic addition algorithms.

Teaching addition of cardinal numbers

Theory

A DEFINITION FOR ADDITION

Addition of whole (cardinal) numbers is a *binary operation*. The idea may be illustrated in the following way:

$$(a, b) \xrightarrow{+} c$$

where a, b, and c are whole numbers. For example:

$$(2, 3) \xrightarrow{+} 5, \qquad (6, 0) \xrightarrow{+} 6, \qquad (8, 4) \xrightarrow{+} 12.$$

Note that the addition operation assigns a whole number to an *ordered pair* of whole numbers, hence the use of the word *binary*.

Since it is possible to define many different binary operations on the same set, S, it is necessary to specify the operation clearly to avoid ambiguity or confusion with other operations. How do we decide what number should be assigned to any particular ordered pair of whole numbers (a, b)? For example, how do we decide what number is assigned to $(3, 4)$? That is, $(3, 4) \xrightarrow{+} \boxed{}$ (or more conventionally, $3 + 4 = \boxed{}$). The following definition shows us how.

Definition of Addition

Let A and B be two disjoint sets such that n(A) and n(B), the number properties of sets A and B, are a and b, respectively. Then,

$$a + b = n(A \cup B).$$

This definition formalizes exactly what we want addition to mean. To determine, for instance, the number that should be assigned to $(3, 2)$, we first identify two sets, say A and B, having the number properties 3 and 2, respectively. Suppose we use sets of blocks to do this. Note that sets A and B are disjoint [i.e., $A \cap B = \emptyset$]. Now, according to the definition of addition, $3 + 2 = n(A \cup B) = 5$.

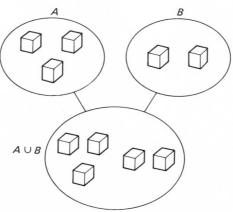

Similarly,
we see that
$4 + 3 = 7$.

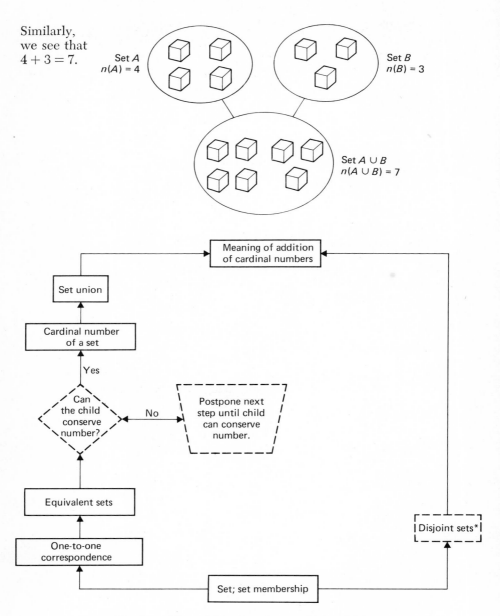

Fig. 4.1 Phase I flowchart for teaching addition.

* It is not customary to teach the concept of disjoint sets prior to teaching the concept of addition since the (disjoint) condition is normally met in practical illustrations of the addition idea.

An analysis of the operation of addition reveals the supporting ideas upon which it is based, for example, *set, set union,* and the *cardinal number of a set.* The child must understand these ideas before he can understand the meaning of addition. The hierarchical relationship of these ideas is given in the Phase I Flowchart for Teaching Addition given in Fig. 4.1. Study it carefully.

The standard terminology for the various components of an addition problem is given here.

$$a + b = c$$

$$\begin{array}{c} a \\ + b \end{array} \Big\rangle \text{addends}$$

$$c \longleftarrow \text{sum}$$

THE BASIC ADDITION FACTS

Altogether there are one hundred basic addition facts to be learned. These facts are suggested by the following table. Study the table to make certain you know how it is constructed.

Table 4.1 The basic addition facts

	Second addend									
+	0	1	2	3	4	5	6	7	8	9
0	0			3						
1					6					
2		3							11	
3				6			9			
4	4								12	
5		6								
6				10						
7								14		
8		9								
9				13				17		

First addend

11 ← 2 + 9 = 11

12 ← 4 + 8 = 12

It is customary to teach the basic addition facts in subsets according to some plan roughly like that given at the top of the next page.

Subset level	Type of problem
1	Sums of 5 or less
2	Sums of 6 to 9
3	Sums of 10 to 14
4	Sums of 15 to 18

The instructional procedures for teaching subsets 1 and 2 of the basic addition facts are fairly straightforward. One procedure frequently used is to develop the facts by working on *sum families,* for example, sums of 5: $0 + 5$, $1 + 4$, $2 + 3$, $3 + 2$, $4 + 1$, and $5 + 0$. It is helpful to students to give special recognition to the commutative property of addition* in learning the basic addition facts.

Fancier maneuvering is often employed to teach subsets 3 and 4. The following example illustrates the basis of one common practice:

$$8 + 5 = 8 + (2 + 3) \qquad [5 = 2 + 3]$$
$$= (8 + 2) + 3 \qquad [\text{Associative property of addition}]\dagger$$
$$= 10 + 3 \qquad [8 + 2 = 10]$$
$$= 13 \qquad [\text{Decimal system of numeration}]$$

Observe that this consists essentially of changing the problem from $8 + 5$ to $10 + 3$, and this new problem is easier to deal with by resorting to the basic ideas underlying the decimal system of numeration. (For instance, the decimal numeral "13" actually stands for $10 + 3$.) Note that the same procedure can be used for any of the basic addition problems whose sum is greater than ten, and that concrete representations are easy to construct.

The foregoing ideas are summarized in the Phase II Flowchart for Teaching Addition given in Fig. 4.2. Observe that this flowchart is an extension of the Phase I flowchart. Note also that the flowchart calls for teaching the special properties of addition during the same period of time that the basic addition facts are being taught. In addition to the associative and commutative properties, the additive identity property of zero should be taught. This property can be stated succinctly in the following way: For all whole numbers n, $n + 0 = 0 + n = n$. Thus, for example, $5 + 0 = 5$, $0 + 7 = 7$, and so on.

---

* The commutative property of addition may be stated as follows: For all whole numbers c and d, $c + d = d + c$. For example, $2 + 5 = 5 + 2$, $4 + 1 = 1 + 4$ and so on. Many elementary school teachers refer to this property as the *order property* of addition.

† The associative property of addition may be stated as follows: For all whole numbers a, b and c, $(a + b) + c = a + (b + c)$. For example, $(3 + 4) + 2 = 3 + (4 + 2)$. Many elementary school teachers refer to this property as the *grouping property* of addition.

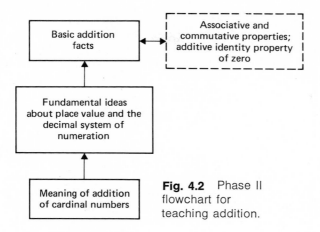

Fig. 4.2 Phase II flowchart for teaching addition.

THE ADDITION ALGORITHM: CASES NOT INVOLVING REGROUPING

The first type of addition problem that is normally taught after the child has learned the basic addition facts is the one that consists of finding the sum of a two-digit number and a one-digit number where no regrouping (i.e., no carry) is necessary. For example, $12 + 5$, $16 + 3$, $13 + 4$, $27 + 2$, and so on. The following example illustrates some of the basic ideas involved in teaching problems of this type.

$$
\begin{aligned}
12 + 5 &= (10 + 2) + 5 && [12 = 10 + 2] \\
&= 10 + (2 + 5) && [\text{Associative property of addition}] \\
&= 10 + 7 && [2 + 5 = 7] \\
&= 17 && [10 + 7 = 17]
\end{aligned}
$$

Observe that the major tactic consists of changing the problem from $12 + 5$ to $10 + 7$, the latter being easier for children to deal with. Observe also the crucial role of the associative property of addition. Two additional examples are given below for purposes of illustration.

$$
\begin{aligned}
21 + 8 &= (20 + 1) + 8 & 53 + 5 &= (50 + 3) + 5 \\
&= 20 + (1 + 8) & &= 50 + (3 + 5) \\
&= 20 + 9 & &= 50 + 8 \\
&= 29 & &= 58
\end{aligned}
$$

When the vertical problem-solving format is introduced, it is customarily developed using a three-step process culminating in the standard form of the algorithm. The following example illustrates the first step in the process.

$$
\begin{array}{r}
13 \\
+6 \\
\hline
\end{array}
\rightarrow
\begin{array}{r}
10 + 3 \\
+\ 6 \\
\hline
10 + 9 = 19
\end{array}
$$

Note that the procedure used is identical to that employed in the horizontal problem-solving format, shown earlier, but the requirement for the use of the associative property of addition is not as obvious.

After the student can deal with problems given in the above format, another refinement is often introduced, such as the following:

$$\begin{array}{c} 26 \\ +3 \\ \hline 9 \\ 20 \\ \hline 29 \end{array} \rightarrow \begin{array}{c} 20+6 \\ +3 \\ \hline \end{array}$$

This procedure is merely an abbreviated version of the earlier method. Note that this refined procedure calls for *adding the ones* and then *adding the tens* in a context similar to that used in the *standard form* of the algorithm:

$$\begin{array}{c} 34 \\ +4 \\ \hline 38 \end{array}$$

Using the intermediate stages of the addition algorithm rather than going directly to its standard form is intended to help assure meaningful learning. Obviously the student must in the final analysis become highly proficient in the use of the addition algorithm in its most refined form.

After the student has mastered addition problems consisting of finding the sum of a two-digit number and a one-digit number where no regrouping is necessary, there are two options for the next problem type to be learned. One is to continue with the problem of finding the sum of a two-digit number and a one-digit number, but to incorporate the cases which require regrouping. The other is to consider the problem of finding the sum of a pair of two-digit numbers where there is no regrouping required. We shall discuss the latter problem type first.

If a horizontal format is used, such problems would look like this:

$$15 + 23 = (10 + 5) + (20 + 3)$$
$$= (10 + 20) + (5 + 3)$$
$$= 30 + 8$$
$$= 38$$

When we analyze this example, we find several new ideas which have not already been discussed. In the second step, for example, moving from $(10 + 5) + (20 + 3)$ to $(10 + 20) + (5 + 3)$ requires application of the associative and commutative properties of addition. For purposes here, such a move will be referred to as the *term rearrangement* principle. Also, in the third step, the subcompetence of being able to determine the sum of multiples of ten is required. Fortunately, as illustrated below, the use of vertical forms like those used earlier helps to avoid some of the difficulty in working with this type of problem. Note how the abacus representation of the example not only reflects the steps that are taken, but also offers an enormous simplification of the process.

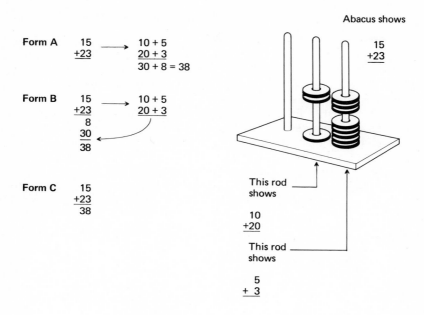

The steps we have discussed are summarized by the Phase III Flowchart for Teaching Addition given in Fig. 4.3.

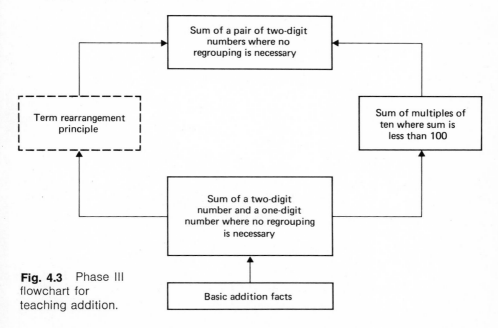

Fig. 4.3 Phase III flowchart for teaching addition.

THE ADDITION ALGORITHM: CASES INVOLVING REGROUPING

After the child has learned how to determine the sum of (1) a two-digit number and a one-digit number, and (2) a pair of two-digit numbers in instances where no regrouping is necessary, we then reconsider these problem types, but this time we use instances requiring the *regrouping* procedure. The ordering of the problem types is the same as before.

An analysis of the first type problem below reveals nothing new in terms of required subcompetencies, so the format used is similar to that used in cases not involving regrouping.

Form A
$$\begin{array}{r} 15 \\ +7 \\ \hline \end{array} \rightarrow \begin{array}{r} 10 + 5 \\ +\ 7 \\ \hline \end{array}$$
$$10 + 12 = 20 + 2$$
$$= 22$$

Observe that the regrouping move occurs in this step. In essence, it consists of changing the 12 ones into 1 ten and 2 ones, and putting the tens together.

Form B
$$\begin{array}{r} 15 \\ +7 \\ \hline \end{array} \rightarrow \begin{array}{r} 10 + 5 \\ +7 \\ \hline \end{array}$$
$$\begin{array}{r} 12 \\ 10 \\ \hline 22 \end{array}$$

Form C
$$\begin{array}{r} 15 \\ +7 \\ \hline 22 \end{array}$$

The vertical format is also used extensively in finding the sum of a pair of two-digit numbers where regrouping is necessary. For example:

Form A
$$\begin{array}{r} 28 \\ +37 \\ \hline \end{array} \rightarrow \begin{array}{r} 20 + 8 \\ 30 + 7 \\ \hline \end{array}$$
$$50 + 15 = 60 + 5$$
$$= 65.$$

Observe that the regrouping move occurs in this step. This time it consists of changing the 15 ones into 1 ten and 5 ones and putting the tens together.

The transition to the standard form of the algorithm is the customary one.

Form B
$$\begin{array}{r} 28 \\ +37 \\ \hline 15 \\ 50 \\ \hline 65 \end{array}$$

Form C
$$\begin{array}{r} 28 \\ +37 \\ \hline 65 \end{array}$$

Observe that the above example required regrouping from ones to tens. The following example requires regrouping from tens to hundreds.

Form A
$$\begin{array}{r} 83 \\ +35 \\ \hline \end{array} \rightarrow \begin{array}{r} 80 + 3 \\ 30 + 5 \\ \hline \end{array}$$
$$110 + 8 = 118.$$

Form B
$$\begin{array}{r} 83 \\ +35 \\ \hline 8 \\ 110 \\ \hline 118 \end{array}$$

Form C
$$\begin{array}{r} 83 \\ +35 \\ \hline 118 \end{array}$$

It is obvious that this example requires the student to be able to add multiples of ten beyond what was needed previously; specifically, the student must be able to add multiples of ten where the sums equal or exceed one hundred. This competence can be developed in several ways. One good procedure is suggested by the following example.

$$60 + 80 = 60 + (40 + 40)$$
$$= (60 + 40) + 40$$
$$= 100 + 40$$
$$= 140.$$

The final problem type is the one in which regrouping is required in both the ones and tens places, as illustrated here.

Form A
$$96 \atop +38 \rightarrow$$
$$90 + 6$$
$$30 + 8$$
$$\overline{120 + 14} = 130 + 4$$
$$= 134.$$

Form B
$$96$$
$$+38$$
$$\overline{14}$$
$$120$$
$$\overline{134}$$

Form C
$$96$$
$$+38$$
$$\overline{134}$$

The ideas in these examples are summarized in the Phase IV Flowchart for Teaching Addition given in Fig. 4.4.

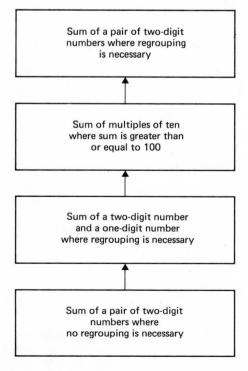

Fig. 4.4 Phase IV flowchart for teaching addition.

THE ADDITION ALGORITHM: OTHER PROBLEM TYPES

All of the basic competencies necessary to apply the addition algorithm to other problem types have been included in the problem types already given. The procedures used need only be generalized, as indicated by the following examples.

a) $\begin{array}{r} 215 \\ +3 \\ \hline \end{array} \rightarrow \begin{array}{r} 210 + 5 \\ +\ 3 \\ \hline 210 + 8 = 218. \end{array}$ Sum of a three-digit number and a one-digit number—no regrouping required.

b) $\begin{array}{r} 357 \\ +9 \\ \hline \end{array} \rightarrow \begin{array}{r} 350 +\ 7 \\ +\ 9 \\ \hline 350 + 16 = 360 + 6 \\ = 366. \end{array}$ Sum of a three-digit number and a one-digit number—regrouping required.

c) $\begin{array}{r} 428 \\ +61 \\ \hline \end{array} \rightarrow \begin{array}{r} 400 + 20 + 8 \\ +\ 60 + 1 \\ \hline 400 + 80 + 9 = 489. \end{array}$ Sum of a three-digit number and a two-digit number—no regrouping required.

d) $\begin{array}{r} 557 \\ +74 \\ \hline \end{array} \rightarrow \begin{array}{r} 500 +\ 50 +\ 7 \\ +\ 70 +\ 4 \\ \hline 500 + 120 + 11 = 600 + 30 + 1 \\ = 631. \end{array}$ Sum of a three-digit number and a two-digit number— regrouping required.

The strategies for using manipulatives (e.g., an abacus, multibase arithmetic blocks, and so on) to teach these types of addition problems are essentially the same as those used earlier.

A Comprehensive Flowchart for Teaching Addition is given in Fig. 4.5. It is a composite of the four partial flowcharts (Phase I–Phase IV) given earlier. Observe, among other things, that it can be used not only as an aid in *diagnosing* the learning states of individual children, but in subsequent *prescription* activities.

ADDITION INVOLVING NEGATIVE INTEGERS

When the cardinal number system is expanded to form the set of integers, we must consider how to perform the operation of addition in instances where negative numbers are involved. There are two new problem types which must be examined, namely, the cases where one or both of the addends are negative.

First, let us consider the case where only one addend is less than zero. The following example illustrates the basic concepts.

$$5 + {}^-3 = (2 + 3) + {}^-3 \qquad [5 = 2 + 3]$$
$$= 2 + (3 + {}^-3) \qquad [\text{Associative property of addition}]$$
$$= 2 + 0 \qquad\qquad [3 \text{ and } {}^-3 \text{ are opposites.}]$$
$$= 2 \qquad\qquad\quad [\text{Zero is the additive identity.}]$$

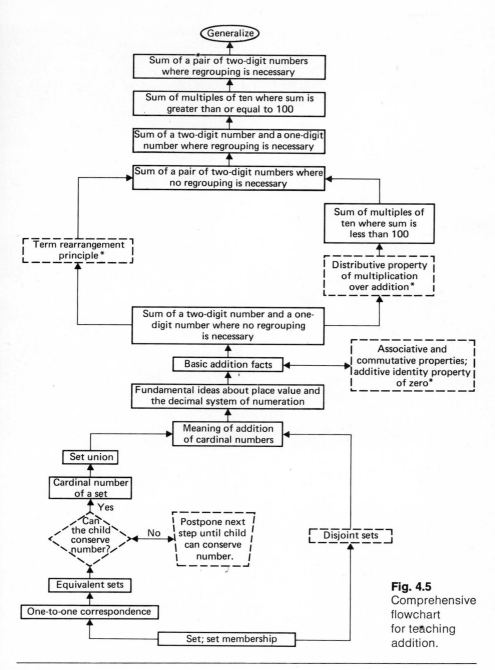

Fig. 4.5
Comprehensive
flowchart
for teaching
addition.

* These topics need not be treated formally.

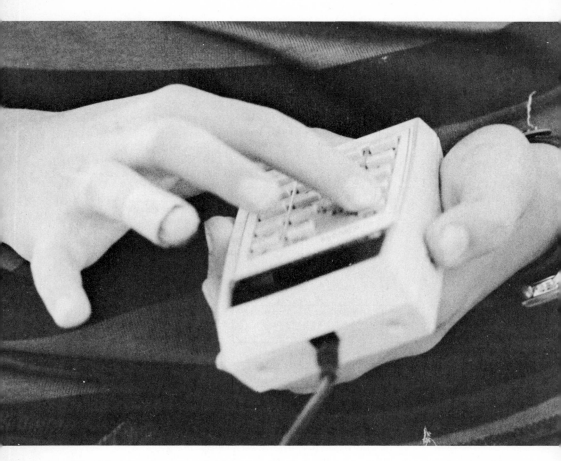

Hand-held calculators add a new and important dimension to the teaching of computational concepts and skills.

Observe how 5 was cleverly renamed as a sum, namely $2 + 3$, so as to form the sum of opposites, $3 + {}^-3$. This is the key to the conceptual strategy for adding numbers with unlike signs.

Next, let us consider the case where both addends are negative:

$$^-4 + {}^-2 = \boxed{}$$

The desired sum is $^-6$. In order to demonstrate that this is the case, consider the following argument. Start with $^-4 + {}^-2$ and add six to it in the form of $4 + 2$, and examine the subsequent steps:

$$
\begin{aligned}
(^-4 + {}^-2) + (4 + 2) &= (^-4 + 4) + (^-2 + 2) \\
&= \quad 0 \quad + \quad 0 \qquad \text{[Term rearrangement]} \\
&= \quad 0
\end{aligned}
$$

Since $(^-4 + ^-2)$ and $(4 + 2)$ have a sum of zero, they must be opposites. Consequently, since $(4 + 2) = 6$, $^-4 + ^-2$ must equal $^-6$.

Number line methods can be used to good advantage to help children learn the procedures that are involved.

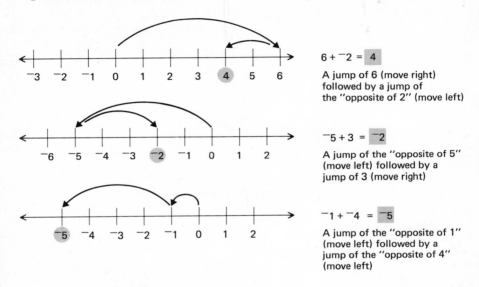

$6 + ^-2 = \boxed{4}$

A jump of 6 (move right) followed by a jump of the "opposite of 2" (move left)

$^-5 + 3 = \boxed{^-2}$

A jump of the "opposite of 5" (move left) followed by a jump of 3 (move right)

$^-1 + ^-4 = \boxed{^-5}$

A jump of the "opposite of 1" (move left) followed by a jump of the "opposite of 4" (move left)

Other practical ideas for teaching addition in instances where negative numbers are involved may be found in the **practice** section and in some of the articles listed in the bibliography.

Practice

This **practice** section shows you how to use Instructional Principle 4 in the design and organization of learning activities. The activities pertain to the addition concepts and skills outlined in the **theory** section.

As suggested by Principle 4, you should be certain that students have an opportunity to examine mathematical ideas embodied in different ways. The principle also suggests that the preferred order of learning experiences is from *concrete* to *semiconcrete* to *abstract* (or symbolic).

ACTIVITIES FOR STUDENT INVOLVEMENT
PHASE I: THE MEANING OF ADDITION

Concrete mode activities

In the initial stages of learning the basic concepts of addition, you should use activities that will help the student to understand the meaning of addition in real-world situations. The following sample activities are presented with this aim in mind.

Sample activity 1 (Orally presented problem situations)

Prepare construction paper cutouts of various kinds of animals so that each student in a small group has a complete set. Provide each student with a small flannel board. Orally present situations such as the following:

> Place three paper dogs on one side of your flannel board and four paper cats on the other. Now describe how you can tell how many animals you have on your flannel board.

Have individual students use their animal cut-outs and individual flannel boards to describe how they arrived at their answer. A variation of this activity would be to have the students create their own problem situations and present them to the group.

Sample activity 2 (Fact finder relay)

Divide the class into two teams, A and B. Give each team two trays of colored beads and a wire rod to place the beads on. Station the bead trays and pupils in the room as indicated by the following diagram. (Note that each team is subdivided into three groups stationed as shown in the diagram below.)

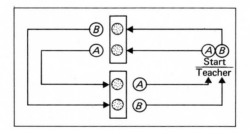

Pupil 1 walks to the first tray and puts nine or fewer red beads on the wire rod and hands it to pupil 2 who goes to the second tray and puts nine or fewer blue beads on the wire rod and hands it to pupil 3. Pupil 3 then takes it to the finish line and tells the teacher how many beads were placed on the rod. A team gets one point for each correct answer. Play continues until the teacher says to stop. The team with the most points at the end of play is the winner.

Semiconcrete mode activities

Following the use of concrete materials you should provide activities in which the actual objects are replaced by pictures or other graphic displays. One possible way to increase interest in these types of activities would be to use snapshot examples in which the students were involved.

Sample activity 1 (Use of a number line)

Provide each student with a number line that he can mark with a grease pencil. Then use a large classroom flannel graph to present situations like the following:

I've placed a set of apples on one side of my flannel graph. Now I'm going to place a set of pears on the other side. Mark your number line to show how many members are in the set of fruit after I join the set of apples with the set of pears.

Next have the students present their number line solutions to show how they got their answer. Encourage a diversity of approaches by recognizing all correct responses. For example:

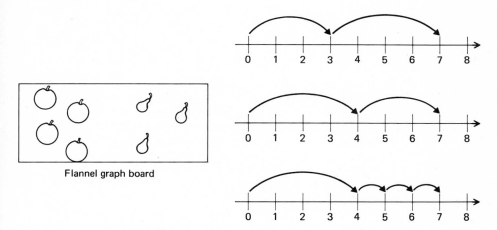

Flannel graph board

Sample activity 2 (Domino bingo)

Make "bingo" cards that have at least three rows and three columns. Write numerals in the squares that describe the total number of spots on a domino. For example:

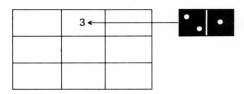

Begin play by flipping a coin to see who goes first. The first player draws a domino from a pile (the "kitty") that is face down in the middle of the playing table. If he can play the domino, he places it on his card; if not, he returns it to the kitty face down. The first player to have three dominoes in a straight line is the winner. If an incorrect play is made and challenged by another player, the player challenged must return all of his dominoes to the pile and begin again.

Sample activity 3 (Set circles)

Have the students construct set circles to illustrate typical classroom events. For example, you've just finished sending three children to the blackboard and send two more to join them. After these students sit down, ask the class to draw set circles to illustrate how many children were at the blackboard.

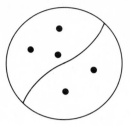

Abstract mode activities

To provide abstract activities the teacher should use situations in which children use only numerals to represent numbers. Since children vary in their rate of development, their ability to move from concrete to abstract activities will vary within a given class. Therefore, abstract activities, such as $4 + 2 = \square$, should be prescribed for individuals only after they have been successful with concrete and semiconcrete activities.

ACTIVITIES FOR STUDENT INVOLVEMENT
PHASE II: BASIC ADDITION FACTS

Concrete mode activities

The primary purpose of using concrete activities is to provide *meaningful* opportunities for the child to discover the basic addition facts and their relationships. Such experiences also help the child learn counting concepts and skills. The following types of activities should be useful ideas for teaching.

Sample activity 1 (Rod families)

Give each student a set of Cuisenaire rods and a table that is structured as follows:

```
        Five    Family

  1. _____ plus _____

  2. _____ plus _____

  3. _____ plus _____

  4. _____ plus _____

  5. _____ plus _____

  6. _____ plus _____
```

The teacher chooses one rod, in this case the five rod. The students are to find all the rod combinations that equal the five rod and record them.

Sample activity 2 (Balance beam)

Provide each student in a small group with a mathematical balance (see adjoining diagram). Direct the student how to place a washer or washers on the sum side of the balance. Each student then uses the other side of his balance to find addends (washers) that will balance the sum. (Notice that the balance beam also can be used as a replacement for the rods in Sample Activity 1).

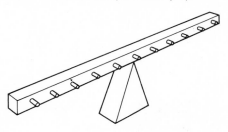

Sample activity 3 (Counters)

Supply each student with twenty counters (e.g., popsicle sticks) and a supply of rubber bands. Teach the students how to bundle the sticks to represent answers to addition problems where the sum is ten or greater. Then provide each pupil with a set of addition facts to be determined. The students should verify their answers by using their counters. (An abacus can be used as a substitute for the counters in this activity.)

Semiconcrete mode activities

To provide semiconcrete practice with the basic addition facts, use graphic displays that represent the number combinations you want the children to learn.

Sample activity 1 (Slide rule)

Give each student two rulers graduated only in centimeters. Show them how to manipulate the top ruler to find the sum of an addition combination. This is done by placing the zero point of the top ruler below the first addend (5) on the bottom ruler. By locating the other addend (4) on the top ruler, the sum (9) can be found directly above it on the bottom ruler.

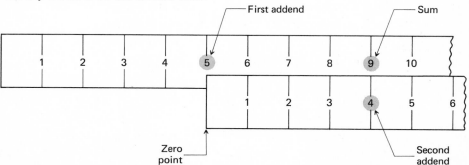

Sample activity 2 (Basic fact dominoes)

Give four students a set of dominoes. They begin the game by each player drawing two dominoes from the kitty (originally the entire set of dominoes) which is face down in the center of the playing surface. The player with the highest domino sum goes first. He lays one of his dominoes on the table and draws another from the kitty. The next player draws another domino and then must either return one to the kitty or play a domino whose sum equals the number of dots on *one* end of any of the dominoes played previously (see illustration below).

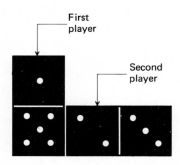

Play continues in this manner until all possible plays have been made. The players get one point for each domino played correctly. The player with the most number of points at the end of the game is the winner. The game can also be played by using the *total* number of dots on the face of the dominoes as the basis for play. This procedure will produce a wider range of number facts.

Abstract mode activities

To provide practice in the abstract mode with the basic addition facts, present students with activities involving only the use of symbolic representations. The use of games is particularly helpful in generating and maintaining interest in mastering the basic addition combinations.

Sample activity 1 (Jigsaw relay)

For troublesome facts make flash cards like the following example.

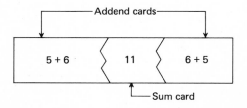

Cut the addend cards so that all the cards that equal a given sum card will fit that card, e.g., 4 + 1, 1 + 4, 0 + 5, 5 + 0, 3 + 2, 2 + 3 all should fit the sum card 5.

These cards can be used for different games. For example, a timed relay can be conducted by scrambling two identical sets of sum and addend cards for each team and placing them face up on separate piles on each team's table. The two teams line up one behind the other at their respective tables. On signal, the first player in the line chooses a card from the sum pile, and then must find an addend card that matches it. All the following players must find an addend card that matches an open sum card, or must choose another sum card and find a match for it. Play continues until all of the cards have been assembled. The first team finished is the winner.

Sample activity 2 (Bean bag toss)
Place a grid like the following on the classroom floor.

9	4	8
5	1	3
6	2	7

—————————————————————— Pitch line

Divide the class into two teams. The first player of one team tosses his two bean bags on the score grid from behind the pitch line. He then scores points if he can correctly add the numbers on which his bags land. The first player on the other team then tosses his bean bags. Play continues with each player adding to his team's score according to his ability to give the answer to the addition facts he selects. In order to get a maximum number of points for his team, players are encouraged to select the facts yielding the largest sums. The game can be varied by using two-digit numerals in the grid.

Sample activity 3 (Addition fact relay)
Give each of two teams (members seated one behind the other) the same dittoed sheet containing a set of basic addition fact problems. At a signal from the teacher the first player on each team answers one of the facts on his team's dittoed sheet and passes the paper to the player behind him. The last player on the team completes the sheet and brings it to the teacher. The team gets one point for each correct answer. The winner is the team with the most points. In case of a tie, the first team to turn in the answer sheet wins. By reusing the same sheet or placing another one into play the teacher can control the type of practice received by the students.

Sample activity 4 (Timed practice drills)

Practice is an essential part of the maintenance of computational skills. To be most effective, practice activities should be well-motivated. To construct a well-motivated practice activity, the material should be organized so as to allow each pupil to work at his own rate and level of achievement.

One good method for helping students learn the basic addition facts is to provide timed practice intervals. During (or immediately after) these timed intervals, pupils should check their own answers—thereby having immediate knowledge of whether their answers are right or wrong. Some recording procedure may be used so that each student can compare his present performance with his previous record—the purpose is to tap the child's natural interest in self-improvement.

ACTIVITIES FOR STUDENT INVOLVEMENT, PHASE III AND PHASE IV: THE ADDITION ALGORITHMS FOR CASES INVOLVING AND NOT INVOLVING REGROUPING

Concrete mode activities

Since the associative property is involved in cases that involve regrouping, we use manipulative aids such as bundles of counting sticks in conjunction with place value charts to assist students in understanding the renaming processes involved in these types of problems. Students most often experience difficulty with the renaming/regrouping process when moving from tens to hundreds and hundreds to thousands—not from ones to tens. In any event, the teacher should choose manipulative devices that indicate the influence place value has on summing numbers, whether regrouping is required or not.

Sample activity 1 (Multibase arithmetic blocks)

Give the student charts labeled like the one below.

Tens	Ones
Longs	Units

Next have the students write a specified pair of addends beside the chart as indicated in illustration 1A or 1B. Then have them represent each addend by placing the correct number of MAB blocks in the appropriate column of the place value chart. Finally ask them to combine the blocks in each column and represent the amount in each column with the correct numerals. For an example without regrouping, see illustration 1A. For an example involving regrouping, see illustration 1B. Note that an extra step is needed to illustrate the regrouping process in illustration 1B.

Illustration 1A (no regrouping required)

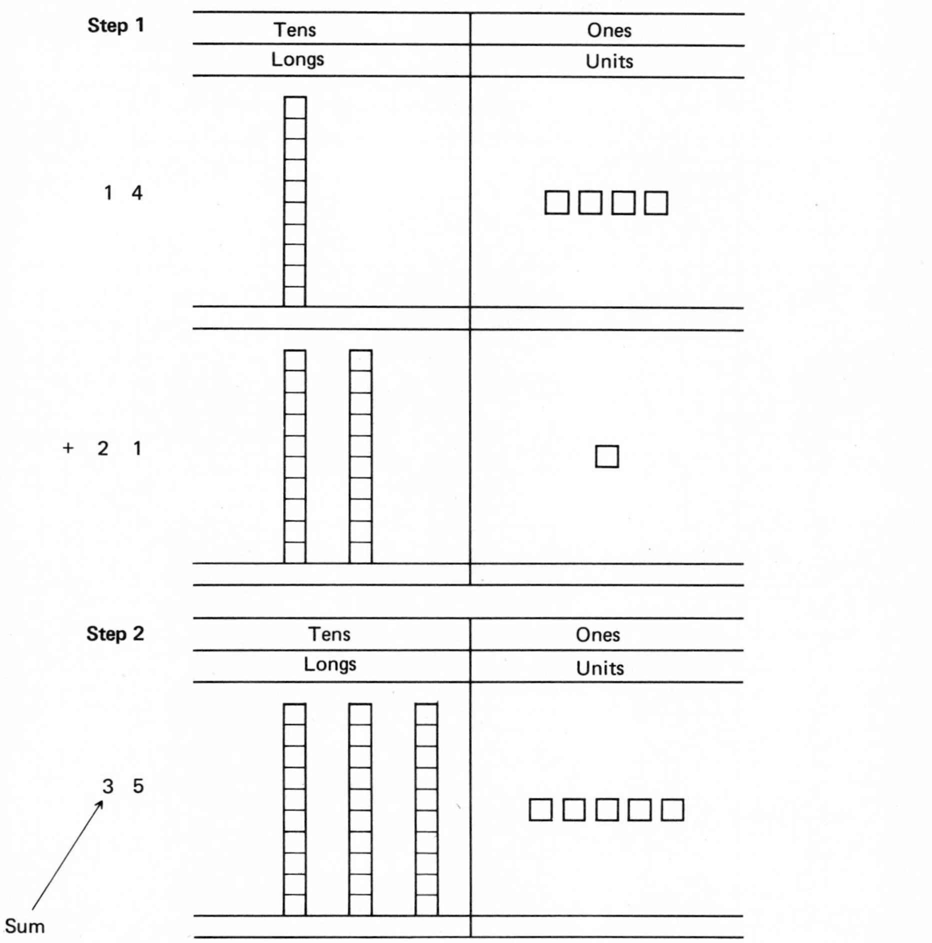

Illustration 1B   (regrouping required)

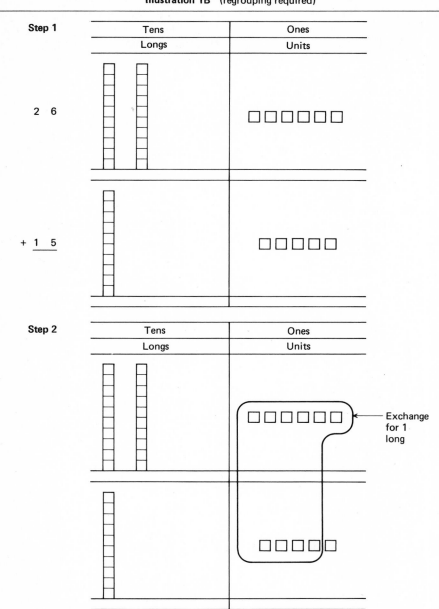

Illustration 1B (continued)

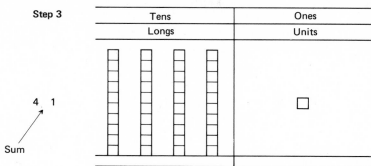

Sample activity 2 (Pocket charts)

Give each of the pupils a pocket chart and counters like those in the illustration below.

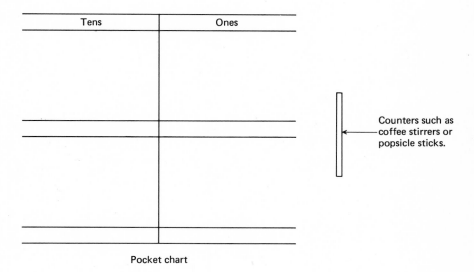

Pocket chart

Place a problem like 12 + 6 = ☐ or 15 + 6 = ☐ on the blackboard. Have each pupil represent each addend by placing counters in the correct pocket of the chart. See illustrations 2A and 2B. Next ask them to combine the counters in each column and represent the number of counters in each pocket with the correct numerals. Illustration 2A shows an example that doesn't involve regrouping. Illustration 2B provides an example that does involve regrouping. Note in the regrouping illustration 2B how the ten counters from the ones pockets are grouped and placed in the tens pocket.

An appropriate algorithm for illustration 2A would be

$$12 + 6 = 10 + (2 + 6) = 10 + 8 = 18.$$

Illustration 2A (no regrouping required)

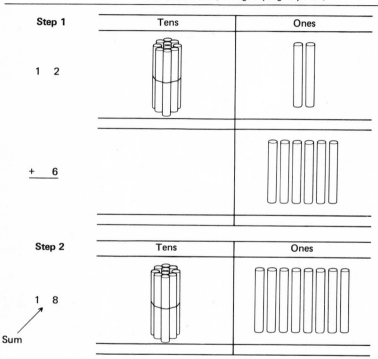

An appropriate algorithm for illustration 2B would be

$$15 + 6 = (10 + 5) + 6$$
$$= 10 + (5 + 5) + 1$$
$$= (10 + 10) + 1 = 20 + 1 = 21.$$

Illustration 2B (regrouping required)

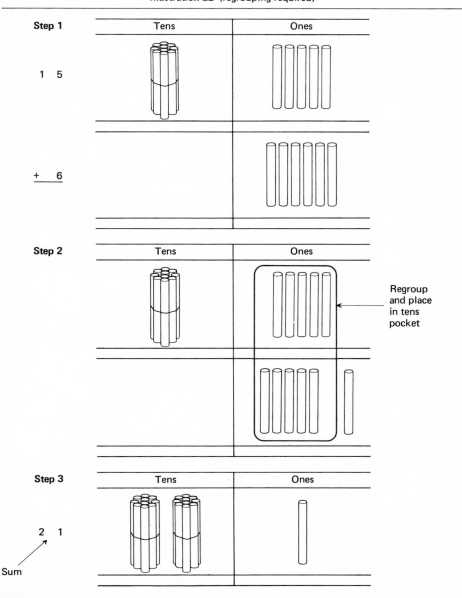

Sample activity 3 (Counters)

Provide each student with at least 50 counters, such as coffee stirrers, and five rubber bands. Place problems like $21 + 4 = \boxed{}$ and $24 + 8 = \boxed{}$ on the blackboard. Have each pupil represent the addends by grouping the counting sticks as indicated in illustrations 3A and 3B. Then ask the students to combine the counting sticks and represent the results with numerals as shown in the accompanying illustrations.

$$(21 + 4) = 20 + 5 = 25$$

Illustration 3A

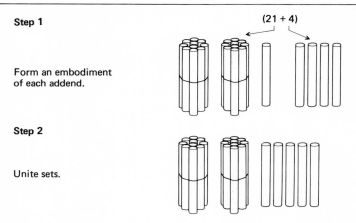

Step 1

Form an embodiment
of each addend.

Step 2

Unite sets.

$$24 + 8 = (20 + 4) + 8 = 20 + (10 + 2) = (20 + 10) + 2 = 32$$

Illustration 3B

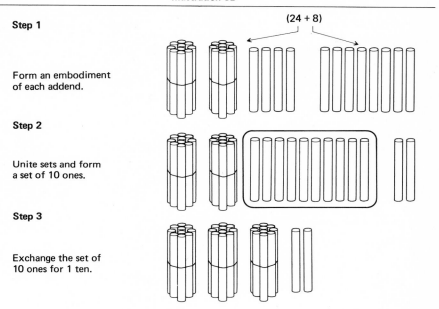

Step 1

Form an embodiment
of each addend.

$(24 + 8)$

Step 2

Unite sets and form
a set of 10 ones.

Step 3

Exchange the set of
10 ones for 1 ten.

Semiconcrete mode activities

Learning activities of a semiconcrete variety should follow the concrete learning experiences. The transition to graphic or pictorial material is a good intermediate stop for concept development. The following sample activities show how to construct such learning experiences.

Sample activity 1 (Abacus representations)

Give each student abacus representations as shown below. Have the students use these diagrams to record the steps in their thinking as they work problems such as $26 + 3 = \boxed{}$ and $38 + 5 = \boxed{}$. Study illustrations 4A and 4B.

The following diagram shows the steps taken in finding the sum

$$26 + 3 = 29.$$

Illustration 4A

Step 1

Represent
26.

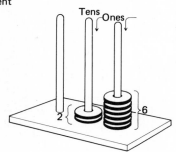

Step 2

Add 3.

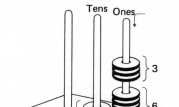

Step 3

The sum
is 29.

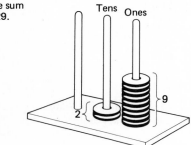

The following diagram shows the steps taken in finding the sum

$$38 + 5 = 43.$$

Illustration 4B

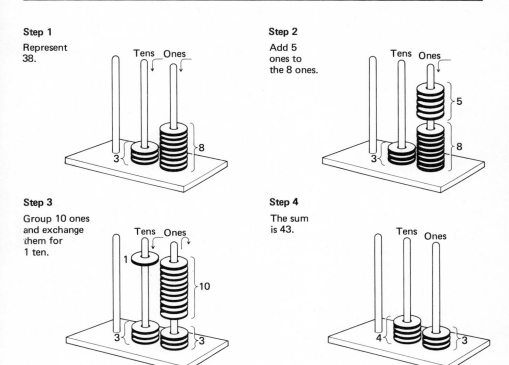

Step 1
Represent 38.

Step 2
Add 5 ones to the 8 ones.

Step 3
Group 10 ones and exchange them for 1 ten.

Step 4
The sum is 43.

Sample activity 2 (Nomograph)

Give each student a nomograph made from graph paper, like the one in the illustration below. Have them use their rulers to solve problems, such as $10 + 15 = \boxed{}$.

For example, have them place one end of their ruler on the addend 10 and the other on the addend 15. Then they read the sum (25) from the center scale.

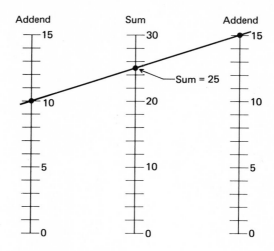

Abstract mode activities

Finally you want to help the student move from expanded forms of the addition algorithm to the shortest and most efficient procedures. The following activities are designed to promote this transition.

Sample activity 1 (Partial sums and place value chart)

Show students how to place partial sums in a place value chart to work problems such as $25 + 16 = \boxed{}$. Provide each student with dittoed forms. For example:

	Tens	Ones	
	2	5	
	+ 1	6	
	1	1	→ (5 + 6)
	+ 3	0	→ (20 + 10)
Sum	4	1	

Sample activity 2 (Expanded notation)

Explain how to use expanded notation for solving an addition problem such as this: $26 + 47 = \boxed{}$ in the manner illustrated below.

$$\begin{array}{r} 26 = 20 + 6 \\ +47 = 40 + 7 \\ \hline 60 + 13 = 73 \end{array}$$

ACTIVITIES FOR STUDENT INVOLVEMENT: ADDITION OF INTEGERS

Sample activity 1 (Darts)

Provide students with a dart board marked like the one shown here.

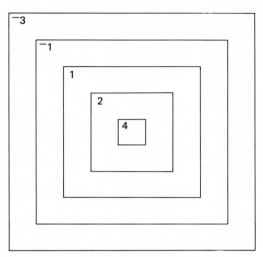

Dart Board

The students are allowed to throw four darts each, and they should keep score on a card like this one.

Name_____	
Positive	Negative
+2	⁻3
+4	⁻1
+1	
Total = 7	Total = ⁻4
Score 7 + ⁻4 = 3	

Sample activity 2 (Miniature golf)

Set up a miniature golf course on a play area. Provide the students with score cards like the one below. Have them play the course and keep score using the card.

Hole	Par/	Number of strokes	Score
1	4	4	O
2	4	3	−1
3	3	3	O
4	2	3	+1
5	5	4	−1
6	3	4	+1
7	4	5	+1
8	6	5	−1
9	4	6	+2
Total	35	37	+2

Date _____

Name _____

Lowest score wins.

Exercise set

1. What basic addition fact is suggested by the following statement about sets?

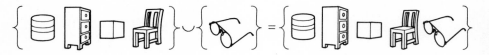

2. Why are the two sets $\{p, q, r\}$ and $\{r, s\}$ inappropriate to use to explain what the sum $3 + 2$ is equal to?

3. What property of addition figures prominently in supporting the claim that

$$9 + 7 = 10 + 6 \, ?$$

4. There are altogether 100 basic addition facts. However, if the commutative property of addition is used so as to treat facts like $3 + 2$ and $2 + 3$ as being essentially the same, then how many basic addition facts remain to be learned?

5. Demonstrate how to use either the multibase arithmetic blocks or an abacus to teach the basic addition facts whose sums are greater than ten.

6. Among other things, the flowcharts for teaching addition serve to identify the major classes of instructional objectives that should be formulated relative to addition. Write an instructional objective corresponding to:

   a) the "Basic addition facts" component of the Phase II Flowchart.

   b) the "sum of a two-digit number and a one-digit number where no re-grouping is necessary" component of the Phase III Flowchart.

   c) the "sum of multiples of ten where the sum is less than 100" component of the Phase III Flowchart.

   d) the "sum of a pair of two-digit numbers where no regrouping is neces-sary" component of the Phase III Flowchart.

   e-h) each component of the Phase IV Flowchart.

7. The following example illustrates the steps that must be taken to find the sum

$$\begin{array}{r} 34 \\ +8 \\ \hline \end{array}$$

using an abacus.

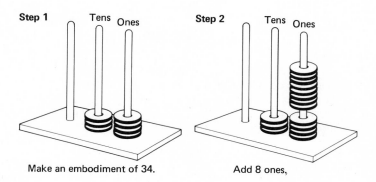

Make an embodiment of 34.   Add 8 ones,

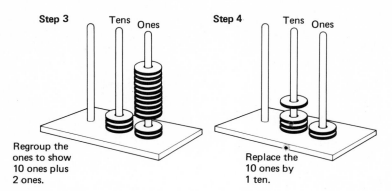

Regroup the ones to show 10 ones plus 2 ones.

Replace the 10 ones by 1 ten.

Demonstrate how to find each of the following sums on an abacus by detailing each step in the manner shown above.

a) 52   b) 78   c) 26   d) 41
    +9   +7   +48   +83

8. Construct a rationale in support of the statement that:

   Children should learn how to use counting sticks, multibase arithmetic blocks, or other similar types of representations for doing addition problems before using an abacus.

9. Use the flowcharts for teaching addition to order the following series of addition problems into the sequence in which they normally would be taught.

   a) 23   14   56   b) 37   82   9
       + 5   +17   +23   + 6   +14   + 7

   c) 47   35   29   d) 37   345   52
       +72   +64   + 9   + 4   + 3   +47

10. Piaget's theory of cognitive development suggests that a child should be a number conserver as a prior condition for beginning the study of addition. Write a brief rationale for this position. Support your explanation with examples where possible.

11. Supply a reason for each step in the following example.

$$5 + 7 = 5 + (5 + 2)$$ _____
$$= (5 + 5) + 2$$ _____
$$= 10 \quad\ + 2$$ _____
$$= 12$$ _____

12. Construct a rationale in support of the statement that:

   To master the addition facts students should be given short, spaced drill and practice sessions rather than long concentrated sessions.

13. Describe what kinds of learning experiences should precede drill and practice exercises.

14. Describe how the flowcharts for teaching can be used as a diagnostic aid. For example, how could a teacher use the comprehensive flowchart in Fig. 4.5 as an aid in determining whether a student has the prerequisites for learning the meaning of addition?

15. Describe how to extend the flowcharts to include the addition of three-digit numbers.

16. In order to illustrate the commutative (order) property of addition to a child, a procedure like the following is often employed.

    Example
    To show that
    $$3 + 2 = 2 + 3$$
    construct a pair of sets to show $3 + 2$:

    ◯ ◯ ◯   ◯ ◯

    Then reverse the positions of the sets to show $2 + 3$:

    ◯ ◯   ◯ ◯ ◯

    Describe a similar approach for illustrating the associative (grouping) property of addition.

17. What instructional principle(s) from Chapter 2 do the flowcharts for teaching addition relate to most directly?

18. What instructional principle(s) from Chapter 2 do the activities described in the **practice** section relate to most directly?

19. Principle 5 suggests the necessity for being able to keep accurate and up-to-date *profiles of achievement* on individual children. One way to handle this requirement is to build an achievement record system which corresponds to the flowcharts for teaching. For example, every component of the flowchart for teaching addition corresponds to a set of specific learnings that you want every child to acquire. This idea can be translated into an addition achievement chart like that shown below. Think of each cell □ as an individual component, and each set of cells as a distinct phase of the flowchart. A cell that is totally shaded means that the child has mastered the associated concepts and skills; a cell that is partially shaded means that some, but not all of the specified competencies have been acquired. Discuss this method for keeping track of student achievement.

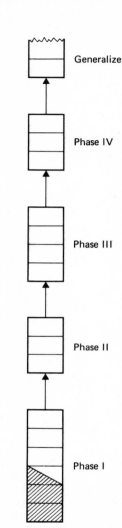

Addition achievement
chart

READINGS FOR ADDITIONAL STUDY

For each of the following topics, select an article from the bibliography which addresses the issue and write a brief *reaction* report.

20. Teaching the meaning of addition.

21. Teaching the basic addition facts.

22. Teaching the properties of addition.

Bibliography

1. Ashlock, R. B. *Error Patterns in Computation.* Columbus: Charles E. Merrill, 1972.

2. Ashlock, R. B. "The number line in the primary grades." *The Arithmetic Teacher* **8** (February 1961): 75–6.

3. Ashlock, R. B. "Teaching the basic facts: three classes of activities." *The Arithmetic Teacher* **18** (October 1971): 359–64.

4. Batarseh, Gabriel J. "Addition for the slow learner." *The Arithmetic Teacher* **21** (December 1974): 714–15.

5. Biggs, Edith. "Trial and experiment." *The Arithmetic Teacher* **17** (January 1970): 26–32.

6. Breed, Frederick S., and Alice L. Ralston. "The direct and indirect methods of teaching the addition combinations." *Elementary School Journal* **37** (December 1936): 283–94.

7. Brumfiel, Charles, and Irvin Vance. "On whole number computation." *The Arithmetic Teacher* **16** (April 1969): 253–57.

8. Buckingham, B. R. "Teaching addition and subtraction facts together or separately." *Educational Research Bulletin* **6** (May 1927): 228–29.

9. Burns, Marilyn. "Ideas: Reinforcement of addition." *The Arithmetic Teacher* **22** January 1975): 34–46.

10. Callahan, John J., and Jacobson, Ruth S. "An experiment with retarded children and Cuisenaire rods." *The Arithmetic Teacher* **14** (January 1967): 10–13.

11. Cohen, Louis S. "Open sentences—the most useful tool in problem solving." *The Arithmetic Teacher* **14** (April 1967): 263–67.

12. Copeland, Richard W. *How Children Learn Mathematics: Teaching Implications of Piaget's Research.* New York: The Macmillan Company, 1970.

13. Cox, L. S. "Diagnosing and remediating systematic errors in addition and subtraction computation." *The Arithmetic Teacher* **22** (February 1975): 151–57.

14. Edmonds, G. F. "Discovering patterns in addition." *The Arithmetic Teacher* **16** (April 1969): 245–48.

15. Flournoy, Frances. "A consideration of the ways children think when performing higher-decade addition." *Elementary School Journal* **57** (January 1957): 204–208.

16. Folsom, Mary. "Frames, frames, and more frames." *The Arithmetic Teacher* **10** (December 1963): 484–85.

17. Fremont, Herbert. "Pipe cleaners and loops—discovering how to add and subtract directed numbers." *The Arithmetic Teacher* **13** (November 1966): 568–72.

18. Gemma, Sister Mary, S. C. "Using parts of ten." *The Arithmetic Teacher* **17** December 1970): 673–75.

19. Golden, Sarah R. "Fostering enthusiasm through child-created games." *The Arithmetic Teacher* **17** (February 1970): 111–15.

20. Gosman, Howard Y. "Mastering the basic facts with dice." *The Arithmetic Teacher* **20** (May 1973): 330–31.

21. Heckman, M. Jane. "They all add up." *The Arithmetic Teacher* **21** (April 1974): 287–89.

22. Hervey, Margaret A., and Bonnie H. Litwiller. "The addition table: experiences in practice-discovery." *The Arithmetic Teacher* **19** (March 1972): 179–81.

23. Hilaire, Paul A. "Addition—not so easy." *The Arithmetic Teacher* **12** (March 1965): 207–11.

24. Immerzeel, George, and Donald Wiederander. "Ideas." *The Arithmetic Teacher* **18** (February 1971): 94–98.

25. Immerzeel, George, and Donald Wiederander. "Ideas." *The Arithmetic Teacher* **18** (January 1971): 30–36.

26. Immerzeel, George, and Donald Wiederander. "Ideas." *The Arithmetic Teacher* **20** (November 1973): 561–72.

27. Immerzeel, George, and Donald Wiederander. "Ideas." *The Arithmetic Teacher* **21** (April 1974): 311–16.

28. Junge, Charlotte W. "Dominoes in the mathematics classroom." *The Arithmetic Teacher* **18** (January 1971): 53–54.

29. King, I. "Giving meaning to the addition algorithm." *The Arithmetic Teacher* **19** (May 1972): 345–48.

30. Lawlis, Frank. "Let's add automatically." *The Arithmetic Teacher* **12** (March 1965): 224–25.

31. MacLatchy, Josephine H. "Counting and addition." *Educational Research Bulletin* **11** (February 1932): 96–100.

32. Macey, Joan M.: "Drill?—Deadly?—Never." *School Science and Mathematics* **73** (October 1973): 595–96.

33. Milne, Esther. "Disguised practice for multiplication and addition of directed numbers." *The Arithmetic Teacher* **16** (May 1969): 397–98.

34. Myers, Donald E. "A geometric interpretation of certain sums." *The Arithmetic Teacher* **18** (November 1971): 475–78.

35. National Council of Teachers of Mathematics. "Number sentences." *Topics in Mathematics for Elementary School Teachers.* Washington, D.C.: The Council, 1964. Booklet 8.

36. Pagni, D. "The computer motivates improvement in computational skills." *The Arithmetic Teacher* **18** (February 1971): 109–12.

37. Rivera, Emilio. "Adding by endings: some important considerations." *The Arithmetic Teacher* **12** (March 1965): 204–206.

38. Sanders, Walter J. "Let's go one step farther in addition." *The Arithmetic Teacher* **18** (October 1971): 413–15.

39. Sawada, Daiyo. "Magic squares: extensions into mathematics." *The Arithmetic Teacher* **21** (March 1974): 183–88.

40. Sherzer, Laurence. "Adding integers using only the concepts of one-to-one corresponding and counting." *The Arithmetic Teacher* **16** (May 1969): 360–62.

41. Van Engen, H., and L. P. Steffe. *First Grade Children's Concept of Addition of Natural Numbers.* Madison, Wisconsin: University of Wisconsin, 1966.

42. Weaver, J. F. "Some factors associated with pupils' performance levels on simple open addition and subtraction sentences." *The Arithmetic Teacher* **18** (November 1971): 513–19.

43. Zalewski, Donald L. "Magic triangles—practice in skills and thinking." *The Arithmetic Teacher* **21** (October 1974): 486–89.

Teaching subtraction of cardinal numbers

5

Synopsis and objectives

Included in Chapter 5 is an opportunity to explore the factors and considerations which should be taken into account in teaching the operation of subtraction. The approach that has been taken places emphasis upon the relationship of subtraction to its inverse operation of addition. Consequently, the **theory** section is developed around the translation of the flowcharts for teaching addition into corresponding flowcharts for teaching subtraction. When the resulting flowcharts are interpreted as intended, they specify the order in which the key concepts and skills of subtraction should be learned, and they also serve as a useful basis for planning teaching strategies.

The **practice** section illustrates how the ideas for learning activities in addition can be modified to teach subtraction, and so is similar in structure to that of Chapter 4.

Also, note that if you have started the activity file for classroom use suggested in Chapter 4, you may want to make a corresponding subtraction activity file.

A careful study of Chapter 5 should enable you to:

1. state the definition of subtraction as the inverse of the operation of addition, and illustrate it;

2. describe the so-called "take-away" interpretation of subtraction, and give concrete illustrations of it;

3. define and illustrate the meaning of the terms *minuend, subtrahend, difference,* and *missing addend;*

4. construct the subtraction number sentence corresponding to a specific set subtraction sentence or illustration, and conversely;

5. translate flowcharts for teaching addition into corresponding flowcharts for teaching subtraction;

6. define the set of basic subtraction facts;

7. classify a difference, $x - y$, as belonging or not belonging to the set of basic subtraction facts;

8. illustrate, by means of examples, the various (written) formats which are popularly used as intermediate steps leading to the standard form of the subtraction algorithm; .

9. order a collection of different types of subtraction problems into a sequence which represents an acceptable teaching arrangement;

10.–12. formulate concrete, semiconcrete, and abstract mode activities for pupil involvement which will facilitate the learning of the meaning of subtraction, the basic subtraction facts, and the basic subtraction algorithms.

Teaching subtraction of cardinal numbers

Theory

SUBTRACTION AS THE INVERSE OF ADDITION

Subtraction is often described as the "undoing" of addition. This idea may be expressed more precisely by stating that subtraction is the *inverse* of addition. This is the basis of the following definition.

> **Definition of Subtraction**
> *For all cardinal numbers a, b, and c,*
> $a - b = c$ *if and only if* $b + c = a$.

To illustrate how this definition operates, suppose that we wish to determine the cardinal number c to associate with, say, $5 - 3$. The definition states that

$$5 - 3 = c \quad \text{if and only if} \quad 3 + c = 5.$$

Since $3 + \boxed{2} = 5$, it follows that $c = 2$. Similarly, we see that $8 - 5 = \boxed{3}$ because $5 + \boxed{3} = 8$, and so on. The standard terminology for subtraction problems is given here.

Observe that subtraction is not always possible in the set of whole numbers. For example, $3 - 7$ does not correspond to a whole number since there is no whole number c such that $7 + c = 3$. This fact is described by stating that the set of whole numbers is not *closed* under the operation of subtraction.*

As suggested by our definition of subtraction, every subtraction sentence is equivalent to an addition sentence. Actually, since addition is commutative, every subtraction sentence can be converted into two equivalent addition sentences. For example:

It follows that every subtraction problem can be converted into an addition problem with a *missing addend.* Such an approach has become a popular strategy for teaching subtraction in the elementary school.

---

* Note that the set of *integers* is closed under the operation of subtraction.

THE "TAKE-AWAY" INTERPRETATION OF SUBTRACTION

There is another, logically equivalent way to think about subtraction of whole numbers. If subtraction is conceptualized as the "undoing" of addition, and addition is thought of in terms of the operation of *set union,* then subtraction can be thought of in terms of *set subtraction.* These ideas are often illustrated in elementary school textbooks in the following way.

Addition

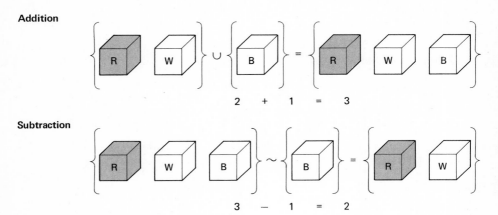

Subtraction

Observe that the set subtraction notion suggests the so-called "take-away" idea.

FLOWCHARTS FOR TEACHING SUBTRACTION

Since addition and subtraction are so closely related, it has become increasingly popular to teach them together; that is, soon after a particular addition competence or skill has been taught, the corresponding subtraction idea is taught. Consequently, the flowcharts for teaching addition can be used as guides for teaching subtraction. Using this approach, an initial flowchart for teaching subtraction would look something like this.

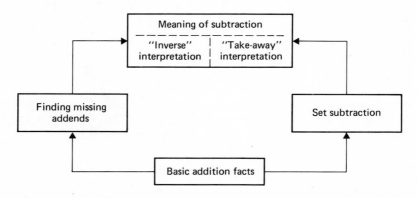

As suggested by the flowchart, both the "inverse" and "take-away" interpretations of subtraction should be, and normally are, taught in elementary programs since each interpretation has its own special advantages. Also, you will note that the flowcharts for teaching subtraction are essentially reflections of the corresponding flowcharts for teaching addition.

THE BASIC SUBTRACTION FACTS

Table 5.1 The basic subtraction facts

Subtrahend

Minuend

−	9	8	7	6	5	4	3	2	1	0
18	9	X	X	X	X	X	X	X	X	X
17	8	9	X	X	X	X	X	X	X	X
16	7	8	9	X	X	X	X	X	X	X
15	6	7	8	9	X	X	X	X	X	X
14	5	6	7	8	9	X	X	X	X	X
13	4	5	6	7	8	9	X	X	X	X
12	3	4	5	6	7	8	9	X	X	X
11	2	3	4	5	6	7	8	9	X	X
10	1	2	3	4	5	6	7	8	9	X
9	0	1	2	3	4	5	6	7	8	9
8	X	0	1	2	3	4	5	6	7	8
7	X	X	0	1	2	3	4	5	6	7
6	X	X	X	0	1	2	3	4	5	6
5	X	X	X	X	0	1	2	3	4	5
4	X	X	X	X	X	0	1	2	3	4
3	X	X	X	X	X	X	0	1	2	3
2	X	X	X	X	X	X	X	0	1	2
1	X	X	X	X	X	X	X	X	0	1
0	X	X	X	X	X	X	X	X	X	0

$12 - 3 = 9$

If you think of subtraction as being the inverse of addition, it is easy to see that there is a basic subtraction fact (BSF) corresponding to every basic addition fact. For example, according to the definition, the BSF which corresponds to $2 + 9 = 11$ is $11 - 2 = 9$. Extending this line of reasoning, it is possible to construct a table (see Table 5.1) of the 100 basic subtraction facts. The teaching of the BSF's, of course, would constitute the next component of the flowchart for teaching subtraction.

A TRANSLATION OF THE PHASE III ADDITION FLOWCHART INTO A FLOWCHART FOR TEACHING SUBTRACTION

After the child has acquired a satisfactory understanding of the meaning of subtraction and has mastered the basic subtraction facts, the teaching of the more complex problem types is begun. We know that the appropriate teaching sequence for subtraction is determined by the teaching sequence used for addition. For example, in the Phase III Flowchart (Fig. 4.3) for Teaching Addition, the first problem type following the basic addition facts involves finding the sum of a two-digit number and a one-digit number where no regrouping is necessary. Examples like $16 + 3$ and $23 + 5$ would fall into this category. The best choice of a corresponding subtraction problem type would be cases where the minuend is a two-digit number, the subtrahend is a one-digit number and no regrouping is required. Thus, in the case of the two addition examples given above, the intended subtraction counterparts would be $19 - 3$ and $28 - 5$, respectively, rather than $19 - 16$ and $28 - 23$ as obtained by a direct application of the definition of subtraction.

Now examine the terminal problem type in the Phase III Addition Flowchart. It calls for summing pairs of two-digit numbers where no regrouping is necessary. Problems like $45 + 23$ and $72 + 13$ would be examples of this case. The subtraction counterpart of this problem type would be cases where both the minuend and subtrahend are two-digit numbers, and no regrouping is required to determine the difference. We have $68 - 45$ and $85 - 72$ as examples of this problem type. Note that the solution of such problems is dependent upon the competence of being able to find the difference of multiples of ten; this problem type would naturally appear in the Flowchart for Teaching Subtraction since it is the subtraction counterpart of the "sum of multiples of ten" component of the Phase III Addition Flowchart.

ALGORITHM DEVELOPMENT

Once the proper teaching sequence of subtraction problem types has been determined, teaching techniques must be developed for each of them. The paper and pencil procedures that are normally used are similar, not only in form but in sequence, to the addition techniques described in Chapter 4. The following examples illustrate the similarities.

	Addition problem type		Corresponding subtraction problem type

A.

```
   15        10 +  5              18       10 +  8
  + 3         +  3              - 3          -  3
             ─────────                    ─────────
             10 +  8 = 18                 10 +  5 = 15
```

B.

```
   37        30 +  7              58       (50 +  8)
  +21        20 +  1             -21      -(20 +  1)
             ─────────                    ─────────
             50 +  8 = 58                  30 +  7 = 37
```

C.

```
   45        40 +  5              54       40 + 14
  + 9         +  9              - 9          -  9
             ─────────                    ─────────
             40 + 14                        40 +  5 = 45
           = 50 +  4 = 54
```

D.

```
   67        60 +  7              95       (80 + 15)
  +28        20 +  8             -28      -(20 +  8)
             ─────────                    ─────────
             80 + 15                        60 +  7 = 67
           = 90 +  5 = 95
```

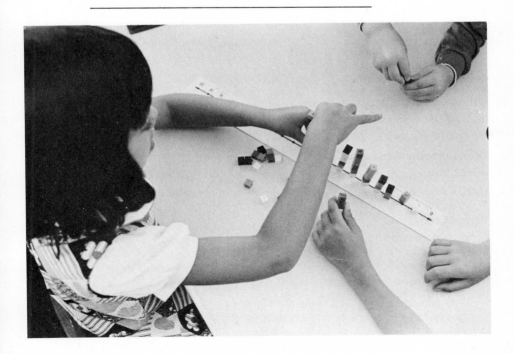

Number lines can be used to good advantage in teaching basic subtraction ideas.

Observe that the standard strategy is to express the problem in a simpler form by using expanded numerals; in some cases, such as examples C and D, a regrouping move is also necessary. These same strategies should form the basis for the use of manipulatives (such as the pocket chart, the abacus, multibase arithmetic blocks, and so on) for solving subtraction problems.

Practice

ACTIVITIES FOR STUDENT INVOLVEMENT, PHASE I: THE MEANING OF SUBTRACTION

Concrete mode activities

Since subtraction is described as the "undoing" of addition, it is suggested that, where possible, the physical world situations used to teach the meaning of addition be modified to show the nature of subtraction's inverse relationship to addition. This means that activities used to teach the meaning of subtraction should be the counterpart of physically combining sets, namely, physically removing subsets or physically completing partially constructed sets.

Sample activity (Orally presented problem situations)
Use the small flannel boards and paper cutouts prepared to teach the meaning of addition and reverse the situation. For example, notice how the addition situation on p. 92 can be modified:

Place 5 paper dogs on one side of your flannel board and 6 paper cats on the other side. Describe how you can tell how many animals you have on your flannel board. Now, remove 6 cats. Describe how you know how many animals are remaining on your flannel board.

Semiconcrete mode activities

To provide semiconcrete activities the teacher should reverse the procedures used with addition and contrast the two sets of graphic displays.

Sample activity 1 (The number line)
Provide students with examples that show how subtraction is the inverse of addition.
Give each student a number line and use the flannel board to present problem situations like the following example.

I've placed a set of 4 peaches on one side of the flannel board. Mark your number line to show how many pieces of fruit are on the flannel board. Now I'm going to place a set of 6 pears on the other side. When I finish, mark your number line to show how many pieces of fruit are on the flannel board.

The students' number lines should look like the following example.

Next reverse the process by saying,

> I am going to remove the set of pears. When I finish, mark your number line to show how many pieces of fruit are left on the flannel board.

The students' number lines should then look like the following:

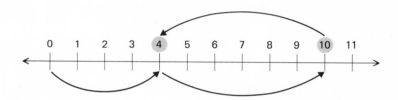

Sample activity 2 (Domino equations)
Make a set of equation cards like the one illustrated below.

Shuffle the cards and place them face down on the playing table. Throw dice to see who goes first. The first player chooses an equation. He then selects a domino which correctly represents the equation and its solution. Each player gets one point for a correct choice. The player with the most points at the end of play is the winner.

Sample activity 3 (Set circles)
Use the same set circles suggested on p. 93. Have the students use them to find the answers to typical classroom situations involving subtraction. For example, suppose that four children are at the classroom aquarium and three sit down. Have someone use set circles to reconstruct how many remained after the three children in the group of four sat down.

Abstract mode activities

Provide symbolic activities by giving the students equations and having them generate verbal problems to match the equation. The inverse of these types of activities are also useful in getting children to operate at the abstract level.

Sample activity (Writing mathematical sentences)

Present problem situations that require the students to write the equation for:

A. "How many are left?" situations. For example,

Bill has five pieces of candy and gives two pieces to Joe. How many does he have left? (Answer $5 - 2 = \boxed{}$)

B. "How many more are needed?" situations. For example,

Jane has completed 6 problems in her math homework. Altogether there are 10 problems in the homework assignment. How many more does Jane have to do to complete the assignment? ($6 + \boxed{} = 10$)

ACTIVITIES FOR STUDENT INVOLVEMENT, PHASE II: THE BASIC SUBTRACTION FACTS

Because the basic subtraction facts are the inverses of the addition facts, it is essential that practice exercises encourage students to use this addition/subtraction relationship to find answers to forgotten or undiscovered subtraction facts. Care should be taken to see that young children try to master the basic subtraction facts only after they show that they can understand inverse relationships.

Concrete mode activities

Give children manipulative devices that can be used when needed to verify the results of their thinking.

Sample activity 1 (Rod families)

Give each student a bag of Cuisenaire rods to be used when working on assignments designed to memorize the basic subtraction combinations.

For example, Bill wants to find answers to the problem $7 - 3 = \boxed{}$. Have him place the light green rod on top of the black rod. Then have him find the rod that completes the equation $7 = 3 + \boxed{}$. This would be the purple rod.

Sample activity 2 (Mathematical balance)

Provide each student in a small instructional group with a mathematical balance like the one illustrated at the top of the next page.

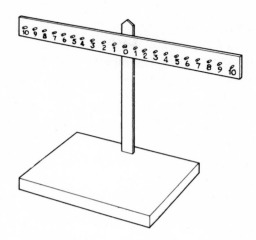

Direct the students to place a washer or washers on the sum (right) side of the balance. Then have them place one washer on the addend (left) side. Each student then tries to find the missing addend that balances the scale.

Sample activity 3 (Counters)
Assuming the children can bundle counters for representing numbers such as 14, have them look for solutions to addition equations such as $14 - 8 = \boxed{}$. Special care should be given to the process of regrouping the tens to ones that is required to understand how place value operates when solving such problems. Also, keep in mind this is the type of readiness needed to solve examples such as $24 - 9 = \boxed{}$, which are taught later.

Semiconcrete mode activities

To provide semiconcrete practice with the basic subtraction facts, use some of the same types of graphic displays that were developed for teaching the basic addition facts. In some cases, slight modification of the materials will be necessary. Observe that graphic displays are particularly useful for representing the three different types of subtraction situations.

Sample activity 1 (Slide rule subtraction)
Using the same slide rule described on p. 95, have students set up the answer to equations like $5 + 4 = \boxed{}$. Then pose the question:

If your ruler shows $5 + 4 = 9$, how can you find the answer to $9 - 4 = \boxed{}$ *without* changing the position of the two rulers?

Present other examples, then ask for solutions to problems such as $8 - 5 = \boxed{}$.
This activity can be extended to a team activity where the team operates against time to obtain answers to subtraction problems.

Sample activity 2 (Dot drawings)

Give students cards with dot drawings like the ones presented below, and have them write the subtraction equations suggested by the cards.

3 − 2 = 1   5 − 3 = 2

Sample activity 3 (Number line)

Place number line drawings like the following on the blackboard.

Have the students write the addition and subtraction equations suggested by the drawing, e.g., 4 + 3 = 7 and 7 − 3 = 4. To place a semipermanent number line on the board, soak yellow chalk in sugar water over night. Use it to draw the number line. After it dries you can erase over the line and it will remain until the board is washed with a wet sponge.

Abstract mode activities

The purpose of abstract activities is to have students commit the basic subtraction facts to memory and to learn how they are related to the basic addition facts. By carefully choosing the facts for the following games, the teacher can make the practice specific or general in nature. These activities can also yield useful diagnostic information. Simply record which cards give which learners difficulty. This strategy is one way to apply Principle 11 which stresses the necessity for designing classroom activities which will help the students remember the basic skills and concepts they have learned.

Sample activity 1 (Puzzle cards)

Make a set of puzzle cards, like the following example, from 5″ × 7″ cards. Cut the cards so that the pieces from one card will not fit the pieces from another card.

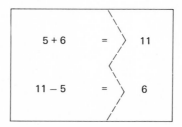

The teacher (or student leader) begins the game by scrambling the pieces face up on a table top. The first player chooses four pieces and then attempts to fit them together. If unsuccessful, he must put all the pieces that do not fit back into play. The second player then chooses four pieces and attempts to fit his pieces together, and so play continues until all cards are assembled. A player gets one point for each card he completes. The player with the most points at the end of play is declared the winner.

Sample activity 2 (A bean bag toss)

Divide the class into two teams. Place a grid on the classroom floor similar to the one shown on p. 97. The first player of one team tosses his two bean bags on the score grid from behind the pitch line. He scores one point for his team if he can correctly subtract the smaller number from the larger number. The first player on the other team then tosses his bags. Play continues with each player adding to his team's score. By varying the numerals written on the grid, all the subtraction combinations can be practiced.

ACTIVITIES FOR STUDENT INVOLVEMENT, PHASE III: THE SUBTRACTION ALGORITHMS INVOLVING AND NOT INVOLVING REGROUPING

Concrete mode activities

To provide concrete activities the teacher should use concrete manipulative devices that highlight the type of strategies involved in the algorithms being taught.

Sample activity 1 (Multibase arithmetic blocks)

Give the students charts labeled like those shown in illustrations 1A and 1B. Have the students write a problem at the right of the chart as indicated in illustrations 1A and 1B. Then have them represent the minuend by placing the correct number of MAB blocks in the appropriate columns of the chart. Finally have the students remove the number of blocks represented by the subtrahend and write the difference. For an example without regrouping see illustration 1A. Notice why an extra step is needed to illustrate regrouping in 1B.

Illustration 1A

First represent the minuend 27 with counters.	Tens (Longs)	Ones (Units)

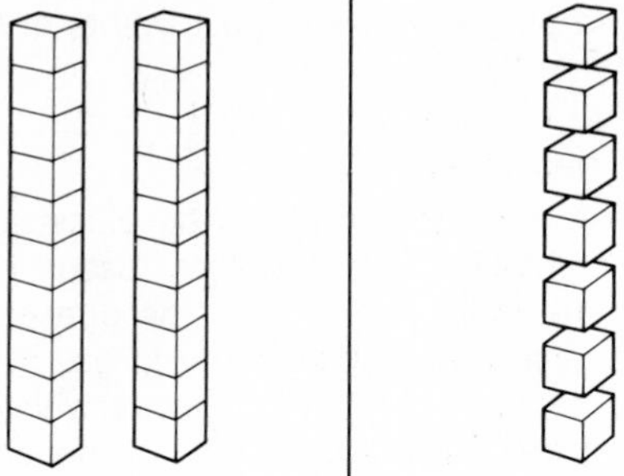

$$27 = 20 + 7$$
$$- 12 = 10 + 2$$
$$10 + 5 = \boxed{15}$$

becomes

Next, remove 1 ten and 2 ones.	Tens (Longs)	Ones (Units)

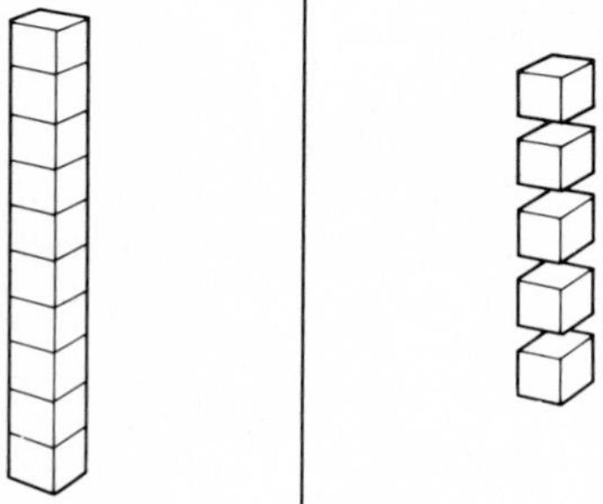

Difference

Illustration 1B

First represent the minuend 34 with counters.	Tens (Longs)	Ones (Units)

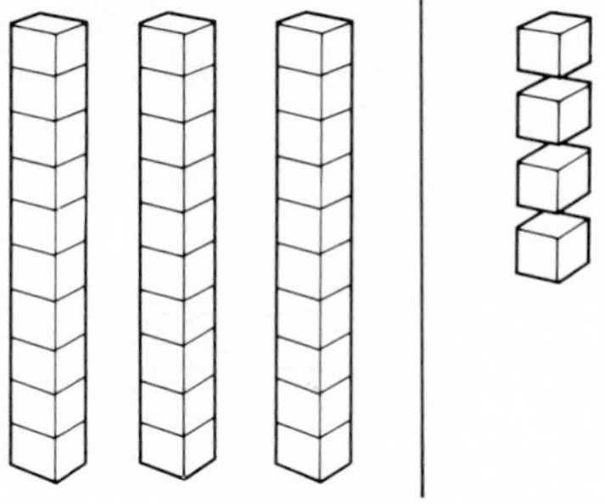

Next exchange 1 ten for 10 ones.	Tens (Longs)	Ones (Units)

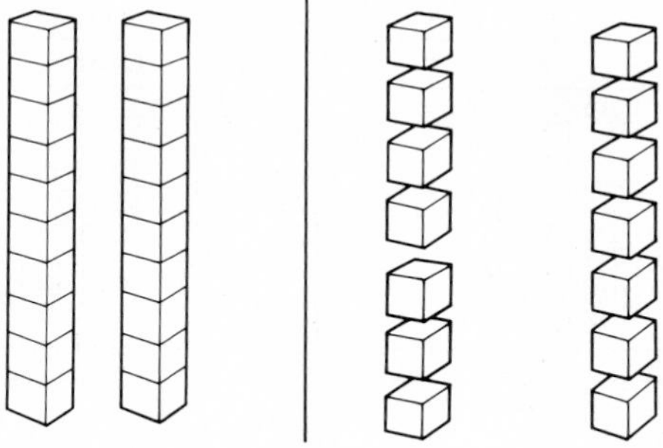

Then remove 2 tens and 7 ones.	Tens (Longs)	Ones (Units)

$$
\begin{array}{r}
34 \\
-27 \\
\end{array}
\longrightarrow
\begin{array}{r}
20 + 14 \\
-(20 + \ 7) \\
\hline
7 \\
\end{array}
$$

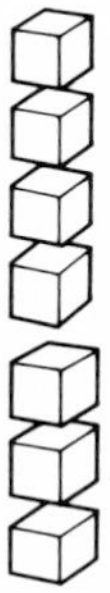

Final result

Sample activity 2 (Pocket charts)

Provide each student with a pocket chart and counters like those shown in illustrations 2A and 2B. Then give the students an equation with a missing addend. Next, have the students represent the given addend by placing counters in the pockets of the chart as necessary. Finally, ask the students how many more counters are needed to obtain the sum. If regrouping is necessary, have the students demonstrate this move. A sample problem that does not require regrouping is given in illustration 2A, and one that does is given in illustration 2B.

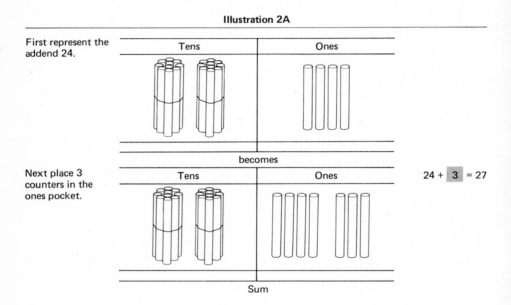

Illustration 2A

First represent the addend 24.

Tens	Ones

becomes

Next place 3 counters in the ones pocket.

Tens	Ones

24 + 3 = 27

Sum

Illustration 2B

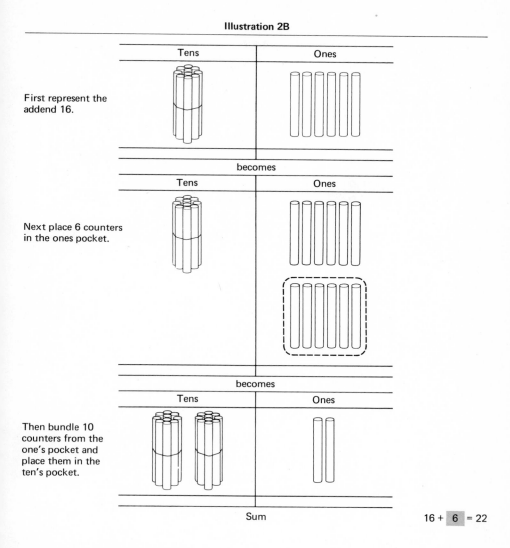

First represent the addend 16.

becomes

Next place 6 counters in the ones pocket.

becomes

Then bundle 10 counters from the one's pocket and place them in the ten's pocket.

Sum   16 + 6 = 22

Semiconcrete mode activities

Give students graphic displays that will help them record the results of each step.

Sample activity 1 (Multibase abacus)

Give each student a multibase abacus like the one in illustration 3A. Have the students use this device to record the steps in their thinking as they mentally work problems such as $45 - 32 = \boxed{}$ or $35 - 26 = \boxed{}$. For example, see illustrations 3A and 3B.

Illustration 3A

Step 1

Represent 45.

Step 2

Remove 3
tens and
2 ones.

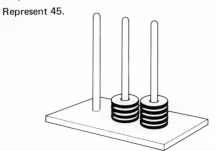

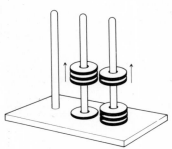

Step 3

The
difference
is 13.

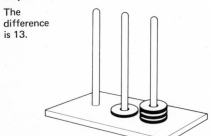

$$\begin{array}{r} 45 \\ -32 \\ \hline 13 \end{array}$$

Illustration 3B

Step 1

Represent 35.

Step 2

Exchange 1
ten for 10
ones.

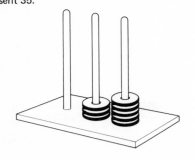

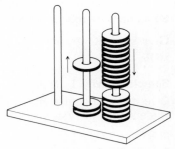

Illustration 3B (continued)

Step 3

Remove 6
ones and
2 tens.

Step 4

The difference
is 9.

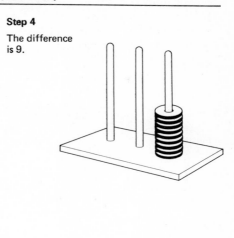

$$\begin{array}{r} 35 \\ -26 \end{array} \longrightarrow \begin{array}{r} 20 + 15 \\ -\ (20 + \ \ 6) \\ \hline \boxed{9} \end{array}$$

Sample activity 2 (Nomograph)

Give each student a nomograph like the one below. First review how to add using the nomograph (place one end of ruler on one side scale, the other end on the other side scale and read the sum from the center scale). Then have the students use their knowledge of the relationship between addition and subtraction to figure out how to use the nomograph to subtract. The following example shows how to place a ruler on the nomograph to find

$$10 + 15 = 25,\ 25 - 10 = 15,\ \text{and}\ 25 - 15 = 10.$$

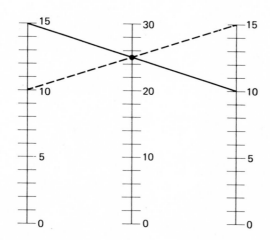

Sample activity 3 (Place value chart and tally marks)

Give each student a ditto sheet containing a place value chart like the one in the illustration below. Also provide two colored pencils, one blue and one red. Have students mark the place value chart to show how they thought through problems such as $22 - 6 = \boxed{}$. Use red for tens and blue for ones.

Step 1

Represent the minuend in

$$\begin{array}{r} 22 \\ -\ 6 \\ \hline \end{array}$$

Tens	Ones
$/\,/$	$/\,/$

Step 2

Rename 22 as 1 ten + 12 ones.

Tens	Ones
$/$	$\cancel{\text{////}}\ \cancel{\text{////}}$ $//$

Step 3

Take away 6 ones.

Tens	Ones
$/$	$\cancel{\text{////}}\ \cancel{\text{////}}$ $\cancel{//}\,/$

Step 4

$$\begin{array}{r} 22 \\ -\ 6 \\ \hline \boxed{16} \end{array}$$

Tens	Ones
$/$	$\cancel{\text{////}}\ /$

Abstract mode activities

To provide abstract activities, teach students to use place value charts and expanded notation to record their thought processes as they work problems such as:

$$\begin{array}{r} 59 \\ -14 \\ \hline \end{array} \quad \text{or} \quad \begin{array}{r} 32 \\ -14 \\ \hline \end{array}$$

Sample activity 1 (Place value chart and expanded notation)

Have students use place value charts to record their computation. Then have them translate their work into expanded notation. This procedure highlights the role place value plays in multidigit subtraction.

Tens	Ones		Tens	Ones
3	2	$\rightarrow$	2	12
-1	4		-1	4
			1	8

$$\text{or} \quad \begin{array}{r} 32 \\ -14 \\ \hline \end{array} \rightarrow \begin{array}{r} 20 + 12 \\ -(10 +\ 4) \\ \hline 10 + 8\ =\ 18 \end{array}$$

Exercise set

1. Use the definition of subtraction to justify the truth of the following statements.
   a) $12 - 8 \neq 7$
   b) $15 - 9 = 6$

2. Translate each of the following subtraction sentences into an equivalent addition sentence.
   a) $13 - 5 = \boxed{}$
   b) $11 - 4 = \boxed{}$

3. Translate each of the following addition sentences into an equivalent subtraction sentence.
   a) $3 + \boxed{} = 7$
   b) $6 + \boxed{} = 10$

4. Construct the subtraction sentences which fulfill the following conditions.

	Subtrahend	Difference	Minuend
a)	x	6	19
b)	r	s	t

5. Complete each of the following set subtraction sentences.
   a) $\{a, b, c\} \sim \{a, b\} = \boxed{}$
   b) $\{u, v, x, y\} \sim \{u, x\} = \boxed{}$

6. Write the number sentence suggested by each of the following set subtraction sentences.
   a) $\{m, n, r, s\} \sim \{r\} = \{m, n, s\}$
   b) $\{a, b, c, x, y\} \sim \{a, y\} = \{b, c, x\}$

7. Identify which of the following are basic subtraction facts.
   a) $9 - 5 = 4$ b) $16 - 3 = 13$
   c) $12 - 1 = 11$ d) $14 - 5 = 9$

8. Use the comprehensive flowchart for teaching addition as a guide for ordering the following types of subtraction problems into the sequence in which they should be taught.

   a)
   $$\begin{array}{r} 27 \\ -\ 3 \\ \hline \end{array} \qquad \begin{array}{r} 35 \\ -21 \\ \hline \end{array} \qquad \begin{array}{r} 13 \\ -\ 5 \\ \hline \end{array}$$

   b)
   $$\begin{array}{r} 54 \\ -\ 9 \\ \hline \end{array} \qquad \begin{array}{r} 58 \\ -21 \\ \hline \end{array} \qquad \begin{array}{r} 63 \\ -48 \\ \hline \end{array}$$

c)   15   54   45
      $-\ 8$ $-\ 9$ -37

d)   67   82   95
      $-\ 5$ -73 $-\ 8$

9. Is subtraction a *commutative* operation? That is, does

$$x - y = y - x$$

for all whole numbers x and y?

10. Is subtraction an *associative* operation? That is, does

$$(x - y) - z = x - (y - z)$$

for all whole numbers x, y, and z?

11. The most commonly used algorithm for subtraction is commonly referred to as the *decomposition* method. There are a variety of other subtraction algorithms which have been developed, and several of these are illustrated below. Study the examples, and then see if you can apply the algorithms to the problem which is given.

a) *Decomposition method*

Example	Step 1	Step 2	Step 3	Practice problem
56 -29	$4\overset{1}{\cancel{5}}6$ -29	$4\overset{1}{\cancel{5}}6$ -29 7	$4\overset{1}{\cancel{5}}6$ -29 27	73 -48

b) *Equal additions method*

56 -29	$\overset{1}{5}6$ $-\overset{3}{2}9$	$\overset{1}{5}6$ $-\overset{3}{2}9$ 7	$\overset{1}{5}6$ $-\overset{3}{2}9$ 27	73 -48

c) *Provident method*

56 -29	56 -29 3	$\overset{1}{5}6$ -29 $\cancel{3}$ 2	$\overset{1}{5}6$ -29 $\cancel{3}$ 27	73 -48

d) *Compensation method*

56 -29 Note the change in problems!	57 -30	57 -30 7	57 -30 27	73 -48

12. In Problem 11, both the equal additions method and the compensation method are direct applications of the principle:

$$x - y = (x + k) - (y + k).$$

Explain.

13. A so-called "comparison" method for subtraction is illustrated by the following example.

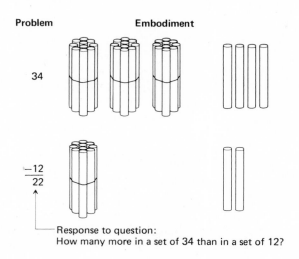

Problem   **Embodiment**

34

−12
——
22
↑

└─── Response to question:
How many more in a set of 34 than in a set of 12?

Use sticks (like those illustrated here) or multibase arithmetic blocks to solve the subtraction problem $46 - 34 = \boxed{}$ by the comparison method.

14. List the types of addition problems which must be mastered as prerequisites to being able to solve $35 - 19 = \boxed{}$. Then describe what implications this has for diagnostic/prescriptive teaching.

15. Use a multibase abacus to show the steps needed to solve the following subtraction problem using the decomposition algorithm. Record the results of each step using expanded notation.

$$\begin{array}{r} 405 \\ -279 \\ \hline \end{array}$$

16. Why is an understanding of place value a prerequisite for teaching subtraction problems such as $35 - 19$?

17. What advantages does a pupil gain when he perceives addition and subtraction as inverse operations?

18. Read W. A. Brownell, "Borrowing in subtraction," *Journal of Educational Research* (February 1940): 415–424 and briefly describe what implications this study has for the use of crutches in teaching subtraction?

19. Consider each of the following subtraction examples which appear in a student text. In each case, tell which interpretation of subtraction is involved.

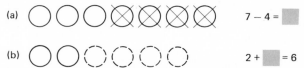

(a) $7 - 4 =$ ▨

(b) $2 +$ ▨ $= 6$

20. Supply reasons for each step in the following example.

$$15 - 7 = 15 - (5 + 2)$$
$$= (15 - 5) - 2$$
$$= 10 - 2$$
$$= \quad 8$$

21. Why is the procedure illustrated below a good subtraction check?

$$\begin{array}{r} 132 \\ -\ 26 \\ \hline 106 \end{array} \qquad \begin{array}{r} \lceil\ \overline{132}\ \rceil \\ | -106\ | \\ \lfloor\ \underline{\ 26}\ \rfloor \end{array}$$

22. Use counting sticks or multibase arithmetic blocks to explain the regrouping processes involved in finding the following difference.

$$\begin{array}{r} 124 \\ -\ 38 \\ \hline \end{array}$$

READINGS FOR ADDITIONAL STUDY

For each of the following topics, select an article from the bibliography which addresses the issue and write a brief reaction report.

23. The use of number lines to teach subtraction concepts.

24. Teaching regrouping procedures in subtraction.

Bibliography

1. Bennett, Albert B., and Gary L. Musser. "A concrete approach to integer addition and subtraction." *The Arithmetic Teacher* **23** (May 1976): 332–336.

2. Brownell, William A., and H. E. Moser. *Meaningful vs. Mechanical Learning.* Durham, North Carolina: Duke University Press, 1949.

3. Buckingham, B. R. "Teaching addition and subtraction facts together or separately." *Educational Research Bulletin* **6** (May 1927): 228–29.

4. Cacha, Frances B. "Subtraction: regrouping with flexibility." *The Arithmetic Teacher* **22** (May 1975): 402–404.

5. Cleminson, Robert A. "Developing the subtraction algorithm." *The Arithmetic Teacher* **20** (December 1973): 634–38.

6. Cox, L. S. "Diagnosing and remediating systematic errors in addition and subtraction computation." *The Arithmetic Teacher* **22** (February 1975): 151–57.

7. Deans, Edwina. "Practice in renaming numbers—an aid to subtraction." *The Arithmetic Teacher* **12** (February 1965): 142.

8. Dye, David. "A different way of subtracting." *The Arithmetic Teacher* **12** (January 1965): 65–66.

9. Easterday, Kenneth, and Helen Easterday. "A logical method for basic subtraction." *The Arithmetic Teacher* **13** (May 1966): 404–406.

10. Fremont, Herbert. "Pipe cleaners and loops—discovering how to add and subtract directed numbers." *The Arithmetic Teacher* **13** (November 1966): 568–72.

11. Hamilton, E. W. "Subtraction by the 'dribble method'." *The Arithmetic Teacher* **18** (May 1971): 346–47.

12. Hoppe, Ruth C. "Research on a 'new' method of subtraction." *The Arithmetic Teacher* **22** (April 1975): 320–27.

13. Hutchings, Barton. "Low-stress subtraction." *The Arithmetic Teacher* **22** (March 1975): 226–32.

14. Ikeda, Hitoshi, and Masue Ando. "A new algorithm for subtraction." *The Arithmetic Teacher* **21** (December 1974): 716–19.

15. Immerzeel, George, and Don Wiederander. "Ideas." *The Arithmetic Teacher* **21** (February 1974): 117–24.

16. Johnson, Paul B. "Finding the missing addend, or checkbook subtraction." *The Arithmetic Teacher* **19** (November 1972): 540–44.

17. Marion, C. "How to get subtraction into the game." *The Arithmetic Teacher* **17** (February 1970): 169–70.

18. Milne, Esther. "Subtraction of integers—discovered through a game." *The Arithmetic Teacher* **16** (February 1969): 148–49.

19. National Council of Teachers of Mathematics. *Topics in Mathematics. Twenty-Ninth Yearbook.* Washington: The Council, 1964, Booklet 2.

20. Silvery, I. M. "Fourth graders develop their own subtraction algorithm." *The Arithmetic Teacher* **17** (March 1970): 233–36.

21. Smith, W. "Subtraction steps." *The Arithmetic Teacher* **15** (May 1968): 458–60.

22. Weaver, J. Fred. "Some factors associated with pupils' performance levels on simple open addition and subtraction sentences." *The Arithmetic Teacher* **18** (November 1971): 513–19.

23. Weaver, J. Fred. "Whither research on compound subtraction." *The Arithmetic Teacher* **3** (February 1956): 17–20.

24. Werner, M. "The case for a more universal number-line model of subtraction." *The Arithmetic Teacher* **20** (January 1973): 61–64.

25. West, T. A. "Diagnosing pupil errors: looking for patterns." *The Arithmetic Teacher* **18** (November 1971): 467–69.

Teaching multiplication of cardinal numbers

Synopsis and objectives

Chapter 6 provides you with the basic theoretical and practical information you need to teach the concepts and principles of the operation of multiplication. The **theory** section is organized around a series of flowcharts showing the order in which the multiplication concepts and computation skills should be learned. The **practice** section contains a variety of instructional activities for classroom use. The activities have been chosen to illustrate selected teaching principles from Chapter 2 and they are also keyed to the flowcharts for teaching multiplication concepts.

Chapter 6 also has a bibliography in which you can find some of the concepts discussed in greater detail. The bibliography can help you expand upon the listing of classroom activities in areas that interest you most.

From a careful study of Chapter 6, you should be able to

1. state and illustrate the definition of multiplication that is based on the notion of Cartesian product;

2. state and illustrate the definition of multiplication that is based on the notion of set union;

3. state and illustrate the definition of multiplication that is based on the notion of repeated addition;

4. define and illustrate the terms *product, factor, multiplier,* and *multiplicand;*

5. classify a product, $a \times b$, as belonging or not belonging to the set of basic multiplication facts (BMF);

6. construct a partial flowchart for teaching multiplication which has the basic multiplication facts as a terminal behavior and a knowledge of the basic addition facts as an entry behavior;

7. demonstrate how to use the distributive property to determine the product of a one-digit number and a two-digit number, whether regrouping is required or not;

8. demonstrate how to use the associative property of multiplication to find the product of two multiples of ten, both of which are less than 100;

9. construct a partial flowchart for teaching multiplication where the terminal behavior calls for being able to find the product of a two-digit number and a one-digit number where no regrouping is necessary, and the entry behavior is a knowledge of the basic multiplication facts;

10. construct a partial flowchart for teaching multiplication where the terminal behavior calls for being able to find the product of a one-digit number and a two-digit number where regrouping is necessary, and the entry behavior is a knowledge of the same problem type but for those cases not involving regrouping;

11. construct sample problems for each component of a comprehensive flowchart for teaching multiplication;

12. given a collection of different types of multiplication problems, order them into a sequence which illustrates an acceptable sequence for teaching;

13. state and illustrate the commutative property of multiplication;

14. state and illustrate the associative property of multiplication;

15. state and illustrate the closure property of multiplication of whole numbers;

16. specify which whole number is a multiplicative identity, and illustrate this property by means of an example;

17. supply missing steps in the application of the various popular forms of the multiplication algorithm for all the basic problem types;

18. justify each step in the application of the various popular forms of the multiplication algorithm;

19. describe how to use the flowcharts for teaching multiplication as an aid in the diagnosis of individual learning states;

20. demonstrate how to use instructional apparatus, such as an abacus, Cuisenaire rods, MAB blocks, and so on, to teach the various basic types of multiplication problems;

21. demonstrate the procedures for finding products in cases where one or both factors are negative;

22.–25. formulate concrete, semiconcrete, and abstract mode activities for pupil involvement which facilitate the learning of the meaning of multiplication, the basic multiplication facts, the properties of multiplication, and the various forms of the multiplication algorithm.

Teaching multiplication of cardinal numbers

Theory

BASIC CONCEPTS

Multiplication of whole numbers, like addition, is a binary operation, and it can be illustrated as follows:

$$(a, b) \xrightarrow{\times} c,$$

where a, b, and c are whole numbers. For example,

$$(2, 3) \xrightarrow{\times} 6, \qquad (7, 1) \xrightarrow{\times} 7, \qquad (8, 0) \xrightarrow{\times} 0.$$

The following definition of the operation of multiplication is based on the notion of the Cartesian product of two sets.

Definition of Multiplication
Let A and B be sets such that $n(A) = a$ and $n(B) = b$. Then

$$a \times b = n(A \times B).$$

For purposes of illustration, suppose we wish to determine the product 2×4. To do this, we think of a pair of sets, say A and B, whose number properties are 2 and 4, respectively. Suppose, for example, that $A = \{m, n\}$ and that $B = \{p, q, r, s\}$. The product 2×4, then, is the number property of the Cartesian product set $A \times B$. Since

$$A \times B = \left\{ \begin{matrix} (m, p), \ (m, q), \ (m, r), \ (m, s) \\ (n, p), \ (n, q), \ (n, r), \ (n, s) \end{matrix} \right\},$$

it follows that $n(A \times B) = 8$. Thus $2 \times 4 = 8$.

The foregoing ideas may appear at first sight to be somewhat pedantic, but they can be treated heuristically in a manner suitable for teaching at the elementary school level. This point is illustrated by the following example.

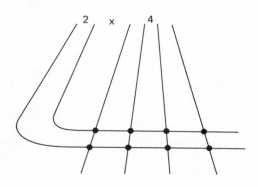

Observe the array of dots; note that the set of dots comprising the array corresponds to the Cartesian product set $A \times B$ given above. Since there are eight dots in the array, we conclude that $2 \times 4 = 8$. In general, every product $a \times b$ can be visualized as an *array,* and vice versa. For example, the arrays associated with the products 3×5 and 4×2 are shown here.

3 x 5   4 x 2

There are other good ways to interpret the operation of multiplication of whole numbers that are more widely known than the Cartesian product approach described above. One of these is to think of multiplication as *repeated addition.* For example,

$$2 \times 4 = 4 + 4 = 8,$$
$$3 \times 2 = 2 + 2 + 2 = 6,$$
$$4 \times 3 = 3 + 3 + 3 + 3 = 12.$$

It is popular in contemporary curriculum materials to develop the idea of multiplication in this way, but to do so by resorting initially to the subordinate idea of uniting equivalent sets. For example, an introductory task for a child might look something like this:

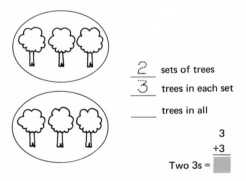

A Phase I Flowchart for Teaching Multiplication is given in Fig. 6.1. It is based on the idea of introducing multiplication as repeated addition, but it is also satisfactory for the Cartesian product approach.

It is understood that the flowchart given in Fig. 6.1 builds upon the *addition* flowcharts given in Figs. 4.1 and 4.2. Note the inclusion in Fig. 6.1 of the component labeled "Skip counting." This competence is related, of course, to the idea of repeated addition, and is widely believed to be a valuable precursor to the development of the multiplication idea, per se.

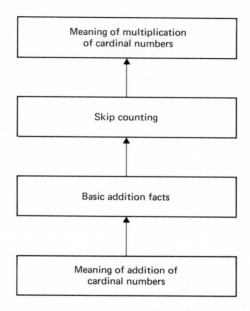

Fig. 6.1   Phase I flowchart for teaching multiplication.

THE BASIC MULTIPLICATION FACTS

Table 6.1   Second factor (multiplicand)

×	0	1	2	3	4	5	6	7	8	9	
0	0			0							
1										9	The standard name for the product 27←3 × 9.
2	0		4				12				
3										27	
4											The standard name for the product
5			10								
6								42			6 × 7
7		7									
8											
9					36						

First factor (multiplier)

As with addition, there are one hundred basic multiplication facts to be learned. They are suggested by Table 6.1. This table is constructed in the same manner as Table 4.1 in which the basic addition facts are tabulated.

Recall that the basic addition facts were learned in subsets; so also are the basic multiplication facts learned. While the subsets are far from standardized, a typical plan might correspond roughly to that given in Table 6.2.

Table 6.2

Subset	Type of problem
1	$a \times b$ where $a \leqslant 5$ and $b \leqslant 5$
2	$a \times b$ where $5 < a \leqslant 9$ and $b \leqslant 5$
3	$a \times b$ where $a \leqslant 5$ and $5 < b \leqslant 9$
4	$a \times b$ where $5 < a \leqslant 9$ and $5 < b \leqslant 9$

The instructional procedures for teaching subset 1 of the basic multiplication facts are fairly straightforward and consist of activities which appeal directly to the basic meaning of multiplication. Typically, the facts are developed in factor families, for example, the set of products having two as a factor (i.e., 2×1, 2×2, 2×3, 2×4, and so on). It is also now common to teach the commutative property of multiplication and use it as an aid to learning the basic multiplication facts.

In attempting to teach subsets 2–4 of the basic multiplication facts, the distributive property may be introduced and used to good advantage. The procedure is illustrated by the following example. Note how the array representing 3×7 can be partitioned into two arrays representing 3×5 and 3×2.

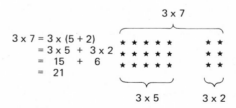

$$3 \times 7 = 3 \times (5 + 2)$$
$$= 3 \times 5 + 3 \times 2$$
$$= 15 + 6$$
$$= 21$$

More sophisticated methods such as these need not be used, of course, since it is always possible to retreat to the repeated addition idea (e.g., $3 \times 7 = 7 + 7 + 7$).

The foregoing ideas are summarized in the Phase II Flowchart for Teaching Multiplication which is given in Fig. 6.2.

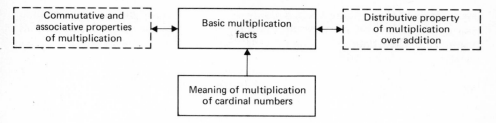

Fig. 6.2   Phase II flowchart for teaching multiplication.

THE MULTIPLICATION ALGORITHM: PROBLEM TYPE 1

The first major type of multiplication problem to be dealt with after the child has learned the basic multiplication facts is the one that consists of finding the product of a two-digit number and a one-digit number where no regrouping (i.e., no carry) is necessary. For example, 3×12, 4×21 and 2×31 are problems of this type.

The following examples illustrate the basic ideas involved in teaching students how to deal with such problems.

$$3 \times 12 = 3 \times (10 + 2) \qquad 4 \times 21 = 4 \times (20 + 1)$$
$$= 3 \times 10 + 3 \times 2 \qquad = 4 \times 20 + 4 \times 1$$
$$= 30 + 6 \qquad\qquad = 80 + 4$$
$$= 36 \qquad\qquad\quad = 84$$

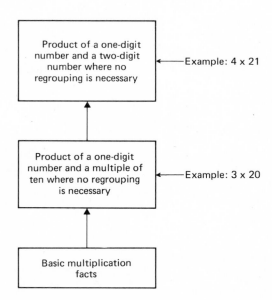

Fig. 6.3   Phase III flowchart for teaching multiplication.

An analysis of these examples reveals the fact that the only new subcompetence required is to be able to compute products like 3×10 and 4×20 (where the products are less than 100). This fact is accounted for by the Phase III Flowchart for Teaching Addition given in Fig. 6.3.

When the vertical problem format is introduced, it is usually developed using a three-step process culminating in the standard form of the algorithm. In the first step, the problems are structured in a form somewhat like that shown in the following example.

$$\begin{array}{r} 21 \\ \times 4 \\ \hline \end{array} \rightarrow \begin{array}{r} 20+1 \\ \times\, 4 \\ \hline 80+4 = 84. \end{array}$$

Observe that the procedure is identical to that used in the horizontal format; only the format has been changed. The second step moves closer to the standard form of the algorithm. Here is an example.

$$\begin{array}{r} 31 \\ \times 2 \\ \hline 2 \\ 60 \\ \hline 62 \end{array} \rightarrow \begin{array}{r} 30+1 \\ \times\, 2 \\ \hline \end{array}$$

The third and final step is to take the shortcut resulting in the desired form of the algorithm.

$$\begin{array}{r} 32 \\ \times 3 \\ \hline 96 \end{array}$$

THE MULTIPLICATION ALGORITHM: PROBLEM TYPE 2

Finding the product of a one-digit number and a two-digit number where regrouping is necessary is the next type of problem to be considered, but, as you will see, this type must be broken into subcategories, depending upon the nature of the regrouping that is required. Study the examples carefully. The teaching sequence should follow the order of the examples.

Example A
$$\begin{aligned}
2 \times 27 &= 2 \times (20+7) \\
&= 2 \times 20 \;+\; 2 \times 7 \\
&= 40 + 14 \left.\right\} \text{Regrouping from} \\
&= 50 + 4 \;\;\left.\right\} \text{ones to tens} \\
&= 54
\end{aligned}$$

Example B
$$\begin{aligned}
4 \times 32 &= 4 \times (30+2) \\
&= 4 \times 30 \;+\; 4 \times 2 \left.\right\} \text{The product } 4 \times 30 \\
&= 120 + 8 \;\;\;\;\;\;\;\;\;\;\left.\right\} \text{requires regrouping} \\
&= 128 \;\;\;\;\;\;\;\;\;\;\;\;\;\;\;\; \text{from tens to hundreds.}
\end{aligned}$$

Example C $5 \times 67 = 5 \times (60 + 7)$

$$= 5 \times 60 + 5 \times 7$$

$$= 300 + 35$$

$$= 335$$

Regrouping required both from ones to tens and from tens to hundreds in this example.

As suggested by Examples B and C, this problem type requires that the subcompetence of being able to find the product of a one-digit number and a multiple of ten must be extended to cover cases where the products are one hundred or greater. A clever paper and pencil procedure for teaching this competence rests upon the associative property of multiplication (assumed to have been learned earlier) and the basic concepts underlying the decimal system of numeration. The procedure is as follows:

$$5 \times 60 = 5 \times (6 \times 10)$$

$$= (5 \times 6) \times 10$$

$$= 30 \times 10$$

$$= 300$$

This example requires still another subcompetence, namely the ability to compute products like 30×10. A common practice for dealing with this type of problem again relies on the associative property of multiplication:

$$30 \times 10 = (3 \times 10) \times 10$$

$$= 3 \times (10 \times 10)$$

$$= 3 \times 100$$

$$= 300$$

When the vertical format is used to find products of Problem Type 2 variety, the sequence of events is analogous to that employed in Problem Type 1. The following examples illustrate the basic ideas.

Form A
$$\begin{array}{r} 27 \\ \times 3 \\ \hline \end{array} \rightarrow \begin{array}{r} 20 + 7 \\ \times 3 \\ \hline 60 + 21 = 81 \end{array}$$

Form B
$$\begin{array}{r} 62 \\ \times 4 \\ \hline \end{array} \rightarrow \begin{array}{r} 60 + 2 \\ \times 4 \\ \hline 8 \\ 240 \\ \hline 248 \end{array}$$

Form C
$$\begin{array}{r} \overset{3}{85} \\ \times 7 \\ \hline 595 \end{array}$$

The standard form of the algorithm

The hierarchical relationship among the foregoing examples is expressed by the flowchart given in Fig. 6.4.

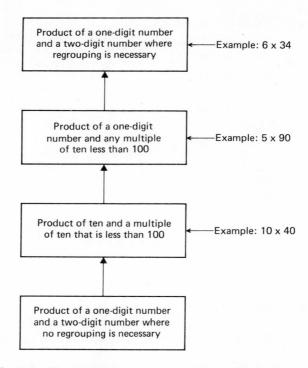

Fig. 6.4 Phase IV flowchart for teaching multiplication.

It is interesting to note that the array interpretation of both Type 1 and Type 2 multiplication problems helps clarify the processes that are involved in the use of the standard algorithm, as shown here.

Example A The following array illustrates the product 3 x 23.

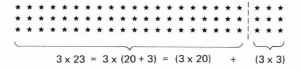

$$3 \times 23 = 3 \times (20 + 3) = (3 \times 20) + (3 \times 3)$$

Example B The following array illustrates the product 5 x 17.

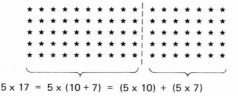

$$5 \times 17 = 5 \times (10 + 7) = (5 \times 10) + (5 \times 7)$$

THE MULTIPLICATION ALGORITHM: PROBLEM TYPE 3

After the student has learned how to find the product of a two-digit number and a one-digit number, the next major type of multiplication problem to be considered is the product of a pair of two-digit numbers where no regrouping is necessary. In this instance, problems would be restricted to the following form:

$$\begin{array}{r} ab \\ \times cd \\ \hline \end{array}$$

where all of the products $d \times b$, $d \times a$, $c \times b$, $c \times a$ are less than ten. Each of the following sample problems falls into this class.

$$\begin{array}{r} 21 \\ \times 42 \\ \hline \end{array} \qquad \begin{array}{r} 40 \\ \times 20 \\ \hline \end{array} \qquad \begin{array}{r} 23 \\ \times 11 \\ \hline \end{array} \qquad \begin{array}{r} 34 \\ \times 20 \\ \hline \end{array}$$

Note that the two following examples do not fall into this class.

$$\begin{array}{r} 56 \\ \times 34 \\ \hline \end{array} \qquad \begin{array}{r} 46 \\ \times 30 \\ \hline \end{array}$$

One of the elementary subclasses of Problem Type 3, namely finding the product of ten and a multiple of ten less than 100 (e.g., 10×50) was included in the Phase IV Flowchart for Teaching Multiplication, and hence would be presumed to be already known. The first new subclass of problems to be learned, therefore, would consist of products of two multiples of ten. A common way for finding such products is shown here.

$$\begin{aligned} 20 \times 30 &= (2 \times 10) \times (3 \times 10) \\ &= (2 \times 3) \times (10 \times 10) \qquad \text{Factors rearranged} \\ &= 6 \times 100 \\ &= 600 \end{aligned}$$

The key to this technique is the rearrangement of factors, as indicated. It will be referred to henceforth as the *factor rearrangement* principle. This principle is rooted, of course, in the associative and commutative properties of multiplication.

Customarily, the next subclass of problems to be considered is that where just one of the factors is a multiple of ten. Two forms of an example of this problem type are illustrated below.

Form A   (Horizontal format)
$$\begin{aligned} 20 \times 32 &= 20 \times (30 + 2) \\ &= 20 \times 30 + 20 \times 2 \qquad \text{Distributive property} \\ &= 600 + 40 \\ &= 640. \end{aligned}$$

Form B   (Initial vertical format)

$$
\begin{array}{r}
32 \\
\times 20
\end{array}
\rightarrow
\begin{array}{r}
30 + 2 \\
\times\ 20 \\
\hline
600 + 40 = 640 \\
\uparrow \qquad \uparrow \\
(20 \times 30)\ (20 \times 2)
\end{array}
$$

After the student has mastered problems of this variety, the more general cases are tackled. The nub of the issue is to enable the child to see that for products like, say, 23×32 four individual products must be calculated and summed. An extremely useful (but unfortunately rarely used) technique for teaching this idea is to resort once again to the array interpretation of multiplication. As illustrated in Fig. 6.5, all four necessary subproducts appear in the array form of 23×32. These four subproducts can easily be identified by constructing expanded forms of the factors, as indicated by the following example.

$$
\begin{array}{r}
32 \\
\times 23
\end{array}
\rightarrow
\begin{array}{r}
30 + 2 \\
\times\ (20 + 3) \\
\hline
6 \leftarrow (3 \times 2) \\
90 \leftarrow (3 \times 30) \\
40 \leftarrow (20 \times 2) \\
600 \leftarrow (20 \times 30) \\
\hline
736
\end{array}
$$

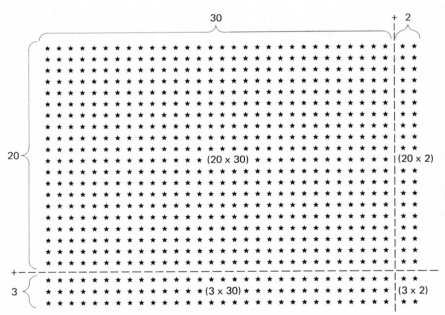

Fig. 6.5 An array form of the product 23×32 which demonstrates that $23 \times 32 = (3 \times 2) + (3 \times 30) + (20 \times 2) + (20 \times 30)$.

The teacher is helping the children use an array to represent the answer to $4 \times 9 = (4 \times 4) + (4 \times 5) = \boxed{}$.

THE MULTIPLICATION ALGORITHM: PROBLEM TYPE 4

After the student has learned how to find products of the form

$$\begin{array}{r} ab \\ \times cd \\ \hline \end{array}$$

where all of the products $d \times b$, $d \times a$, $c \times b$, and $c \times a$ are less than ten, the cases are considered where one or more of these products equals or exceeds ten. These problem types will be designated as products of a pair of two-digit numbers where regrouping is necessary.

In general, within this problem class, the subclasses to be taught parallel those described for Problem Type 3. The following examples illustrate the various broad categories of subproblems which can be encountered, and the order in which they should be taught.

$\quad$ **Subclass A** $\quad$ Both factors are a multiple of ten.

$$
\begin{aligned}
40 \times 30 &= (4 \times 10) \times (3 \times 10) \enspace \rceil \text{ Factor} \\
&= (4 \times 3) \times (10 \times 10) \enspace \llcorner \text{ rearrangement} \\
&= 12 \times 100 \\
&= 1200
\end{aligned}
$$

Subclass B   One factor is a multiple of ten.

$$\begin{array}{r} 32 \\ \times 40 \end{array} \rightarrow \begin{array}{r} 30 + 2 \\ \times\ 40 \\ \hline 1200 + 80 = 1280 \\ \uparrow \qquad \uparrow \\ (40 \times 30)\ (40 \times 2) \end{array}$$

Subclass C   General case.

$$\begin{array}{r} 54 \\ \times 16 \end{array} \rightarrow \begin{array}{r} (50 + 4) \\ \times (10 + 6) \\ \hline 24 \leftarrow (6 \times 4) \\ 300 \leftarrow (6 \times 50) \\ 40 \leftarrow (10 \times 4) \\ 500 \leftarrow (10 \times 50) \\ \hline 864 \end{array}$$

It should be noted that Subclasses B and C can be broken down even further according to the nature of the regrouping which is required (i.e., which sub-products are greater than ten). The details of this procedure are taken up in the exercises at the end of the chapter.

In Fig. 6.6, a Phase V Flowchart is given which summarizes the discussion of Problem Types 3 and 4.

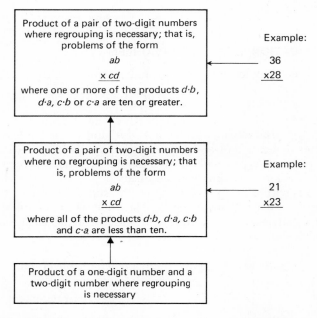

Fig. 6.6   Phase V flowchart for teaching multiplication.

THE MULTIPLICATION ALGORITHM: OTHER PROBLEM TYPES

All of the basic competencies necessary to apply the multiplication algorithm to other problem types have been included in the discussions of the four prob-

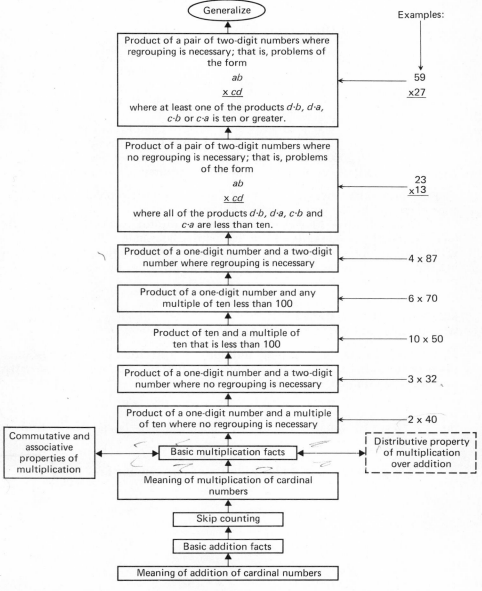

Fig. 6.7 Comprehensive flowchart for the teaching of multiplication.

lem types discussed. The procedures used need only be generalized, as illustrated by the following examples.

a) $3 \times 200 = 3 \times (2 \times 100)$
$\qquad = (3 \times 2) \times 100$
$\qquad = 6 \times 100$
$\qquad = 600$

Product of a one-digit number and a multiple of 100

b) $\begin{array}{r} 214 \\ \times 2 \\ \hline \end{array} \rightarrow \begin{array}{r} 200 + 10 + 4 \\ \times 2 \\ \hline 400 + 20 + 8 = 428 \end{array}$

Product of a one-digit number and a three-digit number, no regrouping required

c) $\begin{array}{r} 438 \\ \times 5 \\ \hline \end{array} \rightarrow \begin{array}{r} 400 + 30 + 8 \\ \times 5 \\ \hline 2000 + 150 + 40 = 2190 \end{array}$

Product of a one-digit number and a three-digit number, regrouping required

The use of manipulatives for teaching these additional problem types are, of course, essentially the same as those used earlier.

A Comprehensive Flowchart for Teaching Multiplication is given in Fig. 6.7. It is simply a composite of the five partial flowcharts (Phase I–Phase V) given earlier. Observe that it can be used as an aid in determining the learning states of individual children, and, consequently, also in prescribing appropriate learning activities.

MULTIPLICATION IN CASES
WHERE ONE OR BOTH FACTORS ARE NEGATIVE

It is possible to use the "repeated addition" interpretation of multiplication to discover the rule for finding the product of a positive number and a negative number. For example, think of

$$4 \times {}^-3 \qquad \text{as} \qquad {}^-3 + {}^-3 + {}^-3 + {}^-3.$$

So, $4 \times {}^-3 = {}^-12$. Similarly, think of ${}^-5 \times 6$ as $6 \times {}^-5$ and it, in turn, as

$$ {}^-5 + {}^-5 + {}^-5 + {}^-5 + {}^-5 + {}^-5 $$

or ${}^-30$. The procedure can be nicely illustrated on a number line.

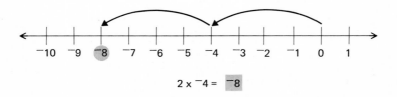

$$2 \times {}^-4 = {}^-8$$

Observe that *the product of a positive number and a negative number is always negative.*

Establishing a meaningful rule for finding the product of a pair of negative numbers is a bit more complicated. One good way for helping children "discover" the rule is to build a pattern similar to the following:

$$4 \times {}^-5 = {}^-20$$
$$3 \times {}^-5 = {}^-15$$
$$2 \times {}^-5 = {}^-10$$
$$1 \times {}^-5 = {}^-5$$
$$0 \times {}^-5 = 0$$
$${}^-1 \times {}^-5 = \boxed{}$$

The pattern suggests the desired result, namely 5. The pattern can be extended to suggest that ${}^-2 \times {}^-5 = 10$, ${}^-3 \times {}^-5 = 15$, and so on. As a result we can make the generalization that *the product of two negative numbers is always positive.*

Practice

In the **practice** section of this chapter you will find activities and learning situations which illustrate how some of the instructional principles presented in Chapter 2 can be applied in classroom settings. As indicated by Principles 2 and 3, for example, initial learning experiences should be based upon the manipulation of concrete embodiments of the concept(s) to be learned. Accordingly, the activities provided in general have been designed to fit nicely into *learning centers* where the laboratory approach to learning is emphasized. The classification of the activities in terms of mode of representation also should encourage the construction of other types of learning centers where the use of semiconcrete and abstract embodiments of concepts are stressed, a practice that would be in conformance with Principle 4.

ACTIVITIES FOR STUDENT INVOLVEMENT, PHASE I: THE MEANING OF MULTIPLICATION

Concrete mode activities

Sample activity 1 (Pencil Lacrosse)

Have students make sets of pencils with one to nine pencils in each set and package each set with a rubber band. Form two teams of students and give each team several sets of pencils.

A member of Team 1 begins by opening and laying down part of one set of pencils on the playing table as indicated below. A member of Team 2 then lays down a set of pencils across Team 1's pencil arrangement. At this time a member of Team 1 must correctly describe the pencil display and count the number of intersections formed by the sets of crossed pencils.

In the example given below the Team 1 player would say, "2 pencils crossed by 3 pencils gives 6 intersections." A team gets one point for each correct description. The team with the most points at the end of play is the winner.

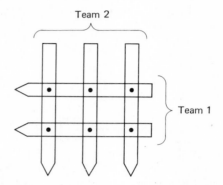

Sample activity 2 (Products as sets)

Give the children a set of blocks and ask them to represent products as shown by the following example.

$$3 \times 2 = \boxed{}$$

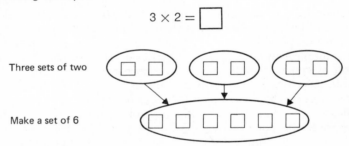

Three sets of two

Make a set of 6

Sample activity 3 (Orally presented problem situations)

As indicated before, presenting problem situations orally provides a way of presenting readiness activities. Give the children play money needed to solve problems such as the following:

1. How much money would you spend if you bought 7 pieces of candy that cost 3 cents a piece?
2. How much would you spend if you bought six 8-cent stamps?
3. Jim earns 5 cents each day for putting out the trash. How much will he have earned at the end of one week?

Semiconcrete mode activities

To provide semiconcrete activities, the teacher should use graphic displays to replace the actual objects used for concrete presentations.

Sample activity 1 (Ordered pair relay)

The teacher should divide the class into two relay teams. Then he should list the same two sets of clothing and the color of each item on the blackboard for each team. For example, see the completed figure below.

Team 1

Shirts : { Blue, Green, Red }

Trousers : { Black, Gray, Yellow }

Team 2

Shirts : { Blue, Green, Red }

Trousers : { Black, Gray, Yellow }

Each team lines up in a single file and the first team member from each team goes to the blackboard and draws a line from one shirt color to one trouser color. He then goes to the end of the line and the other players do likewise. Play continues until one team completes all possible pairings. No two players on the same team may make the same pairing. Each team gets 1 point for each correct pairing. Obviously the team who discovers a systematic way of going about the pairing will win most often. The teacher should have the students share their strategies.

Sample activity 2 (Nonverbal problem setting)

Place the following sketch on the blackboard. Then ask the class to identify the problem Bill has to solve.

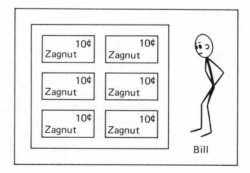

Whenever possible, recast student responses in terms of multiplication ideas.

Sample activity 3 (Jigsaw match)

Using 5″ × 8″ cards, make a set of array-description cards like the one shown. Cut the array cards so that they will fit only one description card. Scramble the array cards and the description cards and ask the students to pair them so that the array cards are matched with the correct description card. A player gets one point for each correct match. The players take turns and the one with the most points when all of the cards have been matched is the winner.

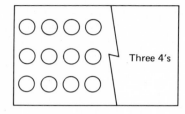

Three 4's

ACTIVITIES FOR STUDENT INVOLVEMENT, PHASE II: BASIC MULTIPLICATION FACTS

Since a knowledge of the basic multiplication facts is a prerequisite for the development of higher computational skills in multiplication, you should establish a schedule for drill and practice activities to make certain students become proficient with them. Such a strategy is an outgrowth of Principle 11. Several of the suggested activities for student involvement should be helpful in this regard.

Concrete mode activities

To provide concrete practice with the basic multiplication facts, give children games to play like those in the following samples.

Sample activity 1 (Rod families)

Give each student a set of Cuisenaire rods, *equation* cards, and *family* cards that are structured as indicated below:

Wrong	Right	Six family	Name _____
		1) 6 _____ rods = one <u>dark green</u> rod 2) 1 _____ rods = one <u>dark green</u> rod 3) 2 _____ rods = one <u>dark green</u> rod 4) 3 _____ rods = one <u>dark green</u> rod	

Family card

A sample equation card for the Six Family would look like the one below. An equation card should be made for each member of each number family to be used in the game.

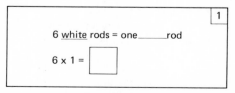

6 <u>white</u> rods = one _____rod

6 x 1 =

1

Equation card

The students should play this game in groups of three or four. Prior to starting the game one person is appointed dealer. The teacher gives the dealer sets of equation cards for the number families that are to be used in the game. Each player is given a corresponding set of family cards.

The dealer shuffles the equation cards and gives each player four cards. The player to the dealer's left plays an equation card and calls on one of the other players to complete the equations. The player so challenged must choose the rod that correctly completes the equation card. He then constructs a rod display to see if he is correct. See check below.

He keeps his own score by marking the right or wrong column of the appropriate family card in the set given to him earlier. At this point, he is required to lay down an equation card and begin the cycle anew. Once a player has been challenged, he cannot be called upon again until everyone in the group has participated. The player with the most points at the end of the game is the winner. Each player turns his family cards over to the teacher who uses the right/wrong information to distribute equation cards for the next round.

Sample activity 2 (Selected factors)

Give a student leader a set of Cuisenaire rods and two sets of factor cards like the ones shown here.

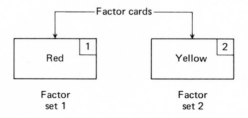

Divide the class into two teams. The first player on Team 1 chooses a factor 1 card. The student leader stands the Cuisenaire rod indicated by this card on end as indicated here.

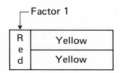

The first player on Team 2 chooses a factor 2 card and the student leader stacks rod(s) indicated by this card on top of each other so that the stack is as tall as the factor 1 rod chosen by Team 1. See the example shown above.

The first player on Team 1 then must select the rod that represents the product. The student leader checks Team 1's product by placing Team 2's factor selection end to end on top of Team 1's product rod. See the example below.

Yellow	Yellow
Orange	

Factor cards answered correctly are paper clipped together and placed in one pile. Factor cards answered incorrectly are clipped and placed in another pile. Play continues until all the factor cards have been used. A team gets one point for each correct product chosen. The team with the most points at the end of play is the winner.

On succeeding rounds of the game, the teacher should include all cards in the incorrect pile as well as some cards from the correct pile. She may also elect to include new factor 1 and factor 2 cards.

Semiconcrete mode activities

To provide semiconcrete mode games, the teacher should use pictures or other graphic displays that represent the basic multiplication facts.

Sample activity 1 (Accordion cards)

Have each student make accordion type cards—like the one shown below from strips of adding machine tape—that illustrate each of the basic multiplication combinations. Number each of the cards according to the number of dots on each section. Then have two students play a guessing game with each other. "If I unfold the 3-strip to show four sections, how many dots will show?" The students may use skip counting (3, 6, 9, 12) to count the dots or check the answer given. Students can also use the accordion cards for individual practice.

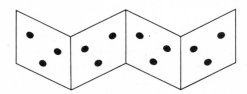

Sample activity 2 (Equation cards)

Make a set of 5″ x 8″ equation cards like the one illustrated below using the basic multiplication combinations, and number them. Next have the students construct graph paper cutouts to illustrate the meaning of the equations on their equation cards. Have them glue their illustrations on tag board. On the back of each illustration place a number in the upper left-hand corner that corresponds to the number assigned to its related equation card.

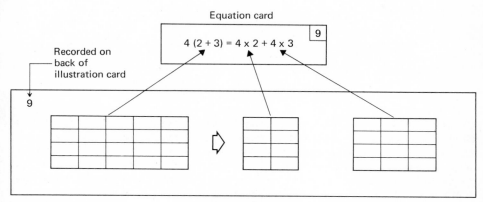

Graph paper illustration

To begin the game, the dealer should shuffle the equation cards and deal each player one card at a time until the deck is exhausted. Next, the illustration cards should be placed in a pile face up in the center of the table. The player to the dealer's left begins the game by deciding whether he can match any of his equation cards with the illustration on the top of the pile. If he can, he places the match in front of him and the game continues. If he cannot, the leader places that illustration on the bottom of the pile and play moves to the next player.

Any player may challenge another player's match. If a challenge is made, the leader checks the numeral on the back of the illustration against the one on the front of the corresponding equation card. If the numerals do not match, the illustration card is placed on the bottom of the deck and the equation card is returned to the player's hand. The first player to empty his hand is the winner.

Abstract mode activities

To provide practice with the basic multiplication facts, present children with a variety of games involving only the use of symbolic representations. The use of games is one application of Principle 10 which emphasizes the need to generate and maintain interest in learning.

Sample activity 1 (Partners)

Each student should construct a set of numbered *player* cards for all of the basic multiplication facts, and the teacher should construct a set of *leader* cards which are numbered (on the front) in a corresponding manner. Note that the leader cards are identical to the player cards, but on the back they contain the commutative form of the factors that are given on the front.

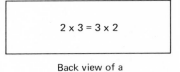

Front view of a
leader and player card

Back view of a
leader card

Distribute the player cards among the students who are to play the game so that each student has an identical set of cards. The student leader is given a corresponding set of leader cards which he or she displays in an order which is preserved. The students who are playing the game must record the number of the partner card and the product. At the end of play, the student leader reads the numbers of the player cards, in order, that the students should have recorded as well as their product. The student with the highest number of correct answers is the winner.

Sample activity 2 (Multiplication roulette)
Students can practice basic multiplication facts by using multiplication table displays such as the one shown.

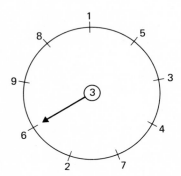

The teacher makes a spinner like the one shown. Two students pair up and challenge each other to a game of Multiplication Roulette. The students spin the pointer

×	0	1	2	3	4	5	6	7	8	9
0	0	0	0	0	0	0	0	0	0	0
1	0	1	2	3	4	5	6	7	8	9
2	0	2	4	6	8	10	12	14	16	18
3	0	3	6	9	12	15	18	21	24	27
4	0	4	8	12	16	20	24	28	32	36
5	0	5	10	15	20	25	30	35	40	45
6	0	6	12	18	24	30	36	42	48	54
7	0	7	14	21	28	35	42	49	56	63
8	0	8	16	24	32	40	48	56	64	72
9	0	9	18	27	36	45	54	63	72	81

and multiply the number on the outside of the wheel by the number located on the hub. Both the numbers on the wheel and the hub can be changed to provide combinations of special interest. The students should write down their answers and check them by using the multiplication table that is provided.

Sample activity 3 (Function machine)
Using a simple desk or pocket calculator, introduce the idea of a "function machine" by showing the student how to enter and process an ordered pair to get a product. Have students place ordered pairs on 3" x 5" cards for each multiplication fact. See the example below.

(3, 5)	◄——————— 3 x 5 = ▓
Ordered pair	Related multiplication fact

The students who need practice should give a set of cards to the student leader. They should predict in writing what number they believe the "function machine" will produce for each card. The student leader enters the ordered pairs, processes the components, and gives the product to the students, who then check their answers.

ACTIVITIES FOR STUDENT INVOLVEMENT, PHASES III AND IV: PRODUCT OF A ONE-DIGIT NUMBER AND A TWO-DIGIT NUMBER, WITH AND WITHOUT REGROUPING

As you examine the Phase III and Phase IV flowcharts and the associated ideas for teaching that were described in the theory section, you should note that considerable use is made of the principle of place value, the commutative and associative properties of multiplication, the distributive property, and renaming moves of the form $34 = 30 + 4$ in order to teach the multiplication algorithm in a meaningful way. Accordingly, you should provide learning experiences which will help children develop a good understanding of these ideas and how they are used.

Concrete mode activities

Sample activity 1 (MAB blocks)

For examples where no regrouping is involved, give each student at least ten long and ten unit blocks and a place value chart like the one below. As an example, consider 2×12. Children represent this product by forming two sets, each of which contains one long block and two unit blocks. See part (a) of the illustration. Have the students record the related computations.

By combining (uniting) the two sets in (a), the children will obtain a set of two long blocks and four unit blocks, as shown in (b). Hence they have illustrated that:

$$2 \times 12 = 2 \times (10 + 2)$$
$$= (2 \times 10) + (2 \times 2)$$
$$= 20 + 4$$
$$= 24.$$

For examples where regrouping is required, another step is added to the procedure to represent the regrouping process. As an example, consider the product 2×16. Children can represent it by forming two sets as shown.

Longs	Units
Tens	Ones
1	6
x	2

(a)

(2×6) 1 2

(2×10) 2 0

(b)

3 2

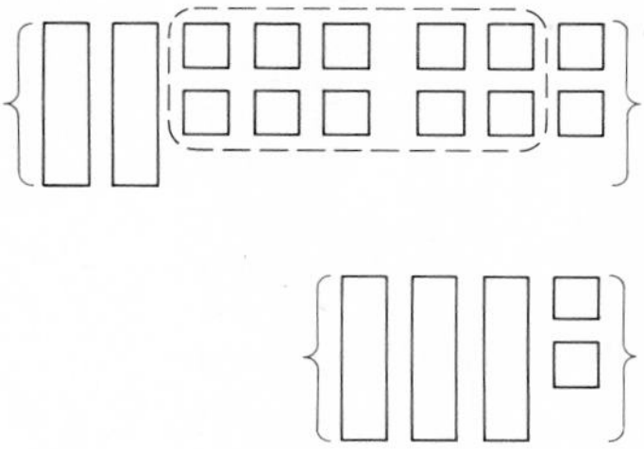

As suggested by diagram (b), ten of the units are grouped and replaced by a long. This process is called *regrouping*.

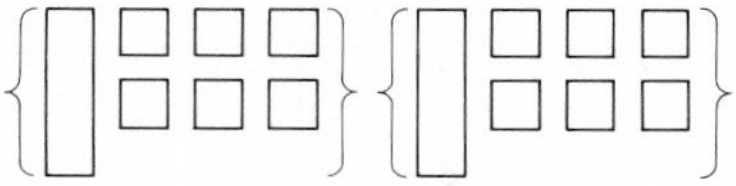

Sample activity 2 (Bundling counting sticks)
Children can interpret the meaning of examples that do not involve regrouping by manipulating counting sticks and recording the results in a place value chart. Give them 100 counting sticks and at least 10 rubber bands. Provide place value charts similar to the one below and demonstrate how to bundle the counting sticks to represent each step of an algorithm.

As one example 2 x 14 can be represented as two sets of counting sticks arranged as indicated below (See a).

(a)

Tens	Ones	
1	4	
x	2	
	8	⟷ 2 x 4
2	0	⟷ 2 x 10
2	8	

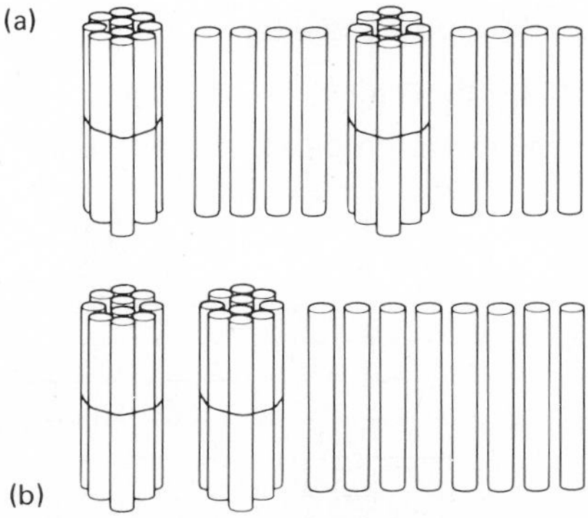

(b)

By combining the two sets children will obtain 2 bundles of ten and 8 single counting sticks.

For cases where regrouping is required another step is added to the previous illustration to represent the regrouping process. As one example, 2 × 17 is represented as two sets of counting sticks arranged as indicated below (see a).

Tens	Ones
1	7
x	2
1	4
2	0
3	4

(a)

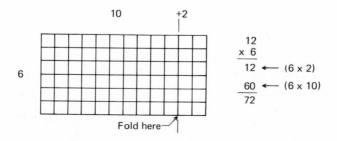

(b)

By combining the two subsets of 7 single sticks the children will obtain one bundle of ten and four sticks, or 14. Finally placing this result with the two bundles of ten or 20 they will obtain the set as shown in illustration (b).

Semi-concrete mode activities

Sample activity 1 (Folding graph paper cards)

Give the students graph paper cards like the following example for 6 × 12.

$$
\begin{array}{r}
12 \\
\times\ 6 \\
\hline
12 \quad \leftarrow (6 \times 2) \\
60 \quad \leftarrow (6 \times 10) \\
\hline
72
\end{array}
$$

10   +2

6

Fold here—

Demonstrate how to fold the graph paper (or array) card to verify the results of the partial products shown in the example. Note that there are other ways to fold the card.

Sample activity 2 (Abacus)

Show the students how to record the partial products for examples such as 6 × 16 on the abacus. See the example below.

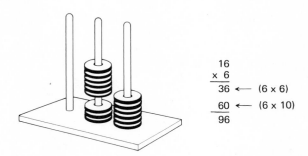

$$
\begin{array}{r}
16 \\
\times\ 6 \\
\hline
36 \\
60 \\
\hline
96
\end{array}
$$

36 ← (6 × 6)

60 ← (6 × 10)

Then have them do similar examples. Construct answer cards with drawings that show the correct arrangement of discs and spacers on the back side of the card. Place the appropriate example on the front side. This arrangement will allow students to check their own answers.

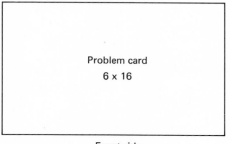

Problem card

6 x 16

Front side

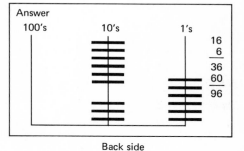

Answer

Back side

Abstract mode activities

Sample activity 1 (Unknown values)

Give the students examples where key numerals are replaced by a place holder such as a ☐. The students pair off in sets of two and alternately fill in a missing numeral. Each player gets one point for each correct replacement. An example is shown on the following page.

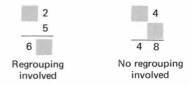

Regrouping   No regrouping
involved   involved

Sample activity 2 (Lattice multiplication)

Often a different arrangement of the place values and factors will help extend the students' understanding of how place value functions in multiplication. The lattice method provides such practice. Provide students with examples like the one below.

(a) 3 x 24 = 72   (b) 3 x 47 = 141

Other related activities can be devised. For example, partially fill in the lattice in some practice exercises and have the students see if they can determine what the missing numerals should be. With example (b) above, the lattice might look as follows:

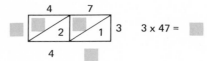

3 x 47 = ▓

You also can provide examples like the ones below and have the students see if they can find and label the various place values.

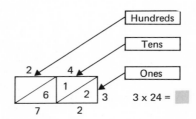

3 x 24 = ▓

ACTIVITIES FOR STUDENT INVOLVEMENT, PHASE V: PRODUCT OF A PAIR OF TWO-DIGIT NUMBERS WITH AND WITHOUT REGROUPING

Concrete mode activities

A representation of the steps in the algorithms for Phase V problems is best illustrated by concrete materials structured like multibase arithmetic blocks.

Materials such as counting sticks are less desirable because of the large number of pieces involved and the difficulty in manipulating them. For this reason the type of concrete mode activities for Phase V problems is more restricted in number and variety than Phases I–IV. Usually when students reach Phase V they can, with a few concrete experiences, easily move on to semiconcrete materials which offer a great deal more variety for instructional purposes.

Sample activity 1 (MAB blocks)

Give each student a place value chart with examples arranged as shown in place value chart (a). Have them compute the partial products and arrange the MAB blocks as indicated in chart (b) to check the meaning of each product. Then have the students combine the blocks in each column to represent the addition required to obtain the final product. See (b).

Hundreds	Tens	Ones	
	2	4	
	x 1	2	
	4	8	2 x 24
2	4	0	10 x 24
2	8	8	

(a)

Flats	Longs	Units

(b)

Sample activity 2 (Multiples of ten)

Give students a set of 3″ x 5″ cards with products that are two-digit multiples of ten like the one below on the front side, and the number and type of MAB blocks needed to represent the product on the back side.

10 x 12 =

Front side of card

Cubes	Flats	Longs	Units
		1	2	0

Back side of card

The students shuffle the cards and place them front side up on the playing surface. The first player begins by representing the product for the top card with MAB blocks. He then checks his response by turning the card over and comparing his block construction with the description given on the back side of the card. If it is correct, he receives one point and play moves to the left. At the end of play the player with the most points is the winner.

Semiconcrete mode activities

To provide semiconcrete mode activities the teacher should use materials that help students make a graphic record of the steps used in their thinking. Both the regrouping and nonregrouping cases should be considered.

Sample activity 1 (Multibase abacus)

Give each student multibase abacus sketches like the ones illustrated below. Have the students use them to record the partial products obtained as they use an algorithm like the one below to solve $25 \times 61 = \boxed{}$.

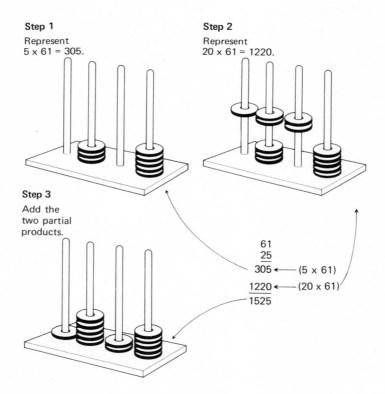

Step 1
Represent
5 x 61 = 305.

Step 2
Represent
20 x 61 = 1220.

Step 3
Add the
two partial
products.

$$
\begin{array}{r}
61 \\
25 \\
\hline
305 \leftarrow (5 \times 61) \\
1220 \leftarrow (20 \times 61) \\
\hline
1525
\end{array}
$$

Sample activity 2 (Accordion cards)

Have each student make accordion-type cards from strips of adding machine tape, and mark them to illustrate multiples of ten. Number each of the cards according to the number of dots on each section.

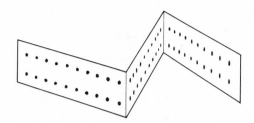

Have several students play a guessing game with each other. "If I unfold the 20 strip to show 12 sections, how many dots will show?" The students may use skip counting {20, 40, 60, 80, 100, 120, . . .} to count the dots and check the answer given.

Abstract mode activities

Sample activity 1 (Place value charts)
Give the students place value charts like the one shown below to help them learn to record the partial products.

Thousands	Hundreds	Tens	Ones	
		2	6	
		7	4	
	1	0	4	← First partial product
1	8	2	0	← Second partial product
1	9	2	4	

This activity will help students in situations where regrouping is required.

Sample activity 2 ("Lightning" multiplication)
Memorize the following procedure and then challenge the class to see if they can obtain the product for examples such as 32 × 46 as fast as you can. When challenged to explain your trick, think out loud for the students as indicated by the diagram and explanation below.

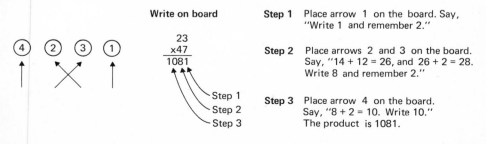

Write on board

```
  23
 x47
1081
```

Step 1   Place arrow 1 on the board. Say, "Write 1 and remember 2."

Step 2   Place arrows 2 and 3 on the board. Say, "14 + 12 = 26, and 26 + 2 = 28. Write 8 and remember 2."

Step 3   Place arrow 4 on the board. Say, "8 + 2 = 10. Write 10." The product is 1081.

Sample activity 3 (Napier's rods)

Using Napier's rods is similar to using lattice multiplication. Cut strips of cardboard 1″ x 10″. One strip is labeled Index. The other ten strips are labeled 0 to 9. See illustration below. In the remaining blocks on each strip, draw diagonal lines and fill in the spaces as in lattice multiplication. To use the rods, the children find the strips which represent the multiplicand and locate the multiplier on the Index. By circling the appropriate columns and making the appropriate additions, the partial products are obtained. Have the students record these products as indicated in the following example. Also have them discuss how this procedure is related to the basic multiplication fact table.

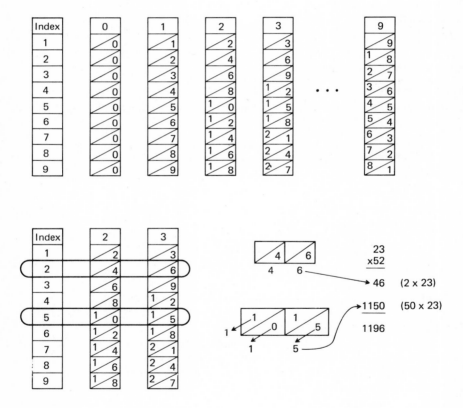

Figure 6.8

Exercise set

1. Write the product, a × b, suggested by each of the following sums.
   a) $4+4+4+4+4$
   b) $2+2+2$
   c) $7+7+7+7+7+7$
   d) $12+12+12+12$

2. Write each of the following products as a sum by using the "repeated addition" interpretation of multiplication.
   a) 2×5 b) 4×8 c) 5×1 d) 7×3

3. Write the product suggested by each of the following arrays.

   a)   b)    c)   d)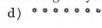

4. For each product listed in Exercise 2, construct an array of dots which corresponds to it.

5. Altogether, there are 100 basic multiplication facts. However, if the commutative property of multiplication is employed so as to treat facts like 4×5 and 5×4 as being essentially the same, then how many basic multiplication facts remain to be learned?

6. What property of multiplication figures prominently in the indicated step of the following procedure?

$$20 \times 40 = (2 \times 10) \times (4 \times 10)$$
$$= (2 \times 4) \times (10 \times 10)$$
$$= 8 \times 100$$
$$= 800$$

7. What property figures prominently in the indicated step of the following procedure?

$$\begin{array}{c} 15 \\ \times 7 \\ \hline \end{array} \rightarrow \begin{array}{c} 10+5 \\ \times\,7 \\ \hline 70+35 = 105 \end{array}$$

8. Several of the components of the Comprehensive Flowchart for Teaching Multiplication can be expanded into miniflowcharts showing not only the different types of problems within a defined, but broader, problem class, but the sequence in which they normally would be taught. For example, consider the component which specifies the task of teaching children how to find the product of a one-digit number and a two-digit number where regrouping is necessary. A miniflowchart for dealing with this problem class might appear as shown on the next page.

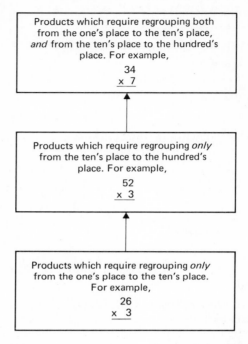

Figure 6.9

Construct miniflowcharts similar to the one shown above for:

a) the component which specifies the task of teaching children the basic multiplication facts. [*Hint*: Use the data given in Table 6.2 on p. 152.]

b) the component which specifies the task of teaching children how to find the product of a pair of two-digit numbers where regrouping is necessary. [*Hint*: Consider the types of regrouping that are possible.]

9. Cut a piece of graph paper to show an array of squares consisting of 25 rows and 34 columns. Then fold the array twice so that when it is opened, the creases set off four subarrays showing that:

$$\begin{array}{r} 34 \\ \times 25 \end{array} = (5 \times 4) + (5 \times 30) + (20 \times 4) + (20 \times 30).$$

10. Construct a teaching plan for using arrays and activities like those hinted at in Exercise 9 to teach children the *standard* algorithm for finding the product of a pair of two-digit numbers. (That is, the ④③②① procedure for finding the product).

11. Use the Comprehensive Flowchart for Teaching Multiplication as an aid in ordering the following types of multiplication problems into the sequence in which they normally would be taught.

a) 15   23   8   b) 76   91   17   c)   42   314   35
    ×5   ×3   ×7   ×4   ×8   ×9   ×21   ×2   ×64

12. How can dot arrays be used to illustrate the commutative property of multiplication?

13. How can sets of blocks be used to illustrate the associative property of multiplication?

14. What addition activities should be used as readiness activities for multiplication? When should these be introduced?

15. Why do some textbooks introduce multiplication and division together? Why do some mathematics educators believe they should be introduced separately?

16. Develop a list of manipulative aids that you should have in your classroom. Tell how each can be used to teach multiplication. Which are the most flexible?

17. Make some cross-number puzzles that can be used as practice exercises with multiplication.

18. What basic terminology do students have to know to understand multiplication? How should these terms be introduced? Why are they important?

19. Why is the ability to make reasonable estimates of products for problems such as $12 \times 25 = \boxed{}$ an important skill?

20. Construct an activity that is designed to help children learn the rules for multiplication in instances where at least one of the factors is negative.

21. Write an instructional objective for each of the components 1 through 9 of the Comprehensive Flowchart for Teaching Multiplication.

22. Construct an achievement record chart for multiplication which is analogous to the one displayed in Exercise 19 of the Exercise Set for Chapter 4.

READINGS FOR ADDITIONAL STUDY

For each of the following topics, read one of the articles listed in the bibliography and write a one- or two-page report which consists of (1) a brief *summary* of the article, and (2) your *reaction* to the positions which have been taken.

23. Multiplication involving negative numbers.

24. Ways of interpreting the operation of multiplication (repeated addition, etc.).

25. The properties of multiplication and how to teach them.

26. Noncommon algorithms for multiplication (e.g., The Russian Peasant Method).

Bibliography

1. Alger, Louisa R. "Finger multiplication." *The Arithmetic Teacher* **15** (April 1968): 341–43.

2. Ando, Masue, and Ikeda Hitoshi. "Learning multiplication facts—more than drill." *The Arithmetic Teacher* **18** (October 1971): 366–69.

3. Bechtel, Robert D., and Lyle J. Dixon. "Multiplication—repeated addition?" *The Arithmetic Teacher* **14** (May 1967): 373–76.

4. Boyer, Lee E. "The distributive property." *The Arithmetic Teacher* **14** (November 1967): 566–69.

5. Boykin, W. E. "The Russian-peasant algorithm: rediscovery and extension." *The Arithmetic Teacher* **20** (January 1973): 29–32.

6. Brownell, W. A. "When is arithmetic meaningful?" *Journal of Educational Research* **38** (March 1945): 481–98.

7. Cacha, F. B. "Understanding multiplication and division of multidigit numbers." *The Arithmetic Teacher* **19** (May 1972): 349–54.

8. Callahan, L. C. "A romantic excursion into the multiplication table." *The Arithmetic Teacher* **16** (December 1969): 609–13.

9. Coon, Lewis H. "Number line multiplication for negative numbers." *The Arithmetic Teacher* **13** (March 1966): 213–17.

10. Deans, Edwina. "Early development of concepts of multiplication and division." *The Arithmetic Teacher* **12** (February 1965): 143–44.

11. Ercolano, Joseph. "Hindu-bobtailed multiplication: an efficient mathematical algorithm." *The Arithmetic Teacher* **21** (April 1974): 318–20.

12. Fennell, Francis M. "Multiplication football." *The Arithmetic Teacher* **17** (March 1970): 236–37.

13. Gibney, T. C. "Multiplication for slow learners." *The Arithmetic Teacher* **9** (February 1962): 74–76.

14. Grafft, William. "A study of behavioral performances within the structure of multiplication." *The Arithmetic Teacher* **17** (April 1970): 335–37.

15. Haines, Margaret. "Concepts to enhance the study of multiplication." *The Arithmetic Teacher* **10** (October 1963): 321–37.

16. Hannon, Herbert. "A new look at the basic principles of multiplication with whole numbers." *The Arithmetic Teacher* **7** November 1960): 357–61.

17. Harvey, Lois F., and George C. Kyte. "Zero difficulties in multiplication." *The Arithmetic Teacher* **12** (January 1965): 45–50.

18. Hervey, Margaret A. "Children's responses to two types of multiplication problems." *The Arithmetic Teacher* **13** (April 1966): 288–92.

19. Hill, Warren H., Jr. "A physical model for teaching multiplication of integers." *The Arithmetic Teacher* **15** (October 1968): 525–38.

20. Immerzeel, George, and Donald Wiederander. "Ideas." *The Arithmetic Teacher* **18** (January 1971): 30–36.

21. Immerzeel, George, and Donald Wiederander. "Ideas." *The Arithmetic Teacher* **21** (February 1974): 117–24.

22. Junge, Charlotte W. "Now try this—in multiplication." *The Arithmetic Teacher* **14** (January 1967): 47.

23. Junge, Charlotte W. "Now try this—in multiplication." *The Arithmetic Teacher* **14** (February 1967): 134–35.

24. McDougall, Ronald V. "Don't sell short the distributive property." *The Arithmetic Teacher* **14** (November 1967): 570–72.

25. Milne, Esther. "Disguised practice for multiplication and addition of directed numbers." *The Arithmetic Teacher* **16** (May 1969): 397–98.

26. National Council of Teachers of Mathematics. *Topics in Mathematics for Elementary School Teachers.* Booklet 2. Washington, D.C. The Council, 1964.

27. Peterson, John C. "Fourteen different strategies for multiplication of integers of why (-1) $(-1) = +1$." *The Arithmetic Teacher* **19** (May 1972): 396–403.

28. Rappaport, David. "Multiplication is repeated addition." *The Arithmetic Teacher* **12** (November 1965): 550–51.

29. Reardin, C. R., Jr. "Understanding the Russian peasant." *The Arithmetic Teacher* **20** (January 1973): 33–35.

30. Schrage, Merry. "Presenting multiplication of counting numbers on an array matrix." *The Arithmetic Teacher* **16** (December 1969): 615–16.

31. Shafer, Dale M. "Multiplication mastery via the tape recorder." *The Arithmetic Teacher* **17** (November 1970): 581–82.

32. Stern, Jane L. "Counting: new road to multiplication." *The Arithmetic Teacher,* **16** (April 1969): 311–13.

33. Traub, Raymond G. "Napier's Rods: practice with multiplication." *The Arithmetic Teacher* **16** (May 1969): 363–64.

Teaching division
of cardinal numbers

7

Synopsis and objectives

Chapter 7 gives you an opportunity to explore the factors to take into account in teaching the operation of division. Considerable emphasis is placed upon relating division to its inverse operation of multiplication. Consequently, the **theory** section is developed around the idea of translating the flowcharts for teaching multiplication into corresponding flowcharts for teaching division. When the flowcharts are correctly interpreted, they specify the order in which the key concepts and skills of division should be learned and they also can be used for diagnostic and prescriptive purposes. Emphasis is placed on the desirability of teaching multiplication and division together in order to take advantage of the logical relationships between these two operations.

The **practice** section is organized in a similar fashion and illustrates how learning activities in multiplication can be modified to form division learning activities. Accordingly, this section is similar in structure to the **practice** section in Chapter 6.

In planning your study of this chapter, we hope you will consult the bibliography to explore particular ideas in greater depth. If you started an activity file for multiplication, you will want to make a related one for division.

When you complete your study of Chapter 7, you should be able to

1. state and illustrate the "inverse of multiplication" definition of division;

2. state and illustrate the definition of division based on the notion of set partitioning;

3. state and illustrate the definition of division based on repeated subtraction;

4. define and illustrate the terms *quotient, missing factor, dividend,* and *divisor;*

5. classify a quotient, $x \div y$, as belonging or not belonging to the set of basic division facts (BDF);

6. translate multiplication number sentences into equivalent division number sentences, and conversely;

7. translate flowcharts for teaching multiplication into corresponding flowcharts for teaching division;

8. order a collection of different division problems into a sequence which illustrates an acceptable order for teaching;

9. describe how to use the flowcharts for teaching division as an aid in the diagnosis of individual learning states and in the prescription of learning activities;

10. demonstrate the use of the repeated subtraction procedure to justify each step in the application of the standard division algorithm;

11. illustrate the various stages of the development of the division algorithm leading up to its refined, standard form;

12. construct examples to show that division is not commutative;

13. construct examples to show that division is not associative;

14. construct examples to show that the set of whole numbers is not closed under division;

15. construct examples illustrating the right distributive property of division over addition;

16–22. state and illustrate the divisibility rules for 2, 3, 4, 5, 6, 8, and 9;

23. demonstrate how to use manipulatives, such as an abacus, balance beam, Cuisenaire rods, MAB blocks, etc., to teach the various basic types of division problems.

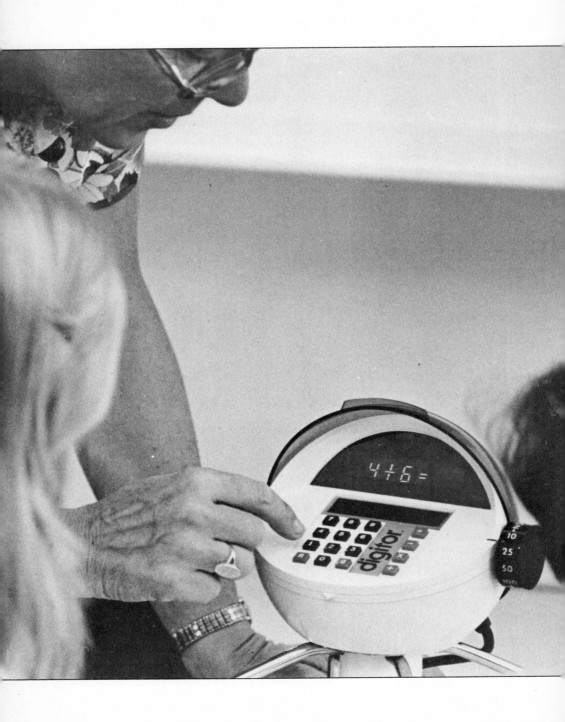

Teaching division of cardinal numbers

Theory

DIVISION AS THE INVERSE OF MULTIPLICATION

Division is related to multiplication in the same way that subtraction is related to addition; that is, division is the *inverse* of multiplication. The following definition states this.

Definition of Division
For all cardinal numbers a, b and c, $b \neq 0$, $a \div b = c$ if and only if $b \times c = a$.

To illustrate how this definition relates division to multiplication, suppose that we wish to determine the cardinal number c to associate with, say $12 \div 3$. The definition states that

$$12 \div 3 = c \qquad \text{if and only if} \qquad 3 \times c = 12.$$

Since $3 \times 4 = 12$, it follows that $c = 4$; that is, $12 \div 3 = 4$. Similarly, we see that $15 \div 5 = 3$ because $5 \times 3 = 15$, and so on. The standard terminology for division problems follows:

$$a \div b = c \leftarrow \text{quotient}$$
$$\text{divisor} \longrightarrow b \overline{)a} \; {}^{c}$$
$$\text{dividend}$$

There are two important observations to make about the definition of division of whole (cardinal) numbers. First, note that division by zero was left *undefined*. This was the purpose of specifying that $b \neq 0$. The reason for this state of affairs is easy to discover by examining an instance where the divisor is zero. For example, consider the problem

$$\frac{5}{0} = \Box.$$

Observe that it has no solution since there is no number which, when multiplied by zero, is equal to five. Second, note that division by nonzero whole numbers is not always possible in the set of whole numbers. For example, consider $1 \div 4$. From the definition of division, we know that

$$1 \div 4 = c \qquad \text{if and only if} \qquad 4 \times c = 1.$$

Since there is no whole number c such that $4 \times c = 1$, it follows that there is no whole number equal to $1 \div 4$.[*] This fact is described by stating that the set of whole numbers is not *closed* under division.

---

[*] Note that such divisions are possible in the set of rational numbers, which are discussed in Chapter 8.

191

The definition of division suggests to us that every division sentence is equivalent to a multiplication sentence. For example, the division sentence

$$15 \div 3 = \boxed{}$$

is equivalent to the multiplication sentence

$$3 \times \boxed{} = 15.$$

So we see that every division problem can be converted into a multiplication problem with a *missing factor*. This is a popular approach to teaching division in the elementary school.

DIVISION AS SET PARTITIONING

If division is conceptualized as the "undoing" of multiplication, and multiplication is thought of in terms of uniting equivalent sets, then division can be thought of in terms of *partitioning* a set into equivalent subsets. There are two basic ways in which the partitioning can occur. Observe that since multiplication is commutative, every division sentence can be converted into two equivalent multiplication sentences. For example,

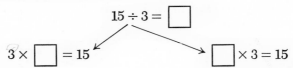

First consider the case on the right. To solve it, we think: "How many sets of 3 make a set of 15?" The following diagram suggests the procedure used to find the answer.

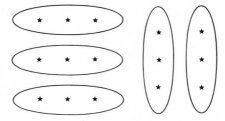

Thus we see that $\boxed{5} \times 3 = 15$. If this problem were solved using blocks or other types of objects, the procedure used is simply to start with a set of 15 and form as many subsets of 3 as possible. This process is often referred to as the *measurement* interpretation for division. This is similar to measuring the length of a room by finding out how many feet there are in the length. Now consider the case on the left. To solve it, we think: "3 sets of how many make a set of 15?" Hence, this time the procedure consists of forming 3 equivalent sets from a set of 15. If this problem is solved using blocks or other objects, the method used is to parcel out the objects, one for each set, and then repeat the process over and over until all 15 are distributed. This procedure is often

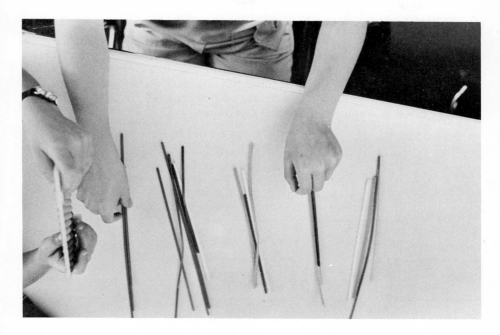

Bundled counting sticks can be used to teach the basic division concepts.

referred to as the *partition* interpretation of division in order to distinguish it from the other, more obvious, form of partitioning.

DIVISION AS REPEATED SUBTRACTION

Just as multiplication can be thought of as repeated addition, division can be thought of as *repeated subtraction*. For example, since

$$2 + 2 + 2 = 6,$$

it follows that $3 \times 2 = \boxed{6}$ (three 2's make 6). When we "undo" this multiplication we get

$$
\begin{array}{cc}
6 & \\
-2 & 1 \\
\hline
4 & \\
-2 & 1 \\
\hline
2 & \\
-2 & \dfrac{1}{3} \\
\hline
0 &
\end{array}
$$

We subtract 2 as many times as we can which is 3. (In 6 there are three 2's.) So, $6 \div 2 = \boxed{3}$. This method is usually used with the more complex forms of division, as we will show later.

FLOWCHARTS FOR TEACHING DIVISION

Since multiplication and division are so closely related, it has become increasingly popular to teach these ideas in tandem; that is, when a particular multiplication competence or skill has been taught, it is followed by the corresponding division idea. Consequently, the flowchart for teaching multiplication can be used as a guide for teaching division. An initial flowchart for teaching division would look like the one shown in Fig. 7.1.

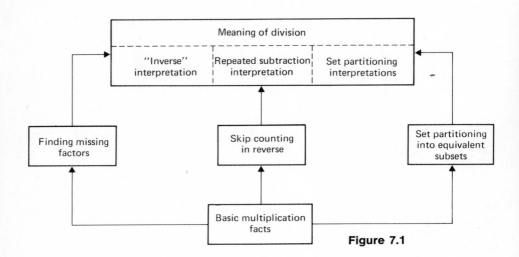

Figure 7.1

The three basic interpretations of division should be, and normally are, taught in elementary school programs since each interpretation has special advantages. Subsequent flowcharts are essentially reflections of the corresponding flowcharts for teaching multiplication.

THE BASIC DIVISION FACTS

If you think of division as being the inverse of multiplication, then you know that there is a basic division fact (BDF) corresponding to every basic multiplication fact, except those having a multiplier of zero. (Remember that division by zero is not defined.) A good way to determine the basic division facts is to examine a table of the basic multiplication facts and "work backwards." Look at Table 8.1. Consider, for example, the BMF $3 \times 9 = 27$. To "undo" a multiplication by 3, we must divide by 3; thus the corresponding BDF is $27 \div 3 = 9$. The general procedure to follow, then, is to first find the *dividend* in the table, next go to the number in the left-hand column for the *divisor,* and finally read the *quotient* in the top row. If you do the same for $42 \div 7 = \boxed{}$, you find the dividend in the top row is 6. So $42 \div 7 = 6$.

Table 8.1

X	0	1	2	3	4	5	6	7	8	9
0	0	0	0	0	0	0	0	0	0	0
1	0	1	2	3	4	5	6	7	8	9
2	0	2	4	6	8	10	12	14	16	18
3	0	3	6	9	12	15	18	21	24	27
4	0	4	8	12	16	20	24	28	32	36
5	0	5	10	15	20	25	30	35	40	45
6	0	6	12	18	24	30	36	42	48	54
7	0	7	14	21	28	35	42	49	56	63
8	0	8	16	24	32	40	48	56	64	72
9	0	9	18	27	36	45	54	63	72	81

The ninety basic division facts can be taught in a variety of ways. To do so, all of the interpretations of division described earlier can be used to good advantage; indeed, it undoubtedly is pedagogically desirable to employ all of them at one time or another in order to enable the student to acquire the broadest possible conceptualization of the division idea.

A TRANSLATION OF THE (PHASE III)
MULTIPLICATION FLOWCHART INTO A FLOWCHART
FOR TEACHING DIVISION

After the student has acquired a satisfactory understanding of the meaning of division and has mastered the basic division facts, you can move on to the more complex problem types. We know the teaching sequence for division is determined by the teaching sequence used for multiplication. In the Phase III Flowchart for Teaching Multiplication (Fig. 6.3), the first problem type following the basic multiplication facts involves finding the product of a one-digit number and a multiple of ten where the product is less than 100. Examples like 4×20 and 3×30 fall into this category. The division counterparts of these examples are $80 \div 4$ and $90 \div 3$, respectively.

Now examine the terminal problem type in the Phase III Flowchart for Teaching Multiplication. Note that it calls for finding the product of a one-digit number and a two-digit number where no regrouping is necessary. Problems like 4×21 and 3×32 are examples of this case. Their division counterparts are $84 \div 4$ and $96 \div 3$, respectively. Similar translations can be made for every component of the Comprehensive Flowchart for Teaching Multiplication (see Fig. 6.7) and thus this flowchart can also function as a Comprehensive Flowchart for Division.

ALGORITHM DEVELOPMENT

Once the proper teaching sequence of division problem types has been determined, instructional techniques must be developed for each of them.

The customary way of teaching the standard division algorithm for the more complex problem types relies on the interpretation of division as repeated subtraction. Generally speaking, the plan calls for the development of the desired (terminal) competence by stages. These stages are discussed and illustrated below.

Stage 1

The process of repeated subtraction is used with no special effort to find shortcuts. For example:

$$(48 \div 4) = \boxed{}$$

$$
\begin{array}{rl}
48 & \\
\underline{-4} & \quad 1 \\
44 & \\
\underline{-4} & \quad 1 \\
40 & \\
\underline{-4} & \quad 1 \\
36 & \\
\underline{-4} & \quad 1 \\
32 & \\
\underline{-4} & \quad 1 \\
28 & \\
\underline{-4} & \quad 1 \\
24 & \\
\underline{-4} & \quad 1 \\
20 & \\
\underline{-4} & \quad 1 \\
16 & \\
\underline{-4} & \quad 1 \\
12 & \\
\underline{-4} & \quad 1 \\
8 & \\
\underline{-4} & \quad 1 \\
4 & \\
\underline{-4} & \quad \underline{1} \\
0 & \quad 12
\end{array}
$$

So $48 \div 4 = \boxed{12}$.

Stage 2
Soon after the basic idea behind Stage 1 has been developed, the child is encouraged to try to find shortcuts. For example:

$$(48 \div 4) = \boxed{}$$

$$
\begin{array}{ll}
48 & \\
-8 \quad 2 & (2 \times 4) \\
\hline
40 & \\
-20 \quad 5 & (5 \times 4) \\
\hline
20 & \\
-20 \quad 5 & (5 \times 4) \\
\hline
0 \quad 12 &
\end{array}
$$

$$\text{So } 48 \div 4 = \boxed{12}.$$

Stage 3
The next step is to try to subtract multiples of ten first, as illustrated by the accompanying examples. Examine them closely.

$$(66 \div 3) = \boxed{} \qquad\qquad (68 \div 2) = \boxed{}$$

$$
\begin{array}{ll}
66 & \\
-30 \quad 10 & (10 \times 3) \\
\hline
36 & \\
-30 \quad 10 & (10 \times 3) \\
\hline
6 & \\
-6 \quad 2 & (2 \times 3) \\
\hline
0 \quad 22 &
\end{array}
\qquad
\begin{array}{ll}
68 & \\
-40 \quad 20 & (20 \times 2) \\
\hline
28 & \\
-20 \quad 10 & (10 \times 2) \\
\hline
8 & \\
-8 \quad 4 & (4 \times 2) \\
\hline
0 \quad 34 &
\end{array}
$$

$$\text{So } 66 \div 3 = \boxed{22}. \qquad\qquad \text{So } 68 \div 2 = \boxed{34}.$$

Stage 4
The technique used in Stage 3 is then generalized as demonstrated by the following examples.

$$(1144 \div 8) = \boxed{} \qquad\qquad (5590 \div 26) = \boxed{}$$

$$
\begin{array}{ll}
1144 & \\
-800 \quad 100 & \\
\hline
344 & \\
-320 \quad 40 & \\
\hline
24 & \\
-24 \quad 3 & \\
\hline
0 \quad 143 &
\end{array}
\qquad
\begin{array}{ll}
5590 & \\
-5200 \quad 200 & \\
\hline
390 & \\
-260 \quad 10 & \\
\hline
130 & \\
-130 \quad 5 & \\
\hline
0 \quad 215 &
\end{array}
$$

$$\text{So } 1144 \div 8 = \boxed{143}. \qquad\qquad \text{So } 5590 \div 26 = \boxed{215}.$$

Stage 5

At this point, or earlier, improvements are also made in formating. Usually this is done in several phases. Study the accompanying examples.

Form A	Form B	Form C

```
   Form A            Form B              Form C

                        6
                       20                    128
    4)148           12)312               31)3968
    120   30           240                  3100     (100 × 31)
    ----             -----                 ------
     28                 72                   868
     28    7            72                   620      (20 × 31)
    ----   --           --                  -----
          37                                 248
                                             248       (8 × 31)
```

So $148 \div 4 = \boxed{37}$.   So $312 \div 12 = \boxed{26}$.   So $3968 \div 31 = \boxed{128}$.

Observe that Form C is the standard form of the division algorithm.

As you examine the five stages above, you can see that they constitute a logical developmental sequence for *meaningful* learning. Keep in mind that stages 1 through 4 are intermediate learning points, and that your objective is to move the student on to the standard, most efficient form of the algorithm as quickly as possible.

The case where nonzero remainders occur

When the students first encounter those problem types which do not result in a remainder of zero, it is a common, though technically questionable, practice to teach them to report a (partial) quotient and a remainder, as illustrated below.

$$25 \div 4 = 6 \text{ R } 1$$

Once the students have learned the basic concepts of fractional numbers, they should then be taught to report quotients correctly. For instance,

$$25 \div 4 = 6\tfrac{1}{4}.$$

**A NOTE ON THE RULES FOR DIVISION
WHEN EITHER THE DIVIDEND OR THE DIVISOR
IS NEGATIVE**

Since multiplication and division are inverse operations, the same rules for working with negative numbers apply to both. It follows, then, that

1. if the divisor and dividend have unlike signs, the quotient is *negative;*

2. if both the divisor and the dividend are negative, the quotient is *positive.*

For example, since $5 \times {}^-3 = {}^-15$, ${}^-15 \div 5 = {}^-3$. And since ${}^-3 \times 5 = {}^-15$, ${}^-15 \div {}^-3 = 5$.

Practice

ACTIVITIES FOR STUDENT INVOLVEMENT, PHASE I: THE MEANING OF DIVISION

Concrete mode activities

Division seems to be the most difficult operation for children to understand and to become proficient with. To counteract this situation, it is a good idea to begin the study with concrete activities that directly relate division to its inverse operation, multiplication. Familiar multiplication situations can be used to show students that division is used to determine a missing factor. For example, $12 \div 3 = \boxed{}$ can be translated into $3 \times \boxed{} = 12$. Consider the following sample activities.

Sample activity 1 (Pencil Lacrosse)

A member of Team 1 begins by reading a problem which is printed on a card.

> 3 pencils crossed by ▮ pencils
> gives 12 intersections?

One of Team 2's players must then lay down a pencil display that identifies the missing factor, 4. See the example below. A team gets one point for each correct factor identified. The team with the most points at the end of play is the winner.

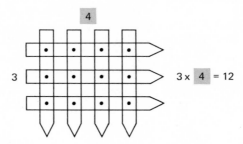

Sample activity 2 (Missing factor)

Give a group of children a set of blocks encircled by red yarn. For example, see the following display.

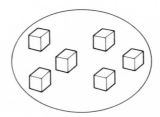

Then give the students, say, two pieces of green yarn. Ask them to divide the set of six blocks into two equivalent subsets, and then tell how many blocks are in each subset, i.e., 2 sets of $\boxed{}$ = 6.

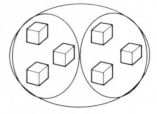

Sample activity 3 (Balance beam)

Give each student a balance beam and nine washers. Ask the students to place one washer on a given number, say 8. See the left-hand arm of the balance beam shown below.

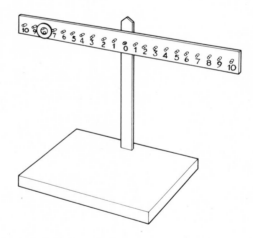

Then ask them to find out how many washers they would need to place on the 2 hook on the right arm of the beam to make it balance. The person identifying the correct number (4) first gets one point.

Semiconcrete mode activities

To provide semiconcrete activities, use graphic displays to replace the actual objects. Since division is the inverse of multiplication, many of the activities described in the multiplication chapter can be altered for teaching division. Having two related activities available in the room at the same time will help the students discover how they can use their knowledge of the multiplication activities to successfully complete the division activities.

Sample activity 1 (Orally presented verbal problems)

Divide the class into problem-solving teams and then present a verbal problem via audio tapes. A set of six-to-eight different tapes with problems at different levels of difficulty would be sufficient for a class of 30 students. Four cassette tape recorders placed at different locations in the room would provide enough listening stations for the teams. Record verbal problems like the following sample and provide the necessary materials for the teams to make drawings that illustrate semi-concrete solutions to the problems.

> Bill wanted to put 24 stamps in his stamp album. If he puts 6 stamps on each page, how many pages will he need? Make a drawing that shows how you got your answer.

Sample activity 2 (Nonverbal problem setting)

Prepare posters like the one below to motivate the search for real-life situations involving division.

Present the poster to the class and ask them to suggest some of the questions that the girl must solve. Focus on problems such as, "How many ice cream bars can the girl buy for $1.00?"

Students who own an inexpensive camera could use it to locate and photograph similar problem situations that they see in their everyday environment. These should be mounted on the bulletin board and possible problem situations identified by the student photographer.

Sample activity 3 (Array description match race)

Using 5″ x 8″ cards, make several sets of cards like the one below.

Cut the encircled array patterns so that they will match only one description card. Give small teams of students identical sets of cards that are scrambled. Tell them they are to match the cards as quickly as they can. The team who finishes first is the winner.

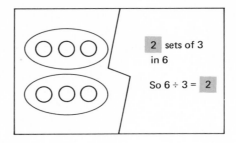

ACTIVITIES FOR STUDENT INVOLVEMENT, PHASE II: BASIC DIVISION FACTS

Concrete mode activities

To provide concrete practice with the basic division facts, give children games to play like those in the following samples.

Sample activity 1 (Rod families)

Give each student a set of Cuisenaire rods, equation cards, and family cards that are structured as indicated below.

Wrong	Right	Eight Family	Name
		1) ———— white rods	= 1 brown rod
		2) ———— brown rods	= 1 brown rod
		3) ———— purple rods	= 1 brown rod
		4) ———— red rods	= 1 brown rod

Family card

Equation cards should be made for each member of the family cards to be used in the game. Each equation card for the eight family would look like the sample here.

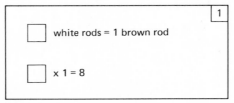

Equation card

Observe that the students are learning the division facts by seeking the missing factor. This seems to be a natural approach for those students who have mastered the multiplication combinations.

The students should play this game in groups of three or four. Before starting the game, appoint one person to be the dealer. The teacher gives the dealer sets of equation cards for the families that he has chosen for the group. Each player is given a corresponding set of family cards.

The dealer shuffles the equation cards and gives each player four cards. The player to the dealer's left lays down an equation card and calls on one of the players to complete the equations by supplying the missing factor. The player so challenged must construct a rod display to check and see if his response is correct.

He keeps his own score by marking the Wrong or Right column of the appropriate family card in the set given to him earlier. At this point, he is required to lay down an equation card and begin the cycle anew. Once a player has been challenged, he cannot be called upon until everyone in the group has participated. The player with the most points at the end of the game is the winner. Each player turns his family cards over to the teacher who uses the marks in the Wrong and Right columns to distribute equation cards for the next game that is played.

Sample activity 2 (Missing factors)

Give a student leader a set of Cuisenaire rods, and a set of factor cards and product cards on each of which is recorded a name of a color of a Cuisenaire rod.

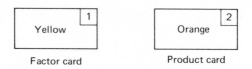

Divide the class into two teams. The first player on Team 1 chooses a product card. The student leader places the rod suggested by this card on the table. See the bottom rod shown below.

The first player on Team 2 takes a factor card given to him by the leader and determines how many rods of that color, laid end-to-end, are as long as the product rod. See the example above. (If no match can be made, the leader gives the player another factor card.) Then he stacks these rods as indicated below and must locate the missing factor rod, the one that is as tall as the stacked factor rods.

Finally the player should tell the multiplication equation which has been illustrated; in this case it would be $\boxed{2} \times 5 = 10$. Play continues back and forth between the teams until all the factor and product cards have been played. A team gets one point for each correct missing factor located. The team with the most points at the end of play is the winner.

Semiconcrete mode activities

To provide semiconcrete mode activities, the teacher should use pictures or other graphic displays that represent the basic division facts.

Sample activity 1 (Accordion cards)
Have each student make accordion-type cards from strips of adding machine tape that illustrate each of the basic multiplication facts. Number each of the strips according to the number of dots on each section.
   Have two students play an estimation game with each other. "If I want to unfold 12 dots using a four-strip, how many sections would I need to display?" The students would use skip counting as they unfold the four-strip to check their estimate. The accordion cards can also be used for individual practice.

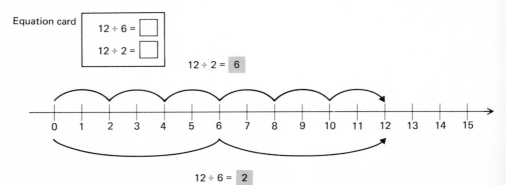

Sample activity 2 (Number line plays)
Provide each student with a number line. The children can use the number line to illustrate the solution to problems like those shown on the equation cards below.

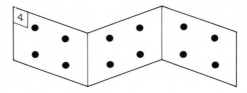

Abstract mode activities

To provide abstract forms of practice with the basic division facts, present students with a variety of games involving only the use of symbolic representations. Help them maintain a positive attitude toward mastering the basic number combinations as this is essential to their future proficiency in calculation.

Sample activity 1 (Partners)

Each student should construct a set of numbered 5″ x 8″ *player* cards for all of the basic multiplication facts, and the teacher should construct a set of *leader* cards which are numbered (on the back) in a corresponding manner. See the following examples.

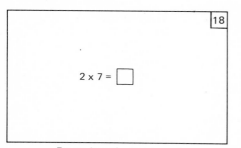

Front view of a player card

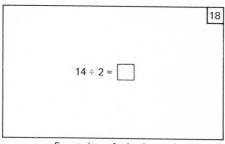

Front view of a leader card

Distribute the player cards among the students who are to play the game so that each student has an identical set of cards. The student leader is given a corresponding set of leader cards which he or she displays in an order which he or she must be careful to preserve. The students who are playing the game must record both the quotients to the division problems as they are shown and the number of the player card that justifies their answer. At the end of play, the student leader reads the numbers of the player cards, in order, that the students should have recorded. The student with the highest number of correct answers is the winner.

Sample activity 2 (Division Roulette)

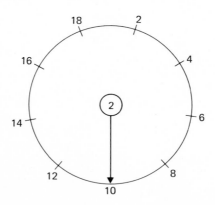

The teacher makes a spinner like the one shown. Two students pair up and challenge each other to a game of Division Roulette. The students spin the pointer and divide the numbers on the outside of the wheel by the number located on the hub. Both the numbers on the wheel and the hub can be changed to provide all 90 combinations. The students write down their answers and check them by using the multiplication matrix. In this example, the procedure for finding the answer to

$10 \div 2 = \boxed{}$ is illustrated by the arrows.

Students can practice basic division facts by using multiplication table displays such as the one below.

X	0	1	2	3	4	5	6	7	8	9
0	0	0	0	0	0	0	0	0	0	0
1	0	1	2	3	4	5	6	7	8	9
2	0	2	4	6	8	10	12	14	16	18
3	0	3	6	9	12	15	18	21	24	27
4	0	4	8	12	16	20	24	28	32	36
5	0	5	10	15	20	25	30	35	40	45
6	0	6	12	18	24	30	36	42	48	54
7	0	7	14	21	28	35	42	49	56	63
8	0	8	16	24	32	40	48	56	64	72
9	0	9	18	27	36	45	54	63	72	81

Sample activity 3 (Function machine)

Using a simple desk or pocket calculator, introduce the idea of a "function machine" by showing the student leader how to enter and process an ordered pair to get a quotient. Have students place ordered pairs on 3″ x 5″ cards for each basic division fact. See the example below.

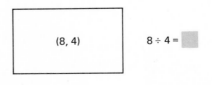

Ordered pair   Related division fact

The students who need practice should give a 3″ x 5″ card containing an ordered pair to the student leader. Then they predict in writing what number they believe the function machine will produce for the ordered pair on their card. The student leader enters the ordered pair, determines the quotient, and gives it to the students who then check their answers.

ACTIVITIES FOR STUDENT INVOLVEMENT, PHASES III AND IV: DIVISION OF A TWO-DIGIT NUMBER BY A ONE-DIGIT NUMBER, WITH AND WITHOUT REGROUPING

Concrete mode activities

When designing concrete activities to teach the initial phases of the division algorithm, the teacher should choose real-life problems and situations which illustrate the basic concepts involved. For example, the task of dividing 23 sheets of paper equally among four students can be used to demonstrate the *remainder* idea. When these basic concepts are well-established at a concrete level, the children are more apt to be able to shift to situations where the same ideas are embodied in semiconcrete and abstract modes.

Sample activity 1 (MAB blocks)

For cases where no regrouping is involved, give each student at least ten long and ten unit blocks.

Now consider the example 2)$\overline{48}$. As the first step, have the children make an embodiment of the dividend, 48, using the blocks. If the *partition* approach is to be taken, the child is asked to form two equivalent subsets out of the set of 48, as shown in the diagram below.

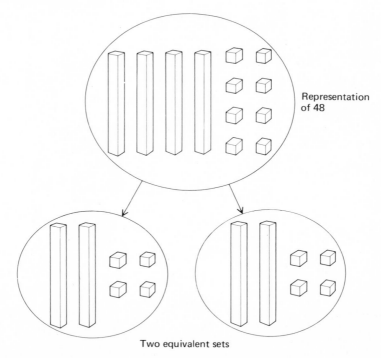

Representation of 48

Two equivalent sets

The procedure for forming the two equivalent subsets is to parcel out the longs, and then the units, using a "one for this set, and one for that set" procedure. Then the children should complete the sentence.

$$\begin{array}{c} \boxed{24} \\ 2\overline{)48} \end{array} \quad \text{because} \quad 2 \times \boxed{24} = 48.$$

The foregoing activity can also be used to illustrate the distributive property, namely $2\overline{)48} \rightarrow (2\overline{)40} + 2\overline{)8})$.

Similar activities can be used in cases where there is a nonzero remainder.

Sample activity 2 (Counting sticks)

Consider the division problem $54 \div 7 = \boxed{}$. In this activity *measurement* approach is employed. The children should first use the counting sticks to make an embodiment of the dividend, 54. Then they should be asked to make all of the subsets of seven they can, after which they should complete the expression

$$\begin{array}{c} \boxed{} \, R \, \triangle \\ 7\overline{)54} \end{array}$$

Semiconcrete mode activities

To provide activities of a semiconcrete nature, use graphic displays that represent how place value and the distributive property influence examples involving regrouping and no regrouping.

Sample activity 1 (Graph paper)

Give the students graph paper examples like the following one for $36 \div 3 = \boxed{}$.

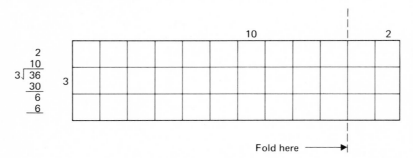

Demonstrate how to fold the graph paper to verify the results of the partial dividends.

Sample activity 2 (Array cards)

Give the students array cards like the following for $34 \div 2 = \boxed{}$.

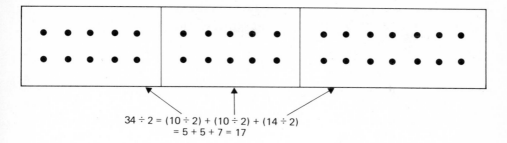

$$34 \div 2 = (10 \div 2) + (10 \div 2) + (14 \div 2)$$
$$= 5 + 5 + 7 = 17$$

Demonstrate how to verify the results of the partial dividends for algorithms like this one which shows the use of the distributive property and renaming. Then give students similar dot displays and have them formulate and connect partial dividends to the dot display as indicated in the illustration.

Abstract mode activities

To provide practice at the abstract level of operation give the children activities involving the use of symbols only.

Sample activity 1 (Unknown values)

Give the children examples where key numerals are replaced by a place holder such as a $\square$, $\bigcirc$, or $\triangle$. The students can pair off and take turns filling in the missing numerals. Each player gets one point for each correct replacement. Use examples like the following.

```
        □                    5
       20                   1△
    4)92                 5)□5
       △0                   50
      ‾1▽‾                  ‾20‾
       ○2                   ▽5
```

Sample activity 2 (Rapid division)

Give the students an incomplete statement of a division rule and some examples which illustrate it. Then ask them to complete the rule and demonstrate to the class how the rule helps them to divide quickly.

Example 1

To divide by 5, multiply the number 2 and divide by $\square$. Look at the example below and complete the rule. Why does it work?

$$325 \div 5 = 650 \div 10 = 65$$

Example 2

To divide by 15, multiply the number by $\square$ and divide by 30. Look at the example below and complete the rule. Why does it work?

$$375 \div 15 = 750 \div 30 = 25$$

ACTIVITIES FOR STUDENT INVOLVEMENT, PHASE V: MULTIDIGIT DIVISION WITH AND WITHOUT REGROUPING

The general form of division is, perhaps, the most complex algorithm for teachers to teach and for pupils to learn and understand. Hence, in teaching it careful attention should be given to checking on prerequisite skills and to providing practice material at the concrete, semiconcrete, and abstract levels. The sample activities that follow represent the types that should be used with each of the algorithms suggested by the flowcharts.

Concrete mode activities

To provide concrete practice with multidigit division algorithms, give the children manipulative materials like those in the following samples.

Sample activity 1 (Counting discs and graph paper)
Give the students large sheets of graph paper marked off into at least 200 large squares as indicated below, and a set of 200 counting discs.

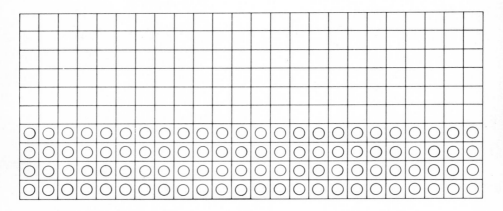

Using the graph paper and counting discs, have the students illustrate the steps in problems such as the following:

$$\begin{array}{r} 4 \\ 24\overline{)96} \\ 96 \\ \hline \end{array}$$

Sample activity 2 (Pocket chart and counting sticks)
Label large cans with the appropriate place values and have the students use counting sticks to illustrate the solution to problems such as this one.

$$12\overline{)132}$$

Have the students begin by arranging the cans and counting sticks to show 132. Next, have them consider what happens when attempting to partition the bundle of

100 sticks into 12 equivalent subsets. Since this obviously cannot be accomplished with the bundle of 100, the rubber band is removed and the 100 is converted into 10 tens which are all placed in the tens can. Now the dividend, 132, is illustrated as 13 and 2 ones. For the next step, remove the 13 tens from the can and separate them into 12 matching subsets. This results in 12 subsets of 10 in each, or 120, with one bundle of ten left over. The partial quotient at this point is ten. Finally the 1 ten that remains cannot be distributed intact, and therefore must be converted into ones and combined with the 2 ones that remain. Now the 12 single sticks can be distributed by placing one stick in each subset. At this point, it can be seen that the quotient is 11 since there are twelve subsets of 11 sticks each.

Semiconcrete mode activities

To provide semiconcrete mode activities, the teacher should use graphic displays that represent the steps in various division problems.

Sample activity 1 (Graph paper)

Have the children color or cut graph paper to illustrate how the distributive property can be used to solve problems such as $156 \div 12 = \boxed{}$.

$$12\overline{)156} = (12\overline{)120} + 12\overline{)36}\,) = (10 + 3) = 13$$

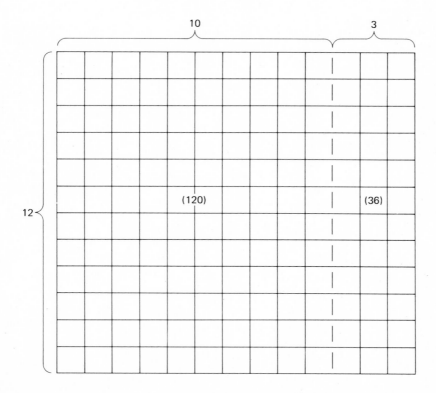

Sample activity 2 (Counting frame)

Give the children problems such as $225 \div 15 =$ ☐ Then show them how to record their thinking as they solve the problem. Consider the procedure used in the example below.

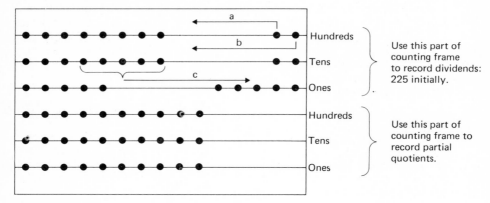

Step 1
Represent the dividend on the top part of the counting frame.

Step 2
Subtract 10 fifteens, or 150, from the dividend:

a) Subtract 100 by moving 1 hundred bead to the left. See arrow (a) above.

b) To subtract 50, move 1 hundred bead to the left. See arrow (b) above. Then move 5 ten beads to the right. See arrow (c). Mathematically this means $50 = 100 - 50$.

Step 3
The frame should now look like the one below. Note there is one tens bead placed on the quotient section to represent the 10 fifteens just removed.

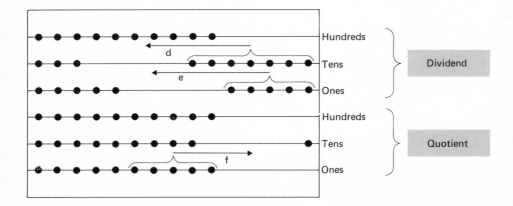

Step 4
Subtract 5 fifteens, or 75, from the dividend remaining:

a) Subtract 70 by moving 7 ten's beads to the left. See arrow (d) above.

b) Subtract 5 by moving the remaining one's beads to the left. See arrow (e) above.

Step 5
Record 5 ones in the quotient section to show the 5 additional fifteens that were removed. See arrow (f).

The completed frame should now appear as shown below.

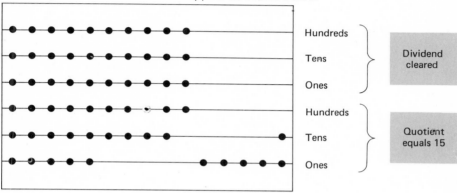

Thus 225 ÷ 15 = 15.

Abstract mode activities

To provide abstract mode activities, focus on using procedures for estimating quotients; also, where possible use the related divisibility rules. A relatively long period of time should be spent on developing the students' ability to efficiently estimate the quotient in various division situations. This competence will be very valuable later on.

Sample activity 1 (Two rule procedures)

Show the students how to round the divisor to the nearest 10, 100, or 1000 as the case may be. Then have them use this number to help estimate partial quotients. For example, have them record their questions and decisions as shown below.

```
      4
     20   ans. 124
    100
26)3224
   2600
   ────
    624
    520
   ────
    104
    104
   ────
```

1. Are there any 26's in 3200?   Yes.
2. How many?   More than 100. So, remove one hundred 26's.
3. Are there any 26's in 624?   Yes
4. How many?   More than 20. So, remove twenty 26's.
5. Are there any 26's in 104?   Yes
6. How many?   4

Sample activity 2 (Divisibility rules)

Present one of the following divisibility rules and have the students practice using the rule. Then see if the students can determine why the rule works.

A whole number is divisible by	Procedure—Check to see:
2	→ if the units digit is even.
3	→ if the sum of the digits is divisible by 3.
4	→ if the last two digits represent a number divisible by 4.
5	→ if the number ends in 5 or 0.
6	→ if the number is divisible by both 2 and 3.
8	→ if the last three digits represent a number divisible by 8.
9	→ if the sum of the digits are divisible by 9.

Exercise set

1. Use the definition of division to justify the truth of the following statements.

   a) $56 \div 9 \neq 6$ b) $72 \div 6 = 12$

2. Translate each of the following division sentences into an equivalent multiplication sentence.

   a) $42 \div 7 = \square$ b) $24 \div \square = 4$

3. Translate each of the following multiplication sentences into an equivalent division sentence.

   a) $5 \times 8 = \square$ b) $3 \times \square = 27$

4. Construct the division sentences using the following information.

	Divisor	Quotient	Dividend
a)	2	x	18
b)	5	14	y

5. Identify which of the following are *not* basic division facts.

   a) $55 \div 5 = 11$ b) $63 \div 7 = 9$ c) $49 \div 7 = 7$ d) $45 \div 3 = 15$

6. As suggested, the Comprehensive Flowchart for Teaching Multiplication can be used as a flowchart for teaching division. In order to demonstrate this fact, construct a sample division problem corresponding to each of the components of the Comprehensive Multiplication Flowchart. [*Hint:* Convert each sample multiplication problem into an equivalent division problem.]

7. Use the Comprehensive Flowchart for Teaching Multiplication (see Exercise 6) as a guide for ordering the following division problems into the sequence in which they normally would be taught.

   a) $24 \div 2$ $35 \div 5$ $132 \div 12$ b) $150 \div 5$ $225 \div 15$ $72 \div 9$

8. Is division a commutative operation? If not, produce a counterexample.

9. Is division an associative operation? If not, produce a counterexample.

10. Among other things, the flowcharts for teaching division serve to identify: (1) the major objectives for division of whole numbers, and (2) the order in which they should be learned. For example, the following objective pertains to the basic facts component of the Comprehensive Flowchart.

    Given
    A balance beam; problems dealing with the basic division facts.

    Required performance
    Use the balance beam to compute the quotients.

    The criterion, of course, is arbitrary. For example, a 3/4 performance for the above objective may be considered satisfactory.
    Use the foregoing ideas to write at least one objective for another component of the flowchart.

11. The division algorithms make use of the other three number operations. How much emphasis should be given to the teaching of division? Check several elementary textbook series. Did they confirm your expectations? Discuss.

12. Explain why it is desirable to teach children both the *measurement* and the *partition* interpretations of division.

13. Write several verbal problems that can be used to introduce division as the inverse of multiplication.

14. How should teachers introduce remainders before pupils have been introduced to rational numbers?

15. Compile a list of practice activities and games that will help pupils develop skill in estimating trial quotients.

16. Consider the following problem $4\overline{)168}$. Explain why the statement "there are no 4's in 1" is misleading to students who are just beginning to learn to estimate quotients, What other procedures could be used?

17. Why are there only 90 basic division facts when there are 100 basic addition, subtraction, and multiplication facts?

18. How important is understanding of the distributive property to a pupil's ability to rationalize the steps used in the long-division process?

19. Illustrate how the number line could be used to help pupils see the inverse relation between multiplication and division.

20. Collect some learning activities beyond textbook exercises that can be used for developing skill with the basic division facts.

21. Develop some learning activities that could be used to teach children how to use a pocket calculator to solve long-division problems.

22. How should problems involving remainders be illustrated with manipulative materials? Give examples.

READINGS FOR ADDITIONAL STUDY

For each of the following topics, read one of the articles listed in the bibliography and write a one- or two-page report which consists of (1) a brief *summary* of the article, and (2) your *reactions* to the positions which have been taken.

23. Fundamental concepts of division.

24. Procedures for teaching the division algorithm.

25. Teaching division in those instances where the remainders are not zero.

Bibliography

1. Ashlock, R. B. *Error Patterns in Computation.* Columbus: Charles E. Merrill, 1972.

2. Bender, Marvin L. "Dividing by zero." *The Arithmetic Teacher* 8 (April 1961): 176–79.

3. Cacha, F. B. "Understanding multiplication and division of multidigit numbers." *The Arithmetic Teacher* 19 (May 1972): 349–54.

4. Capps, Lelon R. "Making division meaningful and logical." *The Arithmetic Teacher* 9 (April 1962): 198–202.

5. Connelly, R., and J. Heddens. "Remainders that shouldn't remain." *The Arithmetic Teacher* 18 (October 1971): 379–80.

6. Deans, Edwina. "Early development of concepts of multiplication and division." *The Arithmetic Teacher* 12 (February 1965): 143–44.

7. Di Spigno, Joseph. "Division isn't that hard." *The Arithmetic Teacher* **18** (October 1971): 373–77.

8. Flournoy, Francis. "Children's success with two methods of estimating the quotient figure." *The Arithmetic Teacher* **16** (March 1969): 100–104.

9. Hilaire, Paul A. "Lets take a look at division." *The Arithmetic Teacher* **8** (May 1961): 220–25.

10. Kurtz, R. "Fourth grade division: how much is retained in grade five." *The Arithmetic Teacher* **20** (January 1973): 65–71.

11. National Council of Teachers of Mathematics. *Topics in mathematics, Twenty-ninth Yearbook.* Washington, D.C.: The Council, 1964, Booklet 2.

12. Rappaport, D. "Grouping—an aid in learning multiplication and division facts." *The Arithmetic Teacher* **8** (January 1961): 27–31.

13. Reeve, O. "The missing factor in division." *The Arithmetic Teacher* **15** (March 1968): 275–77.

14. Ruddell, A. K. "Levels of difficulty in division." *The Arithmetic Teacher* **6** (March 1959): 97–99.

15. Sahagian, Thomas. "An easier way to check long division." *The Arithmetic Teacher* **11** (October 1964): 417.

16. Spitzer, Herbert F. "Measurement or partition division for introducing study of the division operation." *The Arithmetic Teacher* **14** (May 1967): 369–72.

17. Swart, W. L. "Teaching the division-subtraction process." *The Arithmetic Teacher* **19** (January 1972): 71–75.

18. Swart, W. L. "A diary of remedial instruction in division—Grade 7." *The Arithmetic Teacher* **22** (December 1975): 614–622.

19. Tucker, Benny F. "The division algorithm." *The Arithmetic Teacher* **20** (December 1973): 39–41.

20. Van Engen, H. "Teach fundamental operations through problem solving." *Grade Teacher* **8** (April 1962): 58–59.

21. Zweng, M. J. "The fourth operation is not fundamental." *The Arithmetic Teacher* **19** (December 1972): 623–27.

Teaching rational number concepts

8

Synopsis and objectives

Chapter 8 provides you with the basic theoretical and practical information you need to teach the fundamental concepts and principles necessary to understand and work with the rational numbers. The **theory** section is organized around a set of flowcharts showing the main ideas and the order in which they should be taught. Included are treatments of *fractions* and *decimals* and the operations (+, −, ×, ÷) with the rational numbers.

The **practice** section contains practical ideas for classroom use which are keyed to the flowcharts. You are encouraged to use the bibliography provided.

When you have completed a careful study of Chapter 8 you should be able to

1. illustrate the meaning of a proper fraction;

2. define and interpret the terms *fraction, fractional number, numerator,* and *denominator;*

3. state and give meaningful interpretations of the basic principle of equivalence of fractions;

4. describe and provide examples which illustrate the meaning of the terms *standard name* of a fractional number, *primitive* fraction, and *nonprimitive* fraction;

5. describe and illustrate procedures for *direct* comparison of fractional numbers;

6. describe and illustrate the "convert to equivalent fractions" procedure for comparing fractional numbers;

7. state and provide examples of the "cross-product" algorithm for comparing fractional numbers;

8. describe and illustrate procedures for interpreting improper fractions and mixed numerals as well as procedures for converting from one form to the other;

9. construct a flowchart for teaching addition of fractional numbers which reveals the fundamental learning hierarchy of the various problem types;

10. show how to use number lines and regions as aids in the teaching of addition of fractional numbers;

11. describe and give illustrations of how to use concrete learning aids, such as number blocks, to find the *least common denominator* of a pair of fractions;

12. describe and illustrate both the "least common multiple" and the "prime number" techniques for finding the least common denominator of a pair of fractions;

13. use concrete teaching/learning aids, such as number blocks, to demonstrate the commutative and associative properties of addition of fractional numbers;

14. use both number lines and regions to show that zero is an additive identity;

15. define subtraction of fractional numbers as the inverse of addition and illustrate it by means of examples;

16. show how to use number lines and regions as aids in the teaching of subtraction of fractional numbers;

17. translate a flowchart for teaching addition of fractional numbers into a flowchart for teaching subtraction;

18. state and illustrate the basic definition for multiplication of fractional numbers;

19. describe and illustrate the "region" approach for finding the product of a pair of (proper) fractional numbers;

20. construct a flowchart for teaching multiplication of fractional numbers which reveals the fundamental learning hierarchy of the various problem types;

21. define division of fractional numbers as the inverse of multiplication and illustrate it by means of examples;

22. state and explain the "invert and multiply" procedure for dividing fractions;

23. translate a flowchart for teaching multiplication of fractional numbers into a flowchart for teaching division of fractional numbers;

24. explain why the absence of the capability to conserve length or area can serve as an obstacle to learning the basic concepts about fractional numbers;

25. explain how to extend the place value concepts to permit the construction of decimal numerals;

26. demonstrate how to convert decimal numerals to equivalent (common) fraction numerals, and conversely;

27. demonstrate the basic principles involved in performing the four fundamental operations with decimals;

28. formulate concrete, semiconcrete, and abstract activities which will facilitate the learning of fractional number concepts and their uses.

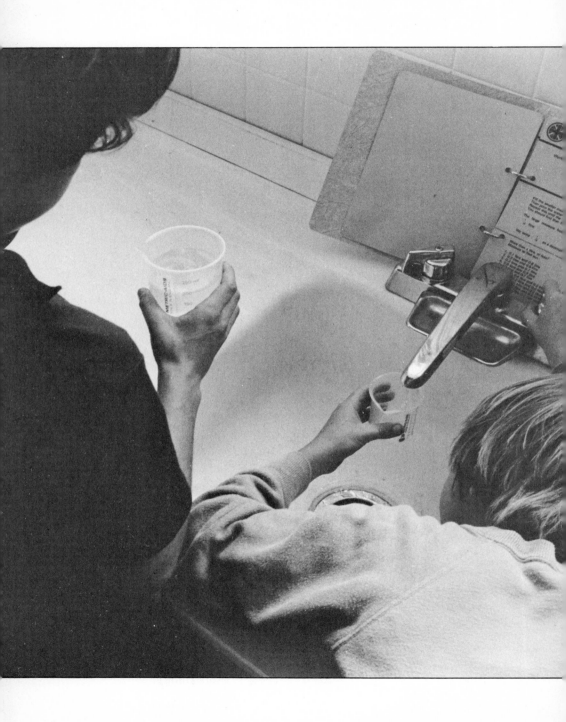

Teaching rational number concepts*

Theory

SOME BASIC CONCEPTS

Symbols like $\frac{2}{3}$ and $\frac{4}{5}$ are called fractions, and fractions are names for rational numbers. In general, every symbol x/y, where x stands for a whole number and y stands for a whole number different from zero, is a name of a rational number. The number above the bar is called the *numerator* and the number below the bar is called the *denominator* of the fraction.

The rational numbers, typically called *fractional numbers* in the elementary school, were invented to describe "whole-part" relationships.

A FLOWCHART FOR TEACHING RATIONAL NUMBER CONCEPTS AND USES

A general flowchart for teaching the key ideas about rational, or fractional, numbers and how to use them is given in Fig. 8.1. In the following sections, each component of the flowchart will be discussed in detail.

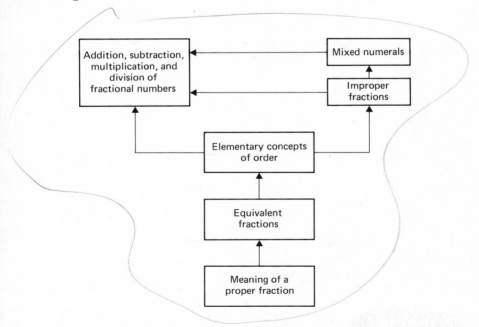

Fig. 8.1 General flowchart for teaching concepts and uses of fractional numbers.

---

* The discussion in this chapter pertains only to the nonnegative fractional numbers.

THE MEANING OF A PROPER FRACTION

As suggested by the flowchart, the development of an understanding of how to interpret a proper fraction constitutes the first step in teaching fractional number ideas.

Those fractions x/y, where x is less than y and $y \neq 0$, are called *proper* fractions. In other words, the proper fractions correspond to the rational numbers between zero and one.

There are several distinct types of situations which give rise to a need for fractional numbers; moreover, each of these situations should be used when helping the student develop an adequate notion of the meaning and use of proper fractions.

One type of situation is illustrated by the following example.

Example. What part of each bar is shaded?

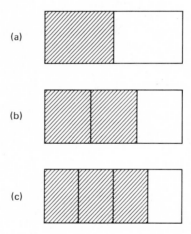

(a)

(b)

(c)

The child must learn that the *denominator* of the fraction tells the total number of equal (congruent) parts into which the region has been subdivided, and that the *numerator* tells the number of those parts which are noted. Thus, for example, in (c) above, since three of the four *congruent* regions into which the bar has been subdivided have been shaded, we say that $\frac{3}{4}$ of the box is shaded. This conceptualization becomes especially important when the converse task is given, namely to shade a certain portion of a region. For instance, suppose you want the student to shade $\frac{5}{6}$ of the following region.

There are, of course, different ways to subdivide the region into six congruent parts, but the student must begin by recognizing the practical necessity of doing this as the first step toward resolving the problem.

A second situation consists of determining fractional parts of a finite set of objects. Here the student would be confronted with a problem like the following:

Example. What fractional part of this set of marbles is red?

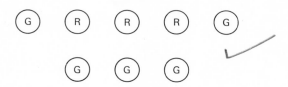

Altogether there are eight marbles, and three of them are red; so we say that $\frac{3}{8}$ of the marbles are red.

The third situation consists of associating the fractional numbers with points on the number line. For example, to find the point on the number line which corresponds to the fractional number $\frac{5}{8}$, we must somehow divide the segment with end points 0 and 1 into 8 parts of equal length. The fifth point of subdivision marks "five-eighths" of the distance from 0 to 1, and so this point corresponds to the fractional number $\frac{5}{8}$.

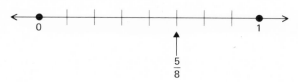

As suggested earlier, all three of the foregoing ways of interpreting proper fractions are important competencies for each child to achieve before proceeding to any more advanced ideas about fractional numbers or how to use them.

THE CONCEPT OF EQUIVALENCE OF FRACTIONS

When children experiment with problems like those above, they soon discover that *different* fractions can be used to specify a particular part of a region or set, or a particular rational number. For example, as the following diagram illustrates, $\frac{1}{2}$, $\frac{2}{4}$, and $\frac{4}{8}$ are all *equivalent* fractions because they specify the same idea about how much of the rod is shaded.

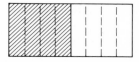

The student learns not only that fractions are symbols and that they are names of rational numbers but also that every rational number can have many names.

The technical term we use when two or more fractions name the same rational number is to say that the fractions are *equivalent.* Associated with every rational number is an *infinite* set of equivalent fractions. For example, consider the rational number $\frac{1}{3}$. Each fraction in the following set is a name of the number $\frac{1}{3}$.

$$\left\{ \frac{1}{3}, \frac{2}{6}, \frac{3}{9}, \frac{4}{12}, \frac{5}{15}, \cdots \right\}$$

It is customary to refer to the fraction that is reduced to lowest terms, that is, the fraction whose numerator and denominator have no common factors, as the *standard name* of the rational number.

The procedures involved in being able to reduce a fraction to lowest terms and of being able to construct fractions equivalent to any specified fraction are outgrowths of the general (equivalence) principle that

$$\frac{a}{b} = \frac{c \times a}{c \times b}.$$

This principle may be interpreted as meaning that if you multiply, or divide, both the numerator and the denominator of a fraction by the same whole number c (where $c \neq 0$), you obtain an equivalent fraction. For example.

$$\frac{5}{7} = \frac{4 \times 5}{4 \times 7} = \frac{20}{28}$$

and, conversely,

$$\frac{12}{30} = \frac{6 \times 2}{6 \times 5} = \frac{2}{5}.$$

Note that in the first example, the first fraction was a *primitive* fraction (one that was expressed in lowest terms) and a *nonprimitive* fraction was produced. In the second example the given fraction was *nonprimitive* and it was reduced to lowest terms. We see that the equivalence principle works both ways.

In general, recognition of the equivalence principle should develop intuitively. Students should have many opportunities to create sets of equivalent fractions and to discover the equivalence principle for themselves. Appropriate learning experiences would include various ways of interpreting fractions: regions, sets, and number lines.

ORDERING FRACTIONAL NUMBERS

After the student has acquired a concept of the meaning of a (proper) fraction and the rudiments of the equivalence idea, the next step is to develop the skills of *comparing* fractional numbers. That is, the student should learn to determine whether one fractional number is larger or smaller than another.

Early learning experiences in the comparison of fractional numbers should consist of direct comparison methods with concrete objects. Suitable materials can be constructed by the teacher for classroom use. For example, it is easy to construct cardboard models of the unit fractions from, say, $\frac{1}{2}$ to $\frac{1}{12}$. Start with some given unit length (about 30 cm is ideal) and then cut out cardboard models of the unit fractional numbers you wish to use.

The availability of models make fractional number comparison fairly easy. For example, to compare $\frac{2}{3}$ with $\frac{3}{4}$ the student should make representations of these fractional numbers, and then place them side-by-side to determine which is larger.

This comparison would reveal the fact that $\frac{3}{4}$ is greater than $\frac{2}{3}$. The use of the number line is a good extension of this strategy.

Comparing fractional numbers by analytical means is a bit more involved, but the most obvious tactic would be to convert the given fractions to equivalent ones which have the same denominator. This procedure is illustrated here.

Example. Which is greater, $\frac{2}{5}$ or $\frac{3}{7}$?

Solution

$$\frac{2}{5} = \frac{7 \times 2}{7 \times 5} = \frac{14}{35}$$

$$\frac{3}{7} = \frac{5 \times 3}{5 \times 7} = \frac{15}{35}$$

$$\text{So, } \frac{3}{7} > \frac{2}{5}.$$

The strategy which was used in the foregoing example provides one good reason why the concept of equivalent fractions appears prior to the concept of order in the general learning hierarchy for fractional numbers (see Fig. 8.1).

Finally, it should be pointed out that perhaps the easiest algorithm for comparing fractional numbers is based on the principal that

$$\frac{a}{b} < \frac{c}{d} \quad \text{if and only if} \quad a \times d < b \times c,$$

or that

$$\frac{a}{b} > \frac{c}{d} \quad \text{if and only if} \quad a \times d > b \times c.$$

For example, consider the problem of comparing the fractional numbers

$$\frac{5}{7} \quad \text{and} \quad \frac{8}{11}.$$

The strategy calls for finding the "cross-products" 5×11 and 7×8. Since

$$5 \times 11 < 7 \times 8,$$

it follows that

$$\frac{5}{7} < \frac{8}{11}.$$

This procedure is difficult to justify, and so it should probably be taught in the more advanced stages of the student's mathematical development.

IMPROPER FRACTIONS AND MIXED NUMERALS

As suggested by Flowchart 8.1, after the child has learned the rudimentary ideas about (proper) fractions, and the basic ideas about equivalence and order, it is then appropriate to begin the study of addition, subtraction, multiplication, and division of fractional numbers. The flowchart also suggests that this is the time to begin the companion activities of teaching the concepts of *improper fractions* and *mixed numerals*. The number line is perhaps the best teaching/learning aid for dealing with these concepts since it permits a natural, easy-to-visualize extension to the fractional numbers which are greater than one. One especially good way of introducing improper fractions—and subsequently mixed numerals—is to ask the student to find the sum of two fractional numbers, say $\frac{3}{5} + \frac{4}{5}$, using the number line approach.

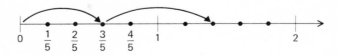

This task involves not only the problem of subdividing the interval between 1 and 2, but also the problem of how to name the sum. Initially, students are most apt to select the improper fraction name. It is important for the teacher to take great care, however, in designing learning experiences that enable the students to become proficient in converting from improper fraction form to mixed numeral form, and vice versa. The key ideas are illustrated by the following examples.

<table>
<tr><td>Converting an improper
fraction to a mixed numeral</td><td>Converting a mixed
numeral to an improper fraction</td></tr>
</table>

$$\frac{7}{5} = \frac{5}{5} + \frac{2}{5}$$

$$= 1 + \frac{2}{5}$$

$$= 1\tfrac{2}{5}$$

$$1\tfrac{2}{3} = 1 + \tfrac{2}{3}$$

$$= \frac{3}{3} + \frac{2}{3}$$

$$= \frac{5}{3}$$

ADDITION OF FRACTIONAL NUMBERS

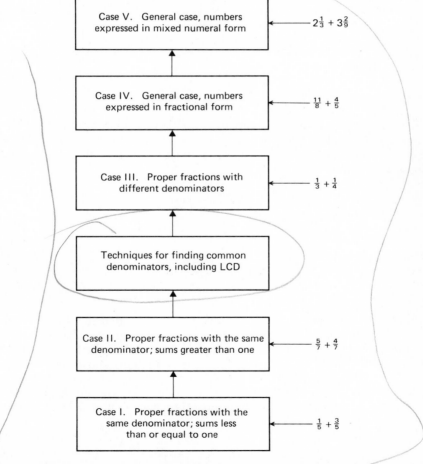

Fig. 8.2 A flowchart for teaching addition of fractional numbers.

A flowchart for teaching addition of fractional numbers is given in Fig. 8.2.

As suggested by the flowchart, the first type of problem for the student to consider should be one like this:

$$\frac{1}{5} + \frac{2}{5} = \boxed{}$$

in which both of the addends are proper fractions having the same denominator, and where the sum is not greater than one.

The fractional number models described earlier involving the use of regions, sets, and number lines can all be used to teach the student the operation of addition of fractions. The uses of region and number line models are especially good. For example, consider the use of regions.

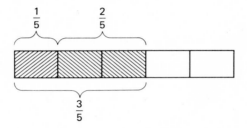

First we have a model of $\frac{1}{5}$ and then another disjoint model of $\frac{2}{5}$. The sum, obviously, is $\frac{3}{5}$. The use of a number line is even better since it graphically shows how to relate the addition of fractional numbers to the addition of whole numbers.

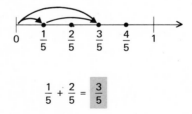

$$\frac{1}{5} + \frac{2}{5} = \boxed{\frac{3}{5}}$$

The second type of addition problem should be that in which the addends are still proper fractions, but where the sum is now greater than one. This case was discussed briefly in the preceding section. As implied there, it also can serve to open the discussion about improper fractions and mixed numerals.

The third type of addition problem involves adding fractions with unlike denominators. In this case the learner must convert the given addition problem to one of the first two kinds, in other words, find a common denominator.

For example, consider the problem

$$\frac{1}{2} + \frac{1}{3} = \boxed{}.$$

As always, the first learning experiences for new problem types should involve the use of concrete learning aids. As illustrated, the student should start by forming a representation of the sum $\frac{1}{2}+\frac{1}{3}$ and comparing it with one.

$\frac{1}{2}$		$\frac{1}{3}$	
1			

The next step is to try to subdivide the unit rod in some way that reveals the sum. The procedure is shown here.

$\frac{1}{2}$			$\frac{1}{3}$		
$\frac{1}{6}$	$\frac{1}{6}$	$\frac{1}{6}$	$\frac{1}{6}$	$\frac{1}{6}$	$\frac{1}{6}$
1					

It is now clear that

$$\frac{1}{2}+\frac{1}{3}=\frac{3}{6}+\frac{2}{6}=\frac{5}{6}.$$

As suggested by this example, emphasis should be placed on finding a common denominator, and children will soon be able to do this in simple cases without resorting to the use of fraction models. When the students have reached this stage, they are prepared to consider the general algorithms for adding fractional numbers which are expressed in (common) fractional form. One of these is:

For all rational numbers a/b and c/d:

$$\frac{a}{b}+\frac{c}{d}=\frac{a \times d}{b \times d}+\frac{b \times c}{b \times d}=\frac{(a \times d)+(b \times c)}{b \times d}.$$

This principle conveys the idea that the product of the denominators of the given fractions can always be used as a common denominator. This procedure does not in general, however, produce the smallest possible common denominator, and often the *least common denominator* (LCD) is what is wanted. One method for finding the LCD of a pair of fractions is to determine the *least common multiple* of the two denominators. For example:

$$\frac{1}{6}+\frac{1}{4}=\boxed{}.$$

Multiples of 6:   6, ⑫ 18, 24, $\cdots$

Multiples of 4:   4, 8, ⑫ 16, $\cdots$

The least common multiple is 12, so it is the desired LCD.

$$\frac{1}{6}+\frac{1}{4}=\frac{2}{12}+\frac{3}{12}=\frac{5}{12}$$

Another more sophisticated method for determining the LCD of two or more fractions involves the procedure of finding the prime factorizations of the denominators. The following example illustrates how the procedure works.

$$\frac{5}{6} + \frac{3}{20} = \frac{5}{2 \times 3} + \frac{3}{2 \times 2 \times 5} \qquad \longleftarrow \qquad \text{First factor each denominator as a product of prime numbers.}$$

$$= \frac{5 \times 2 \times 5}{2 \times 2 \times 3 \times 5} + \frac{3 \times 3}{2 \times 2 \times 3 \times 5} \qquad \longleftarrow \text{Since the LCD must be divisible by both } 2 \times 3 \text{ and } 2 \times 2 \times 5, \text{ it must be } 2 \times 2 \times 3 \times 5 = 60$$

$$= \frac{50}{60} + \frac{9}{60}$$

$$= \frac{59}{60}$$

Since it is a more advanced procedure, it should not be used until the child has become proficient with the more fundamental methods.

PROPERTIES OF ADDITION OF FRACTIONAL NUMBERS

Addition of fractional numbers has many of the same properties as addition of whole numbers. To be specific, addition of fractional numbers is *commutative* and *associative*, and zero is an *identity* element.

The property of commutativity is easy for the student to recognize if number blocks or some other concrete learning aids are used. The technique of teaching is the same as that used for teaching commutativity of whole numbers, as illustrated by the following example.

$$\frac{1}{2} + \frac{1}{3} \qquad\qquad\qquad\qquad\qquad \frac{1}{3} + \frac{1}{2}$$

$\frac{1}{2}$	$\frac{1}{3}$

$\frac{1}{3}$	$\frac{1}{2}$

It should be obvious to students who can conserve length that the *order* in which the fraction models are laid end-to-end has no effect on the overall length, or hence the sum.

The property of associativity can be established in a similar way.

$\frac{1}{4}$	$\frac{1}{3}$	$\frac{1}{8}$

$\frac{1}{4}$	$\frac{1}{3}$	$\frac{1}{8}$

$$\left(\frac{1}{4} + \frac{1}{3} \right) + \frac{1}{8} \qquad\qquad\qquad \frac{1}{4} + \left(\frac{1}{3} + \frac{1}{8} \right)$$

$\frac{1}{4}$	$\frac{1}{3}$	$\frac{1}{8}$

$\frac{1}{4}$	$\frac{1}{3}$	$\frac{1}{8}$

Before using the fact that zero is an identity element for addition, we want to be sure the student knows that zero is a rational number and that every fraction in the set

$$\left\{ \frac{0}{1}, \frac{0}{2}, \frac{0}{3}, \cdots \right\}$$

is a name of zero.

The *identity* property can then be easily established. For example, consider the two approaches given below for

$$\frac{2}{3} + 0 = \frac{2}{3} + \frac{0}{3}.$$

Number line approach

Note that the $\frac{0}{3}$ calls for an "in-place" jump.

Region approach

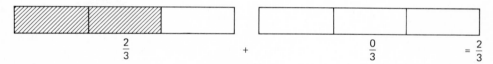

SUBTRACTION OF FRACTIONAL NUMBERS

As with whole numbers, the subtraction of fractional numbers is described as the inverse of addition. That is,

$$\frac{a}{b} - \frac{c}{d} = \frac{m}{n} \quad \text{if and only if} \quad \frac{c}{d} + \frac{m}{n} = \frac{a}{b}.$$

In other words, every subtraction problem can be converted to an addition problem having a missing addend. For example, the subtraction problem

$$\frac{5}{9} - \frac{1}{9} = \boxed{}$$

is equivalent to the addition problem

$$\frac{1}{9} + \boxed{} = \frac{5}{9}.$$

The number line is helpful in illustrating the meaning of these ideas.

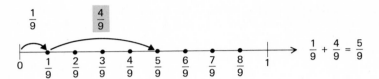

$$\frac{1}{9} + \frac{4}{9} = \frac{5}{9}$$

The foregoing state of affairs is, of course, identical to the relationship which exists between the operations of addition and subtraction of whole numbers. It is not surprising, then, to discover that the so called "take away" interpretation is also extendible to subtraction of fractional numbers. Consider, for example, the problem

$$\frac{4}{5} - \frac{1}{5} = \boxed{}.$$

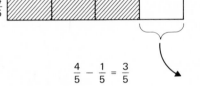

$$\frac{4}{5} - \frac{1}{5} = \frac{3}{5}$$

As with whole numbers, we teach addition and subtraction of fractional numbers in tandem. As the student acquires a particular competence in addition, the corresponding subtraction ideas appear next in the learning hierarchy. *The flowchart for teaching subtraction, then, may be constructed directly from the flowchart for teaching addition.*

MULTIPLICATION OF FRACTIONAL NUMBERS

The definition for multiplication of fractional numbers may be stated as follows:

For all fractional numbers $\frac{a}{b}$ and $\frac{c}{d}$,

$$\frac{a}{b} \times \frac{c}{d} = \frac{a \times c}{b \times d}.$$

Thus, for example,

$$\frac{2}{3} \times \frac{4}{5} = \frac{2 \times 4}{3 \times 5} = \frac{8}{15}.$$

A good strategy for helping children discover this idea is to relate the operation of multiplication of fractional numbers to the array interpretation of the operation of multiplication of whole numbers. For purposes of illustration, note that the product 2×3 can be associated with the following array.

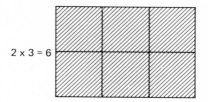

$2 \times 3 = 6$

A conceptually similar procedure can be used to determine the product of a pair of fractional numbers. Consider, for example, the problem

$$\frac{1}{2} \times \frac{1}{3} = \boxed{}.$$

First, draw a unit square. Then shade $\frac{1}{2}$ of the square as illustrated in the diagram on the left; then shade $\frac{1}{3}$ of the square as shown in the diagram on the right. The *intersection* of the two shaded regions corresponds to the product. So, we see that $\frac{1}{2} \times \frac{1}{3} = \frac{1}{6}$.

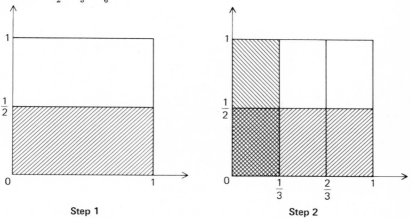

Step 1   Step 2

Note that the product $\frac{1}{2} \times \frac{1}{3}$ can be thought of as "one-half of one-third," or one-sixth.

After the students have become reasonably proficient in finding products in the foregoing manner, they should examine the results of sets of problems they have solved in an effort to discover the multiplication rule:

$$\frac{\square}{\triangle} \times \frac{\triangledown}{\bigcirc} = \frac{\square \times \triangledown}{\triangle \times \bigcirc}$$

Such a procedure, of course, requires considerable teacher guidance.

There are other acceptable alternatives to the "array" procedure described above for teaching children how to find the product of a pair of fractional numbers, but most of them have a special relationship to the nature of the individual problem type under consideration. Before pursuing this matter let us look at the flowchart in Fig. 8.3 which displays in hierarchical form the various types of problems that can be encountered.

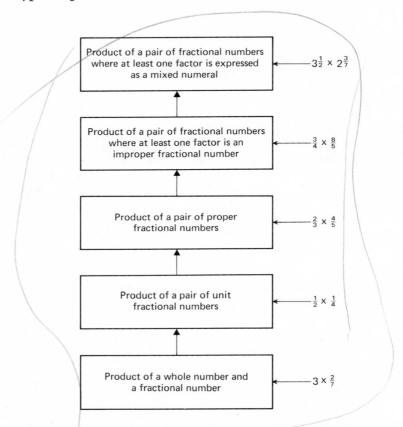

Fig. 8.3 A flowchart for teaching multiplication of the basic fractional number problem types.

As suggested by the flowchart provided in Fig. 8.3, perhaps the easiest and most appropriate problem type to use to introduce the multiplication of fractional numbers is the case where you are trying to find the product of a whole number and a fractional number. This type is selected first since it lends itself to the interpretation of multiplication as repeated addition. It is the only problem type where such an interpretation is useful. Consider the following example.

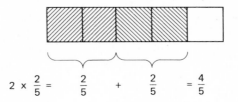

$$2 \times \frac{2}{5} = \qquad \frac{2}{5} \qquad + \qquad \frac{2}{5} \qquad = \frac{4}{5}$$

This problem type leads to an important product rule, namely that

$$a \times \frac{b}{c} = \frac{a \times b}{c}.$$

This principle is often expressed in children's learning materials in the following way:

$$\square \; \times \; \frac{\triangle}{\bigcirc} \; = \; \frac{\square \; \times \; \triangle}{\bigcirc}$$

The "array" procedure described earlier applies directly to the second and third problem types described in Fig. 8.3 flowchart. Modest extensions of the procedure also can be developed to deal with the fourth and fifth problem types, although it is questionable whether such tactics are appropriate for classroom use. The following example reveals the basic ideas.

$$\frac{3}{4} \times \frac{8}{5} = \frac{24}{20}$$

(Three fourths of eight fifths equals twenty-four twentieths.)

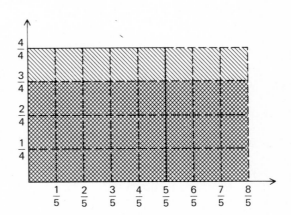

Recognition of the difficulties involved in constructing and conceptualizing such diagrams would seem to argue strongly for the student to develop an understanding of the generalization

$$\frac{a}{b} \times \frac{c}{d} = \frac{a \times c}{b \times d}$$

prior to the introduction of the more complex problem types, and simply use the generalization as the *modus operandi* for dealing with them.

DIVISION OF FRACTIONAL NUMBERS

The division of fractional numbers is related to the operation of multiplication in the same way subtraction is related to addition. Division is the *inverse* of multiplication. That is,

$$\frac{a}{b} \div \frac{c}{d} = \frac{m}{n} \qquad \text{if and only if} \qquad \frac{c}{d} \times \frac{m}{n} = \frac{a}{b}.$$

Every division problem can be converted into an equivalent multiplication problem having a missing factor. For example, the division problem

$$\frac{5}{8} \div \frac{1}{2} = \square$$

is equivalent to the multiplication problem

$$\frac{1}{2} \times \square = \frac{5}{8}.$$

Since the missing factor is $\frac{5}{4}$ it follows that

$$\frac{5}{8} \div \frac{1}{2} = \frac{5}{4}.$$

But the general procedure for solving division problems in this way is not always so easy. For instance, consider the problem

$$\frac{3}{7} \div \frac{1}{2} = \square$$

which can be converted to the form

$$\frac{1}{2} \times \square = \frac{3}{7}.$$

Since 7 is not a multiple of 2, the best strategy to follow here would be to replace $\frac{3}{7}$ by an equivalent fraction which has a denominator that is a multiple of 2. Since $\frac{2 \times 3}{2 \times 7} = \frac{6}{14}$ is such a fraction, we proceed as follows:

$$\frac{1}{2} \times \boxed{} = \frac{6}{14} \, .$$

The missing factor is clearly $\frac{6}{7}$. So, we see that

$$\frac{3}{7} \div \frac{1}{2} = \boxed{\frac{6}{7}}$$

because

$$\frac{1}{2} \times \frac{6}{7} = \frac{6}{14} = \frac{3}{7} \, .$$

The "missing factor" method for solving fractional number division problems is a good strategy for children to learn. Once the basic idea has been mastered, it can also be used to justify the so-called "invert and multiply" method of computing quotients. This method is based on the following principle.

$$\frac{a}{b} \div \frac{c}{d} = \boxed{\frac{a}{b} \times \frac{d}{c}}$$

How

To illustrate the principle, consider the following example.

$$\frac{5}{8} \div \frac{2}{3} = \frac{5}{8} \times \frac{3}{2}$$

Invert divisor and convert to a multiplication problem.

$$= \frac{15}{16}$$

The foregoing principle is easy to justify by using the ideas which have already been developed.

$$\frac{a}{b} \div \frac{c}{d} = \boxed{\frac{a}{b} \times \frac{d}{c}}$$

As in the case of the product rules discussed earlier, the "invert and multiply" method of division can be taught by using a guided discovery teaching strategy.

DECIMAL NUMERALS; SOME BASIC CONCEPTS

The transition from basic common fractions to *decimal fractions* requires an extension of the place value concepts developed for naming whole numbers. The type of extension required is illustrated by the following diagram.

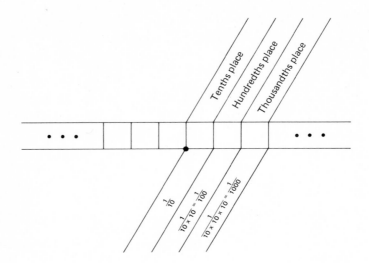

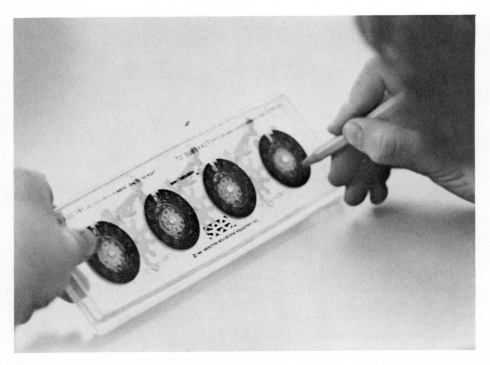

The teacher is helping the student make a place value chart to represent the meaning of decimal numerals.

Accordingly,

$$.3 = 3 \times \frac{1}{10} = \frac{3}{10},$$

$$.05 = 5 \times \frac{1}{100} = \frac{5}{100},$$

$$.007 = 7 \times \frac{1}{1000} = \frac{7}{1000},$$

and so on. Now consider an example like .35. Utilizing standard properties of the place value system, we see that

$$.35 = .3 + .05$$

$$= \frac{3}{10} + \frac{5}{100}$$

$$= \frac{30}{100} + \frac{5}{100}$$

$$= \frac{35}{100}.$$

Similarly,

$$.48 = \frac{48}{100},$$

$$.526 = \frac{526}{1000},$$

$$.9172 = \frac{9172}{10000},$$

and so on.

The first set of competencies that the student needs is being able to read and interpret decimal numerals. Then the student must be able to convert decimal numerals to common fraction numerals, and vice versa.

COMPUTATION WITH DECIMALS

The computational techniques the child has learned for whole numbers transfer directly to the problems of computing with decimals. The only new idea that must be dealt with is locating the decimal point. In addition and subtraction, no new techniques need be learned beyond recognizing the necessity to "line up" the decimal points; that is, add tenths to tenths, hundredths to hundredths, and so on. There are no changes in the rules for regrouping.

Multiplication and division must be examined more closely, however. The following example illustrates the factors which must be taken into account in the case of multiplication. Think through the problem as you would do it.

Observe that, except for the placement of the decimal point, the steps you take are the same as if you were finding the product 7×63.

$$
\begin{array}{r}
63 \\
\underline{\times 7} \\
441
\end{array}
\qquad
\begin{array}{r}
.63 \\
\underline{\times .7} \\
.441
\end{array}
\qquad
\begin{aligned}
.7 \times .63 \\
&= \frac{7}{10} \times \frac{63}{100} \\
&= \frac{7 \times 63}{1000}
\end{aligned}
$$

Hence to find the product $.7 \times .63$, compute the product 7×63 and divide it by 1000. The idea illustrated by this example can, of course, be generalized to produce the common rule for locating the decimal point.

Similar procedures for the division of decimals can be constructed. The following example illustrates the procedure.

$$
\frac{.651}{.3} = \frac{.651 \times 10}{.3 \times 10} = \frac{6.51}{3}
$$

$$
.3\overline{)\,.651} \quad \rightarrow \quad 3.\overline{)\,6.51}
$$

Note that the goal is to convert the problem to an equivalent one where the divisor is a whole number. At this stage the standard division algorithm can be employed.

Practice

ACTIVITIES FOR STUDENT INVOLVEMENT:
MEANING OF A PROPER FRACTION

Sample activity 1 (Flannel board displays)

Students who understand that a whole is equal to the sum of its parts will benefit from making flannel displays to illustrate real-life situations. For example, provide students with cutouts to make proper fractions. Then have the students demonstrate their understanding of statements such as the following by making a bulletin board display.

Judy divided her candy bar into three equivalent parts to share with her two friends, Sharon and Sue. She gave each friend $\frac{1}{3}$ of her candy bar and kept $\frac{1}{3}$ for herself.

Students also can formulate statements to describe flannel board displays presented by their classmates.

Sue	Sharon	Judy
$\frac{1}{3}$	$\frac{1}{3}$	$\frac{1}{3}$

Sample activity 2 (Subset descriptions)

Students who understand subset inclusion will benefit from activities such as the following. Provide the students with red and white poker chips and have them use the chips to follow directions in a statement such as:

Make a set of chips that has $\frac{1}{4}$ red chips and $\frac{3}{4}$ white chips.

This activity can be reversed with the teacher asking students to describe sets containing white and red chips.

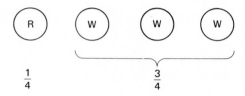

Sample activity 3 (Shading unit regions)

Provide students with dittoed copies of a variety of plane regions and with colored pencils. Have them shade a given fractional part of the plane regions.

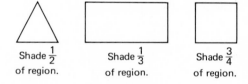

Shade $\frac{1}{2}$ of region.   Shade $\frac{1}{3}$ of region.   Shade $\frac{3}{4}$ of region.

ACTIVITIES FOR STUDENT INVOLVEMENT: THE CONCEPT OF EQUIVALENCE

Sample activity 1 (Centimeter rods)

Have students arrange Cuisenaire rods as shown below to show that the dark green rod can be divided into six parts of the same size and also into two parts of the same size.

Next have them place three white rods and one light green rod on top of dark green rods as shown below, and ask the students:

How much of the dark green rod is covered by the light green rod?

Finally ask the question:

> Since the white rods and the light green rod cover the same amount of the dark green rod, what fractional equivalence do the rod displays show?

In this case, the answer would be $\frac{3}{6} = \frac{1}{2}$

Sample activity 2 (Number line)

Have the student construct number lines like the ones below.

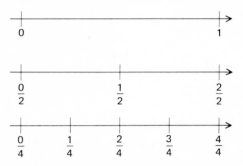

The students can use the number lines to compare two fractions to determine if they are equivalent. They can also develop their own equivalence class like the following one.

$$\left\{ \frac{1}{2}, \frac{2}{4}, \frac{4}{8}, \frac{8}{16}, \cdots \right\}$$

ACTIVITIES FOR STUDENT INVOLVEMENT:
COMPARING FRACTIONAL NUMBERS

Sample activity 1 (Set and subset comparisons)

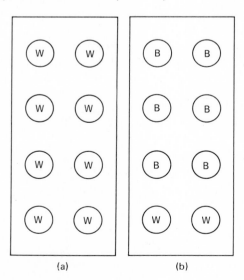

Provide each student with twelve white and twelve blue poker chips. Then have the students use the white and blue chips to make and describe set illustrations like the one shown to compare fractional numbers such as $\frac{6}{8}$ and $\frac{3}{4}$.

    First present the class with an example. Display 8 chips as shown in set (a). Next, replace six of the chips with blue chips. See set (b). It shows that $\frac{6}{8}$ of the chips are blue. Finally, ring this chip display as shown in set (c). This illustration shows that $\frac{3}{4}$ of the chips are blue.

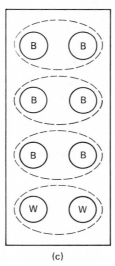

(c)

Sample activity 2 (Shaded unit regions)

Provide each student with centimeter graph paper and a colored pencil. First have the student divide a unit region into thirds. Then tell the students to shade $\frac{1}{3}$ of the region yellow. Next have them divide the same region into sixths as shown by the dotted lines and shade $\frac{1}{6}$ of the region blue.

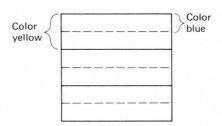

Because only part of the third will turn green, the students will see that $\frac{1}{6}$ of the region is smaller than $\frac{1}{3}$ of the same region.

Sample activity 3 (Geofraction card games)

Provide students with a deck of geofraction cards marked like the ones below.

Construct the cards by selecting a fraction sequence (e.g., $\frac{1}{16}$, $\frac{2}{16}$, ..., $\frac{13}{16}$). Then write the fraction inside the geometric figure located in the center of each card. The fractions replace the normal whole number values found on regular playing cards. Suit values can also be assigned when appropriate. A card deck containing 52 cards would have 13 circle, 13 diamond, 13 square and 13 triangle cards.

Students can use the cards to play any popular card games. By creating different sets of geofractions cards, students will learn to order fractional numbers from smallest to largest and to recognize equivalent fractional numbers. Disputes over which fractional numbers are smallest, largest, or equal can be settled by providing an appropriate fractional number line chart.

ACTIVITIES FOR STUDENT INVOLVEMENT:
MULTIPLICATION AND DIVISION OF FRACTIONAL NUMBERS

Sample activity 1 (Graph paper and cross-hatching)

Provide students with graph paper and colored marking pencils. Have the students mark, label, and shade the graph paper to illustrate the solution to examples such as $\frac{1}{4} \times \frac{1}{2} = \boxed{\frac{1}{8}}$.

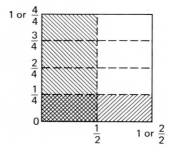

Students should see that the product is shown by the double cross-hatched area; namely, $\frac{1}{4}$ of $\frac{1}{2}$, or $\frac{1}{8}$ of the 1 × 1 area.

In terms of the related division example, $\frac{1}{8} \div \frac{1}{4} = \boxed{}$, students should understand that they are looking for a missing factor. So, they begin by stating the example as $\frac{1}{4} \times \boxed{} = \frac{1}{8}$. The answer, of course, is $\frac{1}{2}$.

Sample activity 2 (Cross products)

Give students a set of fraction number pairs such as $(\frac{1}{3}, \frac{1}{2})$. Write them on the board as shown below and ask students to find the cross products.

$$\frac{1}{3} \diagdown\!\!\!\!\!\diagup \frac{1}{2}$$

Then have the students find the corresponding quotient (e.g., $\frac{1}{3} \div \frac{1}{2} = \frac{2}{3}$) and compare it with the cross-products they obtained. This activity also should help the child learn the "invert and multiply" rule.

ACTIVITIES FOR STUDENT INVOLVEMENT: DECIMALS: CONCEPTS AND OPERATIONS

Sample activity 1 (Place value chart and expanded notation)

Provide students with a place value chart that has been extended as shown below. Have the students interpret the meaning of numerals displayed on the chart.

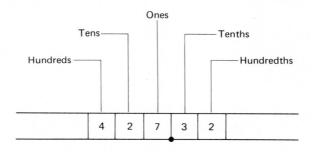

$$427.32 = (4 \times 10^2) + (2 \times 10) + (7 \times 1) + (3 \times \frac{1}{10}) + (2 \times \frac{1}{100})$$

Sample activity 2 (Graph paper)

Provide students with sheets of centimeter graph paper. Have them shade the graph paper to show relationships between fractions and decimals. For example, the following illustration shows the relationship between $.1 = \frac{1}{10}$ and $.01 = \frac{1}{100}$.

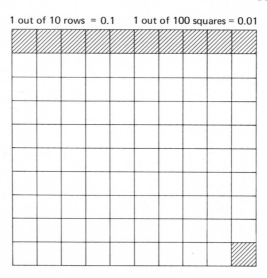

Sample activity 3 (Metric slide rule)

Provide students with two meter sticks. They can use them as shown below to determine answers to addition and subtraction examples such as:

$$.10m + .20m = .30m$$
$$\text{and } .30m - .20m = .10m.$$

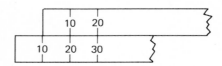

Sample activity 4 (Graph paper)

The results of multiplying by tenths to get hundredths can be shown by using graph paper. Present students with an example such as .5 × .4 = .20. Then have them shade the graph paper to represent the product.

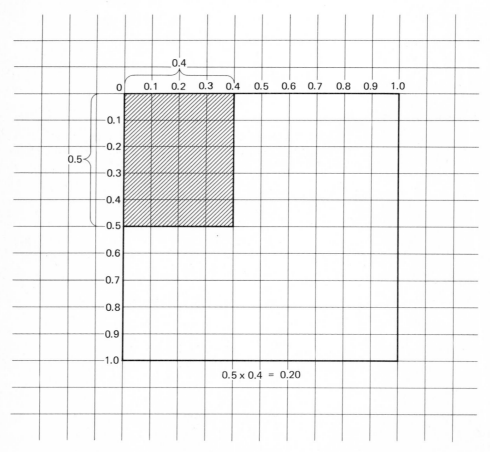

$$0.5 \times 0.4 = 0.20$$

Sample activity 5 (Student-made counters)

Have the students construct counters like the one below out of 5″ x 8″ file cards and paper strips. The file cards should be slit so that the paper strips (wheels) can be inserted and adjusted to place different numerals on the counter. A variety of activities can be used. Students can be asked to count by hundredths or tenths. They can be asked to read the number shown by the counter. They can also be asked to find counters such as those shown on gasoline pumps or pocket counters used in shopping that work the way their counter works.

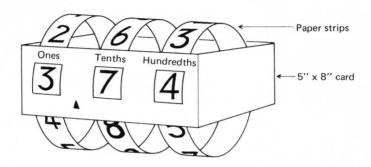

Exercise set

1. Describe the difference between a fraction or decimal and a rational number.

2. Describe now to demonstate the equivalence of each of the following pairs of fractions by using (1) a *concrete* approach which involves teaching/learning aids such as number blocks; and (2) a *semiconcrete* approach using drawings:

    a) $\dfrac{1}{5}, \dfrac{2}{10}$ b) $\dfrac{1}{4}, \dfrac{3}{12}$ c) $\dfrac{2}{3}, \dfrac{4}{6}$ d) $\dfrac{2}{4}, \dfrac{3}{6}$

3. Describe how to demonstrate the equivalence of each of the following pairs of fractions by using (1) the *abstract* approach of converting the given fractions to equivalent ones having the same denominator; and (2) the *abstract* approach which utilizes the "cross-product" algorithm:

    a) $\dfrac{4}{5}, \dfrac{12}{15}$ b) $\dfrac{2}{12}, \dfrac{5}{30}$ c) $\dfrac{3}{9}, \dfrac{5}{15}$ d) $\dfrac{6}{21}, \dfrac{10}{35}$

4. Each of the components of the general flowchart for teaching concepts and uses of fractional numbers can be expanded into "mini-flowcharts" which provide more precise information about teaching/learning sequences. For example, the component which calls for the development of the concept of equivalent fractions would include being able to

   a) determine whether a particular nonprimitive fraction is equivalent to a specified primitive fraction;

   b) determine whether a particular primitive fraction is equivalent to a specified nonprimitive fraction; and

   c) determine whether a particular nonprimitive fraction is equivalent to another nonprimitive fraction.

   Give examples of each type of problem, and then specify a learning hierarchy for these three behaviors along with an explanation.

5. Write the standard name of each of the following fractional numbers (i.e., reduce each fraction to lowest terms).

   a) $\dfrac{3}{24}$ b) $\dfrac{6}{15}$ c) $\dfrac{5}{50}$ d) $\dfrac{15}{27}$

6. For each of the following pairs of fractional numbers, describe how to determine which is greatest by using (1) a *concrete* approach which involves teaching/learning aids, such as number blocks, which permit direct comparison; and (2) the *abstract* approach which consists of converting the given fractions to equivalent ones having the same denominator.

   a) $\dfrac{3}{4}, \dfrac{7}{10}$ b) $\dfrac{4}{5}, \dfrac{5}{8}$ c) $\dfrac{3}{10}, \dfrac{1}{6}$ d) $\dfrac{3}{7}, \dfrac{4}{9}$

7. Demonstrate how to use a number line as an aid for teaching children how to convert improper fractions to mixed numerals and vice versa.

8. One technique for adding fractional numbers that are expressed as mixed numerals is to convert each addend into its equivalent (improper) fractional numeral and proceed as normal. For example,

$$2\frac{1}{3} + 4\frac{1}{2} = \frac{7}{3} + \frac{9}{2} = \frac{14}{6} + \frac{27}{6} = \frac{41}{6} \text{ or } 6\frac{5}{6}$$

Another procedure, which rests upon the fact that addition of fractional numbers is both commutative and associative, is illustrated below.

$$
\begin{array}{c}
2\frac{1}{3} \\
+4\frac{1}{2} \\
\hline
\end{array}
\quad \rightarrow \quad
\begin{array}{c}
2\frac{2}{6} \\
+4\frac{3}{6} \\
\hline
6\frac{5}{6}
\end{array}
$$

Examine a contemporary elementary school textbook series and describe when and how each of these two methods is introduced.

9. The flowchart in Fig. 8.2 specifies a general learning sequence of the various problem types in the addition of fractional numbers. Classify each of the following examples according to the type it best represents.

a) $\frac{3}{7} + \frac{8}{9}$ b) $\frac{1}{8} + \frac{6}{5}$ c) $5\frac{1}{3} + \frac{4}{9}$

d) $\frac{4}{7} + \frac{1}{7}$ e) $\frac{4}{5} + \frac{3}{5}$ f) $2\frac{1}{4} + 1\frac{1}{4}$

10. Use the prime factorization method to find the LCD for each of the following pairs of fractions. Show all steps in the procedure.

a) $\frac{3}{4}$ and $\frac{1}{6}$ b) $\frac{1}{2}$ and $\frac{2}{15}$ c) $\frac{1}{12}$ and $\frac{4}{15}$ d) $\frac{3}{56}$ and $\frac{7}{60}$

11. The following illustration shows that if the orange (Cuisenaire) rod represents 1, then the yellow rod represents $\frac{1}{2}$.

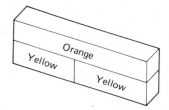

Use similar procedures to answer the following questions.
a) If the brown rod represents 1, what color rod represents $\frac{1}{4}$?
b) If the blue rod represents 1, what color rod represents $\frac{2}{3}$?
c) If the red rod represents $\frac{1}{3}$, what color rod represents 1?
d) If the red rod represents $\frac{1}{5}$, what color rod represents 1?
e) If the dark green rod represents $\frac{2}{3}$, what color rod represents $\frac{1}{9}$?

12. The Flowchart for Teaching Addition of Fractional Numbers (Fig. 8.2) can be used as a guide for teaching subtraction of fractional numbers by simply converting each addition problem type into a corresponding subtraction problem type. For example, the sample addition problem listed for case I in Fig. 8.2 was

$$\frac{1}{5} + \frac{3}{5} = \boxed{\frac{4}{5}}.$$

Since subtraction is the "undoing" of addition, corresponding subtraction problems would be

$$\frac{4}{5} - \frac{3}{5} = \boxed{\frac{1}{5}} \text{ and } \frac{4}{5} - \frac{1}{5} = \boxed{\frac{3}{5}}.$$

Use the foregoing procedure to write subtraction problems which correspond to the sample addition problems listed for cases II, III, IV, and V of Fig. 8.2.

Bibliography

1. Armstrong, Charles. "'Fradecent'—a game using equivalent fractions, decimals, and percents." *The Arithmetic Teacher* **19** (March 1972): 222–23.

2. Arnold, William R. "Reinforce division by learning ratios." *The Arithmetic Teacher* **21** (May 1974): 393–95.

3. Ballew, Hunter. "Of fractions, fractional numerals, and fractional numbers." *The Arithmetic Teacher* **21** (May 1974): 442–44.

4. Beardslee, Edward C., Gerald E. Gau, and Ralph T. Heimer. "Teaching for generalization: an array approach to equivalent fractions." *The Arithmetic Teacher* **20** (November 1973): 591–99.

5. Bell, Kenneth M., and Donald D. Rucker. "An algorithm for reducing fractions." *The Arithmetic Teacher* **21** (April 1974). 299–300.

6. Bohan, Harry. "Paper folding and equivalent fractions—bridging a gap." *The Arithmetic Teacher* **18** (April 1971): 245–49.

7. Botts, Truman. "Fractions in the new elementary curricula." *The Arithmetic Teacher* **15** (March 1968): 216–20.

8. Broussard, Vernon. "Using the subtraction method in dividing decimal fractions." *The Arithmetic Teacher* **10** (May 1963): 288–89.

9. Carlisle, Earnest. "Crazy fractions: an equivalence game." *The Arithmetic Teacher* **20** (April 1973): 303–4.

10. Cohen, Louis S. "The board stretcher: a model to introduce factors, primes, composites, and multiplication by a fraction." *The Arithmetic Teacher* **20** (December 1973): 649–56.

11. Constantine, Deane G. "An approach to division with common fractions." *The Arithmetic Teacher* **15** (February 1968): 176–77.

12. Cook, Nancy. "Fraction bingo." *The Arithmetic Teacher* **17** (March 1970): 237–39.

13. Cunningham, George S., and David Raskin. "The pegboard as a fraction maker." *The Arithmetic Teacher* **15** (March 1968): 224–27.

14. Dilley, Clyde A., and Walter E. Rucker, "Division with common and decimal fractional numbers." *The Arithmetic Teacher* **17** (May 1970): 438–41.

15. Duquette, Raymond J. "Some thoughts on Piaget's findings and the teaching of fractions." *The Arithmetic Teacher* **19** (April 1972): 273–75.

16. Fisher, John W. "Deci-deck." *The Arithmetic Teacher* **22** (February 1975): 149.

17. Geyser, G. W. P. "On the teaching of decimal fractions." *The Arithmetic Teacher* **13** (December 1966): 644–46.

18. Green, George F. "A model for teaching multiplication of fractional numbers." *The Arithmetic Teacher* **20** (January 1973): 5–9.

19. Hales, Barbara B., and Marvin N. Nelson. "Dividing fractions with fraction wheels." *The Arithmetic Teacher* **17** (November 1970): 619–21.

20. Heddens, James W., and Michael Hynes. "Division of fractional numbers." *The Arithmetic Teacher* **16** (February 1969): 99–103.

21. Henry, Boyd. "Do we need separate rules to compute in decimal notation?" *The Arithmetic Teacher* **18** (January 1971): 40–42.

22. Immerzeel, George, and Don Wiederander. "IDEAS." *The Arithmetic Teacher* **18** (October 1971): 397–98.

23. Immerzeel, George and Don Wiederander. "IDEAS." *The Arithmetic Teacher* **21** (February 1974): 123–24.

24. Jacobson, Ruth S. "Fun with fractions for special education." *The Arithmetic Teacher* **18** (October 1971): 417–21.

25. Junge, Charlotte W. "Teaching comparison of common fractions." *The Arithmetic Teacher* **15** (March 1968): 271–77.

26. Larson, H. L. "The structure of a fraction." *The Arithmetic Teacher* **13** (April 1966): 296–97.

27. Moulton, J. P. "A working model for rational numbers." *The Arithmetic Teacher* **22** (April 1975): 328–32.

28. Nelsen, Jeanne. "Percent: a rational number or a ratio." *The Arithmetic Teacher* **16** (February 1969): 105–9.

29. O'Brien, Thomas C. "Two approaches to the algorithm for multiplication of fractional numbers." *The Arithmetic Teacher* **12** (November 1965): 552–55.

30. Olberg, Robert. "Visual aid for multiplication and division of fractions." *The Arithmetic Teacher* **14** (January 1967): 44–46.

31. Pincus, Morris. "Addition and subtraction fraction algorithms." *The Arithmetic Teacher* **16** (February 1969): 141–42.

32. Prielipp, Robert W. "Teaching one of the differences between rational numbers and whole numbers." *The Arithmetic Teacher* **18** (May 1971): 317–20.

33. Richard, Thomas Z. "A game with fraction numbers." *The Arithmetic Teacher* **17** (January 1970): 82–83.

34. Rowland, Rowena. "Fraction Rummy—a game." *The Arithmetic Teacher* **19** (May 1972): 387–88.

35. Sowder, Larry. "Models for fractional numbers—a quiz for teachers." *The Arithmetic Teacher* **18** (January 1971): 44–46.

36. Wassmansdorf, M. "Reading fractions can be easy, maybe even fun." *The Arithmetic Teacher* **21** (February 1974): 99–102.

37. Wilson, Patricia, Delebert Mundt, and Fred Porter. "A different look at decimal fractions." *The Arithmetic Teacher* **16** (February 1969): 95–98.

Teaching the basic concepts of informal geometry

Synopsis and objectives

Included in Chapter 9 are the information and skills you need to teach the basic concepts of informal geometry to young children. We maintain that the introduction to the world of geometry should begin with a study of fundamental topological notions so as to conform to children's initial perceptions of space and the world in which they live. It is also pointed out that study of the more conventional Euclidian concepts should not start until the student can conserve length.

Emphasis is placed on the desirability for creating learning activities in concrete experiences such as geometric model building, paper-folding exercises designed to encourage discovery of geometric properties, and geometric constructions where appropriate.

The bibliography at the end of the chapter contains many interesting articles that will give you additional information about these topics. After a careful study of this chapter you should be able to

1. explain what is meant by Piaget's claim that a child's early conceptualizations of space are topological, not Euclidian, and describe the attendant implications for teaching;

2. explain the significance of the "conservation of length" phenomenon for the teaching/learning of Euclidian concepts such as *square, rectangle,* and so on;

3. describe and provide examples of the basic topological notions of *curve, simple closed curve,* and related concepts;

4. describe and provide examples of the basic Euclidian notions (segment, ray, angle, triangle, and so on) and related concepts;

5. construct paper models of the basic polyhedrons (prisms, pyramids);

6. demonstrate common "paper-folding" techniques which children can use to discover properties of geometric figures;

7. demonstrate the use of geoboards for teaching selected geometrical concepts;

8. demonstrate how to use compasses and a straight-edge for basic geometrical constructions;

9. construct a general flowchart for teaching geometrical concepts which provides a justifiable learning hierarchy for young children;

10. demonstrate how to construct a rectangular coordinate plane;

11.–12. formulate activities for student involvement which will facilitate learning of the elementary *topological* and *Euclidian* concepts.

Teaching the basic concepts of informal geometry

Theory

INTRODUCTION

Geometric concepts are an integral part of everyday life, and in recent years geometry has taken on increased importance in the education of young children.

The pattern of introducing geometry into elementary school mathematics programs used to be to deal with *Euclidian* concepts—in conformance with the historical development of the field. In recent years, however, there has been an increasing tendency to approach the study of the subject from a *topological* perspective. The rationale for this change is largely an outgrowth of the work of Piaget who maintains that a child's first concepts of space are topological, not Euclidian.

It is not possible to discuss the underlying issues here in any detail, but a few pertinent thoughts should prove to be helpful. In the study of topology, figures are not thought to be rigid, or fixed, in shape—this is in sharp contrast to the study of Euclidian geometry. Topology is a sort of "rubber sheet" geometry; length is a meaningless concept. Consider, for example, the following figures.

These figures are all topologically equivalent in the sense that any one of them can be made from any of the others by the processes of *stretching* or *shrinking*. Piaget argues that young children often cannot make distinctions among figures like these; he says that children become conscious of topological relations prior to becoming conscious of Euclidian relations, particularly in those instances where conservation of length is involved.

THE FIRST CONSIDERATIONS FOR TEACHING

The major significance of Piaget's findings regarding the child's initial development of spatial relationships is that the teaching of geometric ideas should begin with the basic topological notions—so as to guarantee that learning tasks conform to the child's expected mental structures.

The construction of a learning hierarchy for geometric concepts must begin, of course, with the development of the entities: *point, line,* and *plane.* To these we should also add the notion of a *curve.*

These ideas should be taught by means of examples and discrimination tasks, activities, and games.

Point

(Normally labeled
by capital letters)

Line

(When we use the word
line, we customarily
mean *straight* line. Notice
the arrows which suggest
that the line is endless.
Normally a line is named
by two of its points.
Pictured here is line *CD.*)

Curve

(We think of a curve as a
path from one point to
another, not necessarily
different, point.)

After these geometric concepts have been mastered, the student should be in a position to learn the concept of a *simple closed curve,* and related ideas. Specifically, if geometric figures are interpreted as sets of points, then it is appropriate to consider the relations: *inside, outside,* and *on,* as illustrated by the simple closed curve shown here.

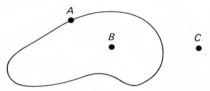

Observe that point *B* is said to be *inside* (i.e., in the interior of) the curve; point *C* is *outside* (i.e., in the exterior of) the curve; and point *A* is *on* the curve. Note also that simple closed curves have only one interior; thus, though the following curve is closed, it would not be classified as being a *simple* closed curve.

Once these topological notions have been acquired and the student can conserve length, the basic concepts of Euclidian geometry can be introduced.

THE INITIAL EUCLIDIAN CONCEPTS

After development of the concepts of point, line, and plane, the student should be taught about (line) *segments* and *rays.*

A *segment* consists of two points, say C and D, and all of the points be-tween them. Here is an example.

Segments are named by specifying their endpoints. In this case we would speak of "segment CD." To specify the segment symbolically we would write $\overline{CD}$.

A *ray*, on the other hand, is a "half-line" together with its endpoint. An example is shown here.

To name a ray, you first specify its endpoint and then some other point of the ray. In the case of this example, we would say "ray AB." To specify the ray symbolically we would write $\overrightarrow{AB}$.

When two rays share a common endpoint, the figure formed is called an *angle*. A sample angle is shown here.

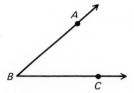

Point B is called the *vertex* of the angle, and the rays BA and BC are called *sides* of the angle. This angle can be named by writing either ∠ABC or ∠CBA. Note that the letter identifying the vertex must be in the middle. Actually, when there is no chance of ambiguity the angle can be named simply ∠B.

The common unit of angle measurement is the *degree*, and students should be taught how to use a *protractor* to determine the magnitude of an angle. The procedure is illustrated below.

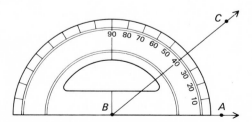

The reading on the protractor indicates that the measure of ∠ABC is 40°. Notice how the protractor is positioned to obtain this measurement.

An angle whose measure is 90° is called a *right* angle.

THE CONCEPTS OF PERPENDICULARITY AND PARALLELISM

The concepts of perpendicularity and parallelism are important in the recognition and determination of properties of common polygons, and therefore are prerequisites for the study of polygonal figures.

Two lines are said to be *perpendicular* if and only if they intersect at right angles. On the other hand, two lines in the same plane are said to be *parallel* if and only if they do not intersect.

One can also speak of parallel and perpendicular segments as well as parallel and perpendicular lines.

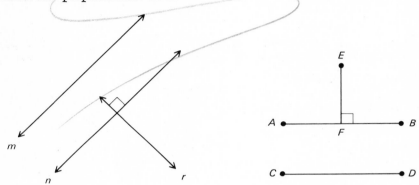

Line *m* is parallel to line *n* (written *m* ∥ *n*), and line *r* is perpendicular to line *n* (written *r* ⊥ *n*).

Segment $\overline{EF}$ is perpendicular to segment AB (written $\overline{EF} \perp \overline{AB}$) and segment AB is parallel to segment CD (written $\overline{AB} \parallel \overline{CD}$).

THE STUDY OF CIRCLES

A circle is defined as being a set of points each of which is *equidistant* from a point in the same plane called the *center* of the circle.

A circle is a simple closed curve. Every circle has an interior and an exterior. Keep in mind that the circle is the curve itself. Children often get confused about this matter and consider a circle to include its interior. Learning tasks involving the identification of points being *on, inside,* or *outside* a circle should help prevent the development of this incorrect interpretation.

The basic terminology regarding circles is illustrated by the following examples.

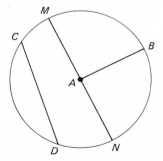

$\overline{AB}$ is a *radius* of the circle *A*. (Note that a circle can be named by specifying its center.)

$\overline{CD}$ is a *chord* of the circle *A*.

$\overline{MN}$ is a *diameter* of the circle *A*.

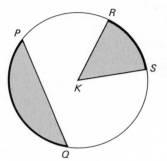

The curve from *R* to *S* is called an *arc* of the circle *K*.

The "pie-shaped" region *RKS* is called a *sector* of circle *K*.

The region bounded by the chord $\overline{PQ}$ and the indicated arc *PQ* is called a *segment* of circle *K*.

THE STUDY OF POLYGONS

After the student has learned about angles, parallel and perpendicular lines, and circles, it is then appropriate to undertake the study of *polygons*.

Triangles, rectangles, pentagons, and so on, are examples of polygons. In general, polygons are comprised of (line) segments. The individual segments which make up a particular polygon are called the *sides* of the polygon.

A triangle has three sides. Triangles are classified according to special characteristics or properties of either their sides or their angles. For example, if two sides of a triangle have the same length (measure), the triangle is said to be *isosceles;* if all three sides have the same length, it is called *equilateral;* and if all three angles of a triangle have the same measure, the triangle is said to be *equiangular*. In elementary school programs, few of these distinctions seem to be necessary for children to learn. The notion of a *right triangle* (a triangle which contains a right angle) probably is one that should be given special consideration, however.

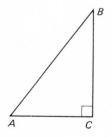

Since *C* is a right angle, *ABC* is called a right triangle.

Four-sided polygons are called *quadrilaterals*. Some of the important types of quadrilaterals, together with a statement of their defining characteristics, are given at the top of the next page.

It should be noted that the endpoints of the sides of a polygon are called *vertices*, and that segments joining any two nonadjacent vertices of a polygon are called *diagonals* of the polygon.

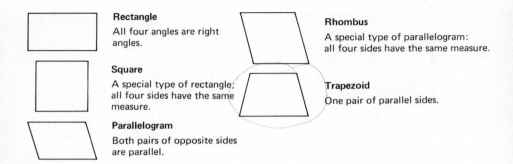

Rectangle
All four angles are right angles.

Square
A special type of rectangle; all four sides have the same measure.

Parallelogram
Both pairs of opposite sides are parallel.

Rhombus
A special type of parallelogram: all four sides have the same measure.

Trapezoid
One pair of parallel sides.

Polygons having more than four sides are generally of lesser importance, but those containing five (pentagons), six (hexagons), and eight (octagons) sides are often included in the learning program. An example of each of them is shown here.

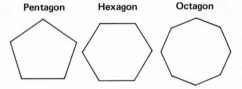

Pentagon   Hexagon   Octagon

Geoboards can be used to good advantage to help students learn to identify the different types of polygons, and some of their properties. A sample geoboard display is illustrated below.

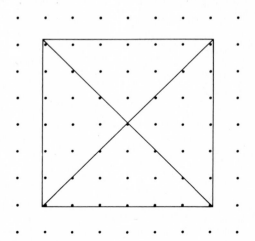

Through a display like this, the child might hypothesize, for instance, that the diagonals of a square are congruent. Many exploratory learning activities of a similar nature can be created by the use of geoboards.

Geoboards can be used to help children of different ages represent their under-standing of geometric figures.

THREE-DIMENSIONAL FIGURES

Students in the middle grades should learn the names of some of the more common three-dimensional figures, some of the technical vocabulary associated with them, and some of their properties. The *sphere* is one of these. A sphere

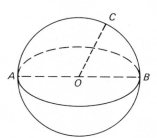

is defined as a set of points that are equidistant from some fixed point, say 0. Note that the sphere itself is a *surface*. Given any point in space, the point is *on* the sphere, *inside* the sphere, or *outside* it. In the case of the example shown above, $\overline{OC}$ is called a *radius* of the sphere and $\overline{AB}$ is called a diameter. Two additional solids which are common to the child's environment are the *cylinder* and the *cone*.

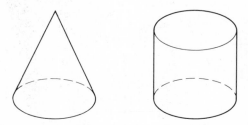

Space figures that are comprised of portions of plane surfaces are called *polyhedrons*. One type of polyhedron is called a *prism*. Some examples of prisms are shown below.

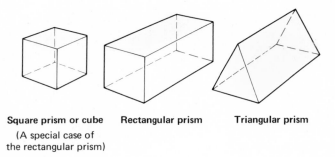

Square prism or cube   **Rectangular prism**   **Triangular prism**
(A special case of
the rectangular prism)

The plane surfaces of prisms are called *faces*. Note that a square (or rectangular) prism has six faces. How many faces does a triangular prism have?

Another type of polyhedron is the *pyramid*. Consider the following examples.

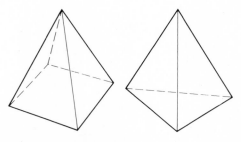

The *sides* of pyramids are triangles.

Model building activities are useful aids in helping students learn about common solids and their properties. Many models can be easily constructed by using graph paper, as illustrated by the following examples. Try making them yourself.

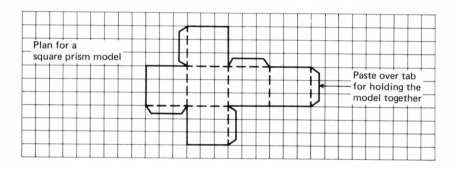

Plan for a
square prism model

Paste over tab
for holding the
model together

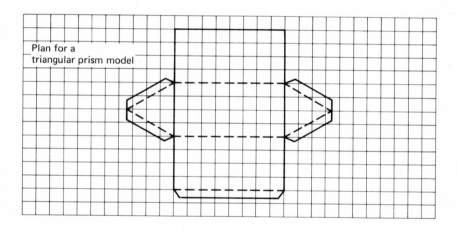

Plan for a
triangular prism model

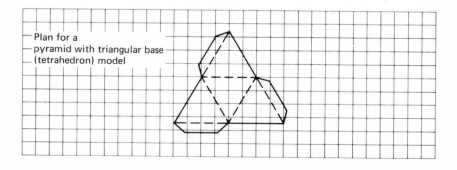

Plan for a
pyramid with triangular base
(tetrahedron) model

GEOMETRIC CONSTRUCTIONS

The construction of geometric figures which requires only the use of a straight-edge can be undertaken with primary age students, but those requiring the use of (a pair of) compasses probably should be withheld until the intermediate grades. Most younger children have not yet developed the manual dexterity needed to manipulate such an instrument.

When the use of compasses is introduced, the construction of arcs and circles are first-order concerns. Tasks such as the following are appropriate at this stage of development:

- Construct a circle with a given point as the center.
- Construct a circle whose center is a given point A and which passes through a specified point B.
- Construct a circle whose center is a given point A and whose radius is equal (congruent) to a given segment CD.
- Construct a segment that is equal (congruent) to a given segment.
- Construct an equilateral triangle.

There are certain construction skills that may be considered to be "building blocks" for more complicated construction tasks. These include being able to

1. *construct a bisector of a segment AB* (i.e., determine the midpoint of a segment);

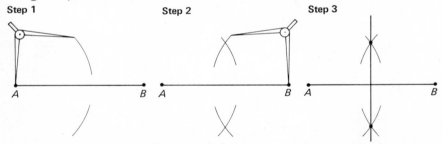

2. *construct a perpendicular to a line at a specified point P on the line;*

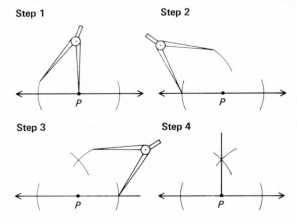

3. *construct a perpendicular to a line from a point S not on the line;*

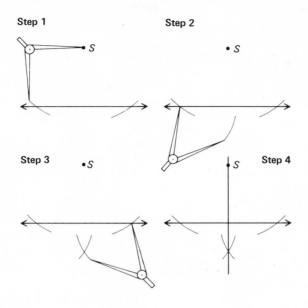

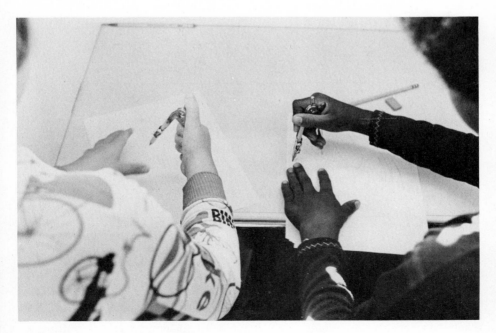

Here these children are practicing how to manipulate a pair of compasses.

4. *construct an angle Q that is equal (congruent) to a given angle B;*

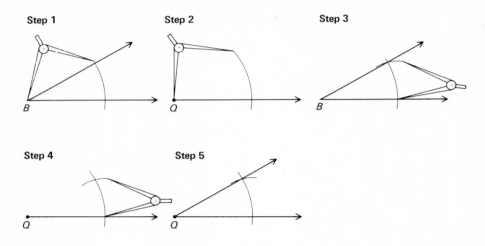

5. *construct the bisector of a given angle P.*

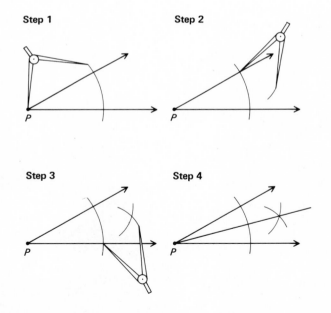

THE COORDINATE PLANE

When you construct a number line, technically speaking you are putting a *coordinate system* on a line. You are creating a one-to-one correspondence between the points of a line and the set of *real** numbers. Just as it is possible to construct a coordinate system on a line, so it is possible to construct a coordinate system on a *plane*, and such a procedure forms a crucial link between the study of geometry and the study of arithmetic. As a result, the basic concepts in making a coordinate system on a plane are often included in elementary school mathematics programs.

The procedure for constructing a *rectangular* coordinate system on a plane consists of imagining a network of number lines which intersect as illustrated below.

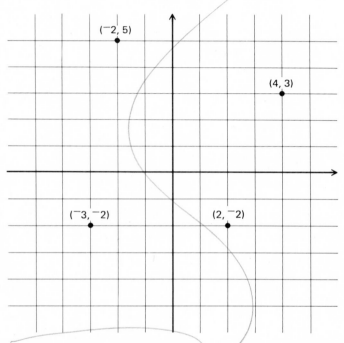

Observe that this procedure establishes a one-to-one correspondence between the points of a plane and the set of *ordered pairs* of real numbers.

In order to see how such a coordinate system can be employed to relate geometric notions to other concepts which the children will be learning, consider the equation:

$$\square + \triangle = 6.$$

As the table on the next page reveals, there are a variety of solutions to this equation. Note also that a solution consists of an *ordered pair* of numbers, the first being a replacement for $\square$ and the second being a replacement for $\triangle$

---

* The real number system consists of the rational numbers together with the so-called *irrational* numbers (numbers like $\sqrt{2}$, π, and so on).

□	△
6	0
4	2
3	3
2	4
0	6
−1	7
7	−1
.	.
.	.
.	.

The solutions listed in the table are plotted on the following coordinate system. Observe that they all appear to fall on the same line. This is no accident. Actually *every* point of the line that has been indentified corresponds to a solution of the equation, and conversely. In other words, the line represents the *solution set* of the equation.

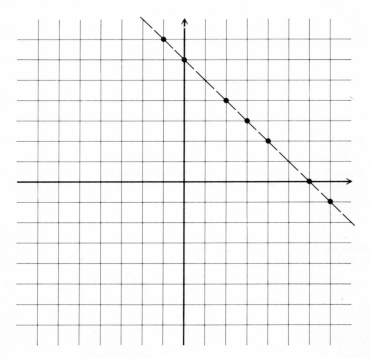

As suggested by the above example, the study of the connection between certain types of equations and their graphs provides opportunities for rich learning experiences which may help the child gain a better perspective of geometry and its ties to other mathematical ideas.

Practice

ACTIVITIES FOR STUDENT INVOLVEMENT: SOME ELEMENTARY TOPOLOGICAL NOTIONS

Sample activity 1 (Types of curves)

Provide each student with eight thumb tacks that have different colored heads, a piece of cork tile and five pieces of colored string or yarn. Then have each student use the thumb tacks, string, and cork tile to form as many different types of curves as possible. See the example below.

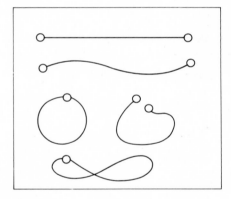

Next have the students use paper and pencil and draw all the different types of curves displayed by the class and label the endpoints. Follow up this activity by helping the students classify the curves.

Sample activity 2 (Rubber sheet curves)

Provide students with rubber sheets cut from different-colored balloons. Have the students make different types of simple open and closed curves on the rubber sheets with magic markers. Next have them describe what happens to their figures if they stretch or shrink their sheet. Ask them questions such as:

1. Can you make an open curve from a closed curve by stretching (tearing not permitted) or shrinking your rubber sheet?

2. Can you make a closed curve from an open one by stretching or shrinking your rubber sheet?

Sample activity 3 (Rubber sheet shapes)

Provide students with sheets of rubber that have figures like the following drawn on their surface.

Also provide each student with a ditto sheet containing true-false questions like the ones below. Have students stretch or shrink the sheet to verify their predictions.

1. △ can be made to look like ▢ . Ⓣ F

2. ▷ can be made to look like ◁ . Ⓣ F

3. ⌐ can be made to look like ○ . T Ⓕ

4. ▢ can be made to look like ⬠ . Ⓣ F

Sample activity 4 (Rubber band orders)

Provide students with material such as wide rubber bands that can expand and shrink without breaking. Have the students use different colored magic markers and place spots on their bands .Then have them test to see whether the order of the spots can be changed by stretching, shinking or changing the shape of the band. Ask the following types of questions:

1. What happens to the order of the spots on the rubber band when you stretch it?

2. What dots do you pass over when you move your pencil from the red to the black dot? Does the order change when you stretch the band?

Sample activity 5 (Inside, outside, on)

The distinction between *inside, outside,* and *on* a simple closed curve are concepts involved in games like marbles, penny pitch, hopscotch, shuffle board, and so on. Have the students play such games and answer questions like "Is the marble outside, inside, or on the boundary of the playing area?"

ACTIVITIES FOR STUDENT INVOLVEMENT: SOME EUCLIDIAN NOTIONS

Sample activity 1 (Planes)

Provide groups of five students with sharpened pencils and a sheet of cardboard. Have the groups experiment to determine the smallest number of pencil points required to balance the cardboard and the positions in which these pencils must be held. See the example below. This activity leads to verification that it takes three noncollinear points to identify (determine) a plane.

Sample activity 2 (Geometry games)

Use a commercial checkerboard. Mark small labels as shown below and put them on the board over the red squares. The students follow the rules used for the game of checkers, but to move they must name the shapes in the square on which their player lands. A student loses his turn if he names a shape incorrectly.

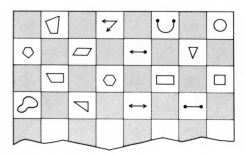

There are other commercial games that you can adapt to help teach geometric concepts. These include:

1. Rummy
2. Dominoes
3. Bingo

Sample activity 3 (Geoboards)

Supply each student with a geoboard and several activity cards like the one below. The students, on their own, can do what the work cards specify and then look on the back of the card to verify that they have made the correct response.

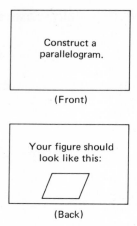

(Front)

(Back)

The geoboard can be used to teach concepts such as classifying shapes, measuring area, changing from one shape to another, and others. It is a very flexible teaching aid.

Sample activity 4 (Recording, observing, describing)

The precision of language and concepts that comes from the study of geometry should be a long-range developmental process. This process should include tasks that require students to refine their recording and observation skills concerning the common types of geometric shapes. Provide students with a chart like the one below and a set of large geometric shapes.

Shape	Name	Number of equal (congruent) sides	Number of parallel sides	Number of angles	
				less than 90°	greater than 90°

Have the student fill in the chart and make comparisons among the various types of triangles, quadrilaterals, and so on, that point out their likenesses and differences.

Sample activity 5 (Paper folding)

An effective way to introduce a geometric concept is through paper folding. For example, to develop the idea that the sum of the measures of the angles of a triangle is 180°, ask the students to fold an isosceles triangle as shown below.

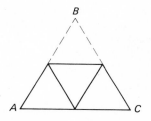

Step 1

Fold at midpoints of sides so that the vertex *B* touches side *AC* as shown:

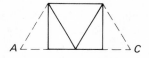

Step 2

Finally fold *A* and *C* over to *B* and crease as shown

Point out to the student that the sum of the three angles (*A*, *B*, and *C*) is 180°. Note that care in folding is necessary for the result to be of value.

Sample activity 6 (Symmetry)

Examples of the use of symmetry are all around us. These uses include man-made structures such as in buildings and art. We also find symmetry in nature.

We can speak of symmetry about a point, a line, or a plane. These ideas are illustrated below.

Have students locate examples of line symmetry and point symmetry in newspapers, magazines, and so on. Then have them verify their choices.

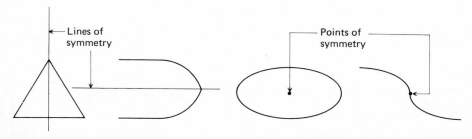

Examples of symmetry about a line   **Examples of symmetry about a point**

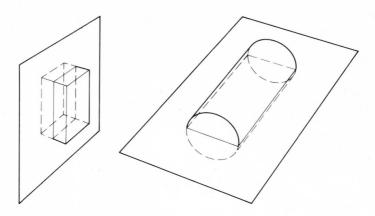

Examples of symmetry about a plane

Sample activity 7 (Three-dimensional models)

The study of three-dimensional figures should follow the development of points, lines, and plane figures.

Models of common three-dimensional figures can be constructed using graph paper, as suggested earlier. It is also possible to obtain commercially prepared models specifically designed for classroom use.

The features of the common three-dimensional geometric shapes can be studied by using charts similar to the one shown below. Have the students examine the different models to determine how they are alike and how they differ.

Shape	Name	Number of edges	Number of vertices	Number of angles	Number of faces	· · ·
·						
·						
·						

ACTIVITIES FOR STUDENT INVOLVEMENT: THE COORDINATE PLANE

Sample activity 1 (Capture a point)

For this activity the players should be given a sheet of graph paper and different colored pencils. The object of the game is to "claim" as many points on the coordinate grid as possible by correctly giving the ordered pairs which specify their locations.

Play begins by having the students roll dice to see who goes first. Using the coordinate grid the first player attempts to claim a point on the coordinate plane by giving its location (e.g., in the case of point P it is (4, −4)). If the point is correctly identified, the player circles the point with his/her colored pencil. Play moves to the left with each player attempting to claim a point. The player with the most number of points claimed at the end of play would be the winner.

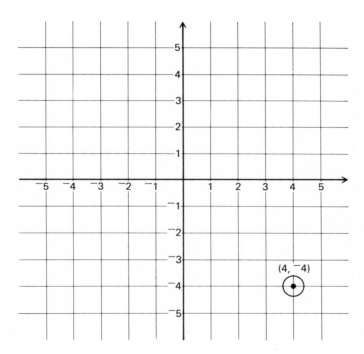

Sample activity 2 (Battleship)

A variation of the children's game called Battleship can be used to teach students how to identify points on a coordinate plane.

Provide two players with their own pieces of peg board and a set of golf tees that are of different colors. Each player, without allowing the other player to observe, locates his golf tees so as to represent different types of ships such as aircraft carriers, battleships, destroyers, and so on. The object of the game is to sink the other person's ships by calling out its locations on the coordinate plane.

The teacher decides who goes first by having the players roll dice. The highest roll goes first. The first player begins by calling out two locations such as (−5, 5) and (−2, +2). The other player then must tell whether any of his ships were hit, marked as ⊗ in the example. A ship is out of the game (sunk) when all of its locations are called by the opposing player. Play continues by the players alternating turns until all the ships of one player are sunk. The game can be played by more than two players.

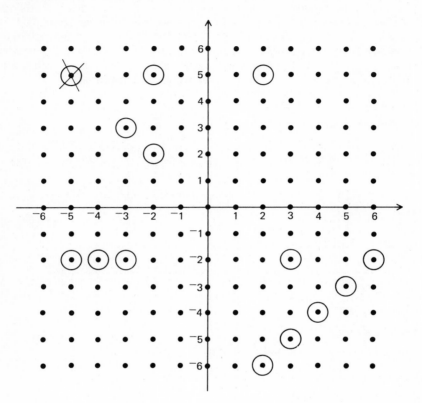

Exercise set

1. Make a rubber sheet out of a balloon, draw the following figures on it, and demonstrate that they are topologically equivalent.

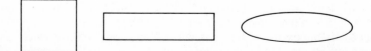

2. Write a set of instructional objectives which encompass the topological ideas that you think are appropriate for a young student to acquire.

3. Develop a game whose purpose is to help students develop the concepts of
   a) point, line, plane, segment, ray;
   b) perpendicular and parallel lines;
   c) the basic polygons;
   d) sphere, cylinder, cone;
   e) the common polyhedrons.

4. Construct paper models of some of the common polyhedrons. Include those described in the text. Also consult the bibliography for additional ideas on this topic.

5. Secure a pair of compasses and a straight-edge and make each of the constructions outlined on pages 266–268.

READINGS FOR ADDITIONAL STUDY

For each of the following topics, read one of the articles listed in the bibliography and write a one- or two-page report which consists of (1) a brief *summary* of the article, and (2) your *reaction* to the positions which have been taken.

6. Teaching basic topological concepts.

7. Paper folding as a technique for learning geometrical ideas.

8. Classroom construction of geometric models.

9. Classroom uses of the geoboard.

10. Teaching the basic concepts of symmetry.

11. Teaching the Cartesian coordinate system and related ideas.

Bibliography

1. Alspaugh, Carol A. "Kaleidoscopic geometry." *The Arithmetic Teacher* **17** (February 1970): 116–17.

2. Aman, George. "Discovery on a geoboard." *The Arithmetic Teacher* **21** (April 1974): 267–72.

3. Backman, Carl A., and Seaton E. Smith. "Activities with easy-to-make triangle models." *The Arithmetic Teacher* **19** (February 1972): 156–57.

4. Beamer, James E. "The tale of a kite." *The Arithmetic Teacher* **22** (May 1975): 382–86.

5. Bell, William R. "Cartesian coordinates and battleship." *The Arithmetic Teacher* **21** (May 1974): 421–22.

6. Brumbaugh, Douglas K. "Isolation of factors that influence the ability of young children to associate a solid with a representation of that solid." *The Arithmetic Teacher* **18** (January 1971): 49–52.

7. Brune, Irvin H. "Some K–6 geometry." *The Arithmetic Teacher* **14** (October 1967): 441–47.

8. Bruni, James V. "A 'limited' approach to the sum of the angles of a triangle." *The Arithmetic Teacher* **19** (February 1972): 85–87.

9. Bruni, James V., and Helene Silverman. "Using geostrips and 'angle-fixers'." *The Arithmetic Teacher* **22** (April 1975): 256–68.

10. Bruni, James V., and Helene Silverman. "Graphing as a communication skill." *The Arithmetic Teacher* **22** (May 1975): 354–66.

11. Brydegaard, Marguerite. "Flight to reality." *The Arithmetic Teacher* **19** (February 1972): 83–84.

12. Burrows, Darryl B. "Alan's geo-igloo." *The Arithmetic Teacher* **21** (February 1974): 95–97.

13. Busch, Mary T. "Seeking little Eulers." *The Arithmetic Teacher* **19** (February 1972): 105–107.

14. Coltharp, Forrest L. "Properties of polygonal regions." *The Arithmetic Teacher* **19** (February 1972): 117–22.

15. D'Augustine, Charles H. "Factors relating to achievement with selected topics in geometry and topology." *The Arithmetic Teacher* **13** (March 1966): 192–97.

16. Denmark, Tom. "An intuitive introduction to the Euclidean concept of betweenness." *The Arithmetic Teacher* **15** (December 1968): 685–86.

17. Dickoff, Steven S. "Paper folding and cutting a set of tangram pieces." *The Arithmetic Teacher* **18** (April 1971): 250–52.

18. Egsgard, John C. "Geometry all around us." *The Arithmetic Teacher* **16** (October 1969): 437–45.

19. Forseth, Sonia D., and Patricia A. Adams. "Symmetry." *The Arithmetic Teacher* **17** (February 1970): 119–21.

20. Garner, R. C. "Manipulative materials, geometric interpretation, and discovery." *The Arithmetic Teacher* **16** (May 1969): 401–3.

21. Gogan, Daisy. "A game with shapes." *The Arithmetic Teacher* **16** (April 1969): 283–84.

22. Grant, Nicholas, and Alexander Tobin. "Let them fold." *The Arithmetic Teacher* **19** (October 1972): 420–25.

23. Hall, Gary D. "A Pythagorean puzzle." *The Arithmetic Teacher* **19** (January 1972): 67–70.

24. Henderson, George, and C. P. Collier. "Geometric activities for later childhood education." *The Arithmetic Teacher* **20** (October 1973): 444–53.

25. Ibe, Milagros D. "Better perception of geometric figures through folding and cutting." *The Arithmetic Teacher* **17** (November 1970): 583–86.

26. Immerzeel, George. "Geometric activities for early childhood education." *The Arithmetic Teacher* **20** (October 1973): 438–43.

27. Inskeep, James E. "Primary-grade instruction in geometry." *The Arithmetic Teacher* **15** (May 1968): 422–26.

28. Junge, Charlotte W. "Dots, plots, and profiles." *The Arithmetic Teacher* **16** (May 1969): 371–78.

29. Liedtke, W., and T. E. Kieren. "Geoboard geometry for preschool children." *The Arithmetic Teacher* **17** (February 1970): 123–26.

30. Liedtke, W. "Experiences with blocks in kindergarten." *The Arithmetic Teacher* **22** (May 1975): 406–12.

31. Liedtke, W. "Geoboard mathematics." *The Arithmetic Teacher* **21** (April 1974): 273–77.

32. Lulli, Henry. "Polyhedra construction." *The Arithmetic Teacher* **19** (February 1972): 127–30.

33. Meggison, Glynn W. "Rays and angles." *The Arithmetic Teacher* **21** (May 1974): 433–35.

34. Moulton, J. P. "Some geometry experiences for elementary school children." *The Arithmetic Teacher* **21** (February 1974): 114–16.

35. Orans, Sylvia. "Kaleidoscopes and mathematics." *The Arithmetic Teacher* **20** (November 1973): 576–79.

36. Page, Robert L. "Old MacDonald builds a fence." *The Arithmetic Teacher* **20** (February 1973): 91–93.

37. Perry, E. L. "Integration geometry and arithmetic." *The Arithmetic Teacher* **20** (December 1973): 657–62.

38. Rea, Robert E., and James E. French. "Fun with geometry through straw construction." *The Arithmetic Teacher* **20** (November 1973): 587–90.

39. Robinson, E. G. "Geometry." *Mathematics Learning in Early Childhood.* NCTM, 1975.

40. Schloff, Charles E. "Rolling tetrahedrons." *The Arithmetic Teacher* **19** (December 1972): 657–59.

41. Sullivan, John J. "Polygons on a lattice." *The Arithmetic Teacher* **20** (December 1973): 673–75.

42. Swadener, Marc. "Activity board—the board of many uses." *The Arithmetic Teacher* **19** (February 1972): 141–44.

43. Swadener, Marc. "Pictures, graphs, and transformations—a distorted view of plane figures for middle grades." *The Arithmetic Teacher* **21** (May 1974): 383–89.

44. Vance, Irvin E. "The content of the elementary school geometry program." *The Arithmetic Teacher* **20** (October 1973): 468–77.

45. VanEngen, Henry. "Geometry in the elementary school." *The Arithmetic Teacher* **20** (October 1973): 423–24.

46. Vaughn, Ruth K. "Investigation of line crossing in a circle." *The Arithmetic Teacher* **18** (March 1971): 157–60.

47. Wahl, M. Stoessel. "Easy-to-paste solids." *The Arithmetic Teacher* **12** (October 1965): 468–71.

48. Waters, William M. "Separation in Euclidean space: an intuitive introduction for informal geometry." *The Arithmetic Teacher* **21** (May 1974): 458–61.

49. Wells, Peter. "Creating mathematics with a geoboard." *The Arithmetic Teacher* **17** (April 1970): 347–49.

50. Witt, Sarah M. "A snip of the scissors." *The Arithmetic Teacher* **18** (November 1971): 496–99.

Teaching measurement concepts and skills

Synopsis and objectives

Chapter 10 provides you with the basic information and competencies you need to teach the foundations of measurement to young children. The **theory** section is built around four flowcharts which deal with the teaching of *linear* measurement, *area* measurement, *volume* and *capacity* measurement, and *weight* or *mass* measurement. Key developmental issues, including *conservation of length, area,* and *volume,* are discussed, and special attention is given to the basic considerations involved in teaching the *metric system.*

The **practice** section contains ideas for teaching measurement concepts and skills, and these ideas are organized so as to conform to the learning hierarchies represented by the flowcharts.

The teaching of measurement is a popular topic for discussion, so there are many references for further study. At the completion of your study of Chapter 10 you should be able to

1. describe the major principles of linear measurement;

2. describe and provide illustrations of why all measurements are approximations;

3. arrange a given set of linear (area, volume, weight) measurement tasks in an acceptable order for teaching;

4. determine whether a child is or is not a conserver of length (area, quantity, volume);

5. describe what role the student's ability to conserve length (area, quantity, volume) plays in his or her ability to develop measurement skills;

6. demonstrate how to use basic measurement tools as laboratory aids for teaching measurement concepts and skills;

7. describe how to use the flowcharts for teaching measurement concepts and skills as aids in the diagnosis of individual learning states;

8. formulate activities that can be employed in the classroom for helping children develop measurement concepts and skills;

9. describe and illustrate the basic principles upon which the metric system has been founded;

10. name the basic metric prefixes and relate them to their corresponding place values in the decimal system of numeration;

11. make conversions from one metric unit to another;

12. describe how the measurement of area, volume, and weight in the metric system relates to the key concept of linear measurement.

Teaching measurement concepts and skills

Theory

SOME BASIC CONSIDERATIONS

The understanding of measurement in everyday affairs is very important. We constantly have need to ascertain "how much" or "how big" something is. As a result, the study of measurement concepts is a basic subject in the elementary school mathematics program.

In recent years, considerable light has been shed on the problem of teaching measurement concepts to young children as a result of Piaget's research on cognitive development. We learn from him that children of elementary school age are in or near the concrete operational stage of cognitive development. We will discuss the practical aspects of this later.

It should also be noted that the imminent change-over from the English system of weights and measures to the metric system poses additional considerations which must be taken into account in designing up-to-date curriculum materials and measurement learning experiences for children.

A GENERAL HIERARCHY FOR TEACHING MEASUREMENT COMPETENCIES

A general (macro) flowchart for teaching measurement concepts and skills is given in Fig. 10.1. As you can see, linear measurement concepts constitute the "bedrock" upon which all other forms of measurement are ultimately based.

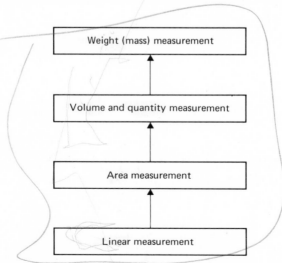

Fig. 10.1   General (macro) flowchart for teaching measurement concepts and skills.

The successive components of the learning hierarchy for measurement concepts are, in order, area measurement, volume and quantity measurement, and finally the measurement of weight (mass).

BASIC CONCEPTS OF LINEAR MEASUREMENT

The use of linear measurement is based on the following ideas:
1. In theory, for every pair of points, P and Q, there is a real number, d, called the distance between them. Furthermore, the distance between two points, P and Q, is always a positive number except when $P = Q$, in which case we say the distance between P and Q is zero.
2. The actual real number that is assigned as the distance between a pair of points is *unit-dependent*. For example, consider the points P and Q.

$\bullet\, Q$

$P\, \bullet$

If in inches the distance $PQ = 5$, then in centimeters the distance is 12.7.
3. In practice, all measurements are *approximations*. The precision of our estimates is a function both of the accuracy we desire and of the accuracy of our tools for measurement. For example, when we say that the distance from Miami to Los Angeles is 2856 miles, we are not saying that this is the exact distance between these cities, but rather a reasonable approximation.
4. Fundamentally, the procedure for assigning a measure of the distance between a pair of points, P and Q, may be illustrated as follows:

Centimeters

Observe that the placement of the ruler side-by-side with the pencil is tantamount to establishing a coordinate system on the ray PQ. The point P is matched with the number zero, the unit selected is the centimeter, and the remainder of the pairings are determined in the customary fashion. Since point Q is matched with the number 7, the length of the pencil is reported as 7 cm. Note that the ruler need *not* be placed so that the zero point corresponds with P (or Q). For example, consider the following ruler placement:

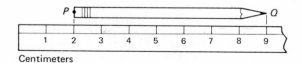

Centimeters

In a case like this the length of the pencil is determined by computing $9 - 2 = 7$ cm. In general, if the two ruler readings are x and y, then the distance is equal to $|x - y|$. The important point to recognize is that when a ruler is placed side-by-side with a segment PQ, a coordinate system is being established on the line PQ, and it is this maneuver that provides the key to linear measurement.

A FLOWCHART FOR TEACHING LINEAR MEASUREMENT CONCEPTS AND SKILLS

An analysis of the competence needed to engage in meaningful activities involving linear measurement suggests the flowchart for teaching in Fig. 10.2.

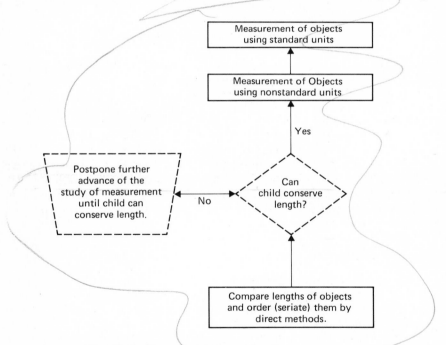

Fig. 10.2 Flowchart for teaching linear measurement.

As suggested by this flowchart, at the base of the plan for teaching linear measurement is the development of the ability to compare two objects and identify the shorter (or longer) of the two. After this comes the ability to order a set of objects from shortest to longest, or vice versa. Ordering a set of Cuisenaire rods would be an example of this sort.

These competencies are simple but the attainment of them is not possible unless the student can *conserve* length. A standard Piagetian procedure for making such a determination is to structure a task for the student similar to the following.

Suppose the child is shown two sticks of equal length that are placed side-by-side, as in the figure below, and is asked: "Which is longer or are they the same?" Suppose the student says they are the same. Then one of the sticks is moved as shown, and the question is asked: "Now which one is longer or are they the same?"

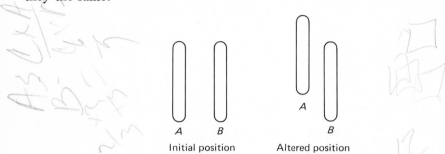

Initial position   Altered position

The student who responds that they are still the same is not influenced by the altered position and is thus considered to be a conserver of length. On the other hand, if the student's response to the altered position is that A (or B) is now longer, then his thinking is influenced by his perception of which appears to be longer. Such a child is a nonconserver of length, and is not ready to engage in linear measurement tasks.

Once evidence is available that a student is a conserver of length, linear measurement may be tackled. As suggested by the flowchart, initially we use nonstandard units of measure to work with rather than standard units. We do this to provide the student with an opportunity to develop personal units of measure, to compare their results with units selected by other students, and, finally, to discover the need for standard units.

BASIC CONCEPTS OF AREA MEASUREMENT

A careful analysis of the competence to engage in meaningful activities involving area measurement suggests the following flowchart for teaching. It, of course, is predicated on the assumption that linear measurement is a logical precursor of area measurement.

As suggested by the flowchart in Fig. 10.3, at the base of the plan for teaching area measurement is the development of the ability to compare two regions and identify the larger (or smaller) of the two. The procedure for comparison should consist of superimposing one region upon the other. The same stratagem can be used to order three or more regions according to their relative sizes. This is the natural next step to take.

As in the case of linear measurement, the attainment of these competencies is complicated by developmental factors. To be specific, we want to know if the student can conserve area. A standard Piagetian procedure for making such a determination is described in the following paragraph.

The student is shown two rectangular pieces of green poster paper which have the same size and shape, and is told that each represents a pasture for

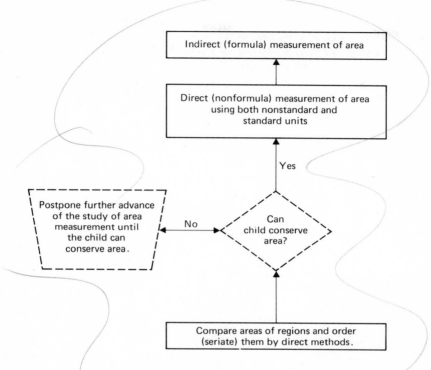

Fig. 10.3   Flowchart for teaching area measurement.

a cow. A model of a cow is then placed on each sheet of paper. After the child agrees that each cow has the same amount of grass to eat, he is then told that the farmers who own these pastures decide to put houses on them. A model house is placed on the corner of one sheet and near the middle of the other, and the student is asked if the two cows still have the same amount of grass to eat. Then, houses are added one by one to each pasture where on one of them the houses are placed adjacent to each other and on the other the houses are spread out, as illustrated.

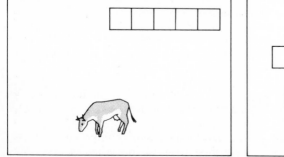

After each addition of houses, the child is asked whether the two cows still have the same amount of grass to eat. The child who thinks the cow has less to eat on the pasture where the houses are spread out is a nonconserver of area.

Once we know that a student is an area conserver, we can proceed with the teaching of area measurement. At the beginning we use direct methods.

Example 1
About how many square regions of the given size are needed to cover the given region?

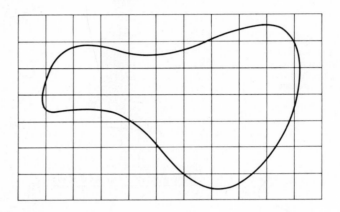

Example 2
About how many small square regions of the given size are needed to cover the given region?

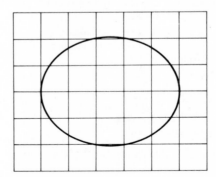

Learning experiences of the foregoing type are intended to enable the child to develop an adequate conceptualization of a unit of area, and to provide the basis for area interpretation.

As indicated by the flowchart, the very last class of competences to be taught is that dealing with the development and use of formulas for computa-

Here the teacher is making use of a practical situation to teach the concept of area.

tion of area. For example, the formula for the area of a rectangle is

$$Area = length \times width.$$

Note that the use of formulas constitute "indirect" methods of measurement and should not be used until direct methods have been mastered.

BASIC CONCEPTS OF THE MEASUREMENT OF VOLUME AND QUANTITY

A careful analysis of the competence to engage in meaningful activities involving volume and quantity measurement suggests the following flowchart for teaching. The flowchart is, of course, predicated on the assumption that volume and quantity measurement is a logical successor of area measurement.

```
        ┌─────────────────────────────┐
        │      Compute volumes by     │
        │ indirect (formularized) methods.│
        └─────────────────────────────┘
                       ▲
        ┌─────────────────────────────┐
        │   Compute volumes by direct │
        │     (nonformula) methods.   │
        └─────────────────────────────┘
                       ▲
                      Yes
                       │
   ┌ ─ ─ ─ ─ ─ ─ ─ ┐        ◇
   │ Postpone further │  No   ╱ Can child ╲
   │ study of volume  │◄─────◇ conserve quantity and ◇
   │ measurement.     │       ╲    volume?   ╱
   └ ─ ─ ─ ─ ─ ─ ─ ┘        ◇
                       ▲
        ┌─────────────────────────────┐
        │    Compare volumes and      │
        │  quantities by direct methods.│
        └─────────────────────────────┘
```

Fig. 10.4   Flowchart for teaching volume and quantity measurement.

As indicated by the flowchart, the strategy for teaching volume and quantity concepts follows the same general lines as the strategy for teaching area concepts.

Initial learning tasks should involve direct comparison of quantities and volumes. For example, to compare two liquid quantities in different-sized containers,

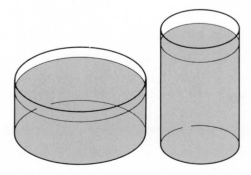

the tactic of transferring the two quantities to transparent containers of the same size should be employed. On the other hand, to compare volumes such as those illustrated below,

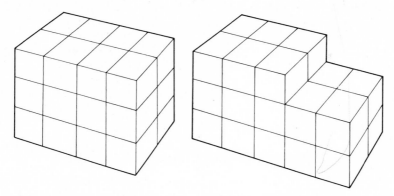

the blocks may either be disassembled or reassembled to permit a direct comparison.

As in the cases of linear and area measurement, volume and quantity measurement instruction should not proceed beyond this first stage until the child can demonstrate conservation of these notions. A standard Piagetian procedure for ascertaining whether a child is a conserver of quantity was described on page 4 of Chapter 1 and should be reexamined at this time.

In the case of volume, the child is provided with a block structure, and is asked to make one like it. After the task has been completed and the student agrees that the two structures have the "same amount" of room, the teacher then alters the original model so that it will appear long or tall, as illustrated below, and then asks the student if the structure he/she built has the same amount of room as the new model.

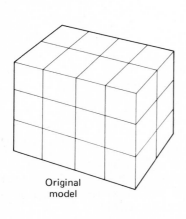

Original
model

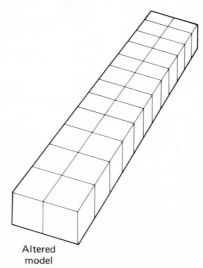

Altered
model

Nonconservers will think not, their judgment being influenced by their perception of which structure now looks bigger.

In any event, once evidence has been obtained to suggest that a child is able to conserve quantity and volume, the formal aspects of these types of measurement may be undertaken. As with area measurement, the initial activities should rely on direct (nonformularized) methods. Subsequently such activities can then be employed as procedures for helping children discover some of the basic formulas for volume and quantity measurement, and thus provide them with a proper basis for this more abstract level of intellectual involvement.

BASIC CONCEPTS OF TEACHING MEASUREMENT OF WEIGHT

An analysis of the competence to engage in meaningful activities involving weight (mass) measurement suggests the flowchart for teaching in Fig. 10.5.

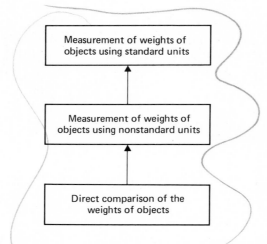

Fig. 10.5   Flowchart for teaching weight measurement.

The first experience with weight measurement, as suggested by the flowchart, should consist of directly comparing (and ordering) the weights of two or more objects. The execution of this maneuver should involve the use of a *balance scale*. A balance scale also must be used to measure the weights of objects using nonstandard units (erasers, chalk, and other classroom objects will serve this purpose). For measurement using standard units, such as ounces or grams, either a balance scale or a *spring scale* may be used.

A simple balance scale is the best tool to introduce the measurement of mass.

THE METRIC SYSTEM: SOME BASIC CONCEPTS

Virtually every country in the world either already has converted to the use of the metric system or is now in the process of doing so. The metric system is a *decimal* system of weights and measures, and presumably was first proposed in the seventeenth century. France was the first country to adopt the metric system, taking official action about 1795.

The basic unit of length in the metric system is the *meter*, which originally was defined as one ten-millionth of the distance from the North Pole to the equator but has since been redefined in more precise scientific terms. Roughly speaking, a meter is slightly longer than a yard and is a convenient unit of measure.

All other metric units are directly or indirectly related to the meter. The basic scheme for doing this is the use of decimal-related prefixes. For example, a *centi*meter is one-hundredth of a meter (note that a cent is one-hundredth of a dollar); similarly, a *milli*meter is one-thousandth of a meter (note that a mill is a thousandth of a dollar). All of the basic prefixes used in the metric system are shown in Table 10.1.

Table 10.1 Prefixes employed in the metric system

Prefix	Meaning
milli	one-thousandth
centi	one-hundredth
deci	one-tenth
deca	ten
hecto	one hundred
kilo	one thousand

Accordingly, a *deci*meter is one-tenth of a meter; a *deca*meter is ten meters; a *hecto*meter is one hundred meters; and a *kilo*meter is one thousand meters. All *linear* measurement in the metric system is, of course, based on the meter.

AREA AND VOLUME MEASUREMENT IN THE METRIC SYSTEM

Area is defined in terms of square units, regardless of the measurement system being employed; thus in the metric system the square centimeter, the square meter, the square kilometer, and so on, are units of area. See the following samples.

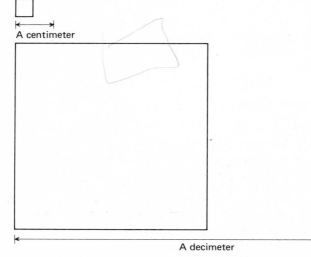

A centimeter

A decimeter

Similarly, the cubic centimeter, the cubic meter, and so on, serve as units of volume, as illustrated below.

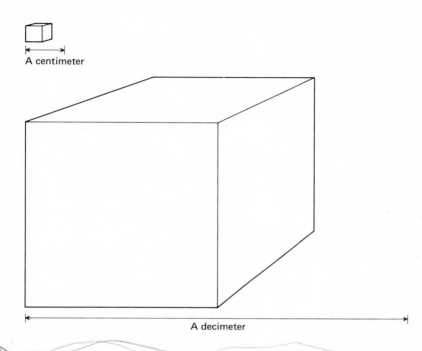

A centimeter

A decimeter

The measurement of the volume of liquid quantities is customarily based on a unit called a *liter*. A liter is defined as one thousand cubic centimeters, or equivalently as one cubic decimeter. Hence if you imagine the amount of liquid it takes to fill the cubic decimeter shown above, you know how much a liter is. If you experiment, you will discover that a liter is only slightly larger than a quart, and so it is a convenient unit of liquid measure.

THE MEASUREMENT OF WEIGHT (MASS) IN THE METRIC SYSTEM

The basic unit for the measurement of weight (more properly, mass) is the *gram*. A gram is defined as the weight of one cubic centimeter of pure water. As you can imagine, therefore, a gram is a relatively delicate unit of measure. An ounce, for example, weighs nearly 30 grams. The kilogram is, perhaps, the most convenient unit for weight (mass) measurement. Roughly, a kilogram weighs slightly more than two pounds. For extremely heavy objects, the *metric ton* unit is employed. A metric ton is 1000 kilograms; it weighs slightly more (approximately 2200 lb) than the conventional ton.

Practice

ACTIVITIES FOR STUDENT INVOLVEMENT: COMPARISON OF LENGTHS OF OBJECTS

As indicated in Fig. 10.2, the first type of learning involvement in linear measurement should consist of activities in which children directly compare lengths of objects. The focus of these activities should be to teach the meaning and concepts underlying the vocabulary of comparison generally related to linear measurement situations—*longer than, shorter than, taller than,* and so on. The purpose of children's activities should be the correct use of this basic vocabulary as they experiment and try to solve measurement problems for themselves in a variety of concrete situations.

The ability to measure the length of one object by comparing it with another is the beginning step of measurement. Free-play activities should include situations that encourage students to directly compare lengths and order objects. The following activities illustrate how this might be done.

Sample activity 1 (Yarn comparison)

Materials. Assorted pieces of yarn of different lengths placed in envelopes for each student.

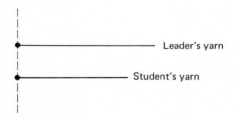

Procedure. A group leader shows a piece of colored string and says, "Find a piece of yarn that is shorter than mine." The leader has each student check his or her selection(s) by laying the yarn beside the model. Care should be taken to help each student see how to make accurate comparisons, such as shown above.

A student gets one point for a correct selection. An increase in score as the student continues to engage in this activity shows improvement with "shorter than" type comparisons.

Variations. Teach other comparisons such as "longer than" or "same length as."

Sample activity 2 (Hot wheels distance competition)

Materials.

1. Pieces of string.
2. "Hot wheel" racers.

3. An incline that will support hot wheel racers, as shown here.

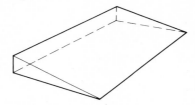

Procedure. The students run their racers down the incline and across the floor. They use the string or tape to decide whose car travels the farthest distance. They should compare the distances by laying their strings side-by-side to see which is the longest.

Variations. By making the incline steeper the students can make the cars go farther and this will lead to using the string as a nonstandard unit of length. Students can be asked to order the strings from longest to shortest distance traveled. A bulletin board display can be created to promote interest in this activity.

Sample activity 3 (Metric rod Rummy)

Materials. Metric rods of varying lengths between 1 cm and 10 cm.

Procedure. A dealer gives seven rods to each of three or four players. The remaining rods should be placed in the center of the playing surface. The player to the dealer's left begins by laying down one rod. The next player then attempts to form as many matches as possible of the rod just played. A match may consist of more than one rod laid end-to-end. After all possible matches have been formed, the player completes his/her turn by drawing a rod from the pot and then choosing the next rod to be put into play. The first person to play all of his rods says, "Rummy." Score is calculated by counting the number of matches made and subtracting the number of rods left in the player's possession.

Variation. By changing the rules students can be asked to make rod displays that are smaller than or larger than the rods in play.

ACTIVITIES FOR STUDENT INVOLVEMENT: MEASUREMENT OF OBJECTS

After students can conserve length, systematic instruction where they use arbitrary and standard units to find the length of objects should begin. The instructional activities also should actively involve pupils in estimation processes. The most commonly employed units should be used. "Personal reference" measures are helpful in this regard.

Sample activity 1 (Personal reference measures)

Materials

1. Metric tape measure.
2. Objects to be measured.

Personal reference unit	Length in centimeters
Index finger	2 cm
Index + middle finger	4 cm
Index + middle + ring finger	6 cm
Index + middle + ring + little finger	8 cm
Hand span	10 cm

Procedure. Have students measure the width of their index finger, and middle finger; index, middle, and ring fingers; index, middle, ring, and little fingers, and their hand span in centimeters. Have them record these body units in a chart.

Have the students use this personal reference to measure some objects in the room and check them with the tape measure.

Variation. Have the students derive other reference units for linear measurement.

Sample activity 2 (Track and pack games)

Materials

1. A track like that shown below.
2. A centimeter ruler.
3. A set of dice.
4. A set of estimation and measurement task cards.
5. Button men for each player and a score card.

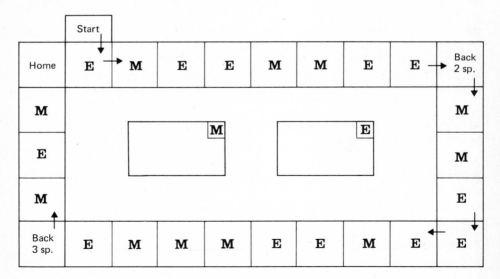

Procedure. Roll the dice to see who goes first. Highest roll is first. All players start with their buttons in the Start box. This first player rolls one die and moves his button the number of spaces shown on the die. If he lands on an "E" or "M" space he must choose the top card in the correct card deck located in the center of the playing board and complete the indicated task. (A student leader checks each player's answer.) The player records the card number, his answer, and the points awarded. He places that card on the bottom of the deck and play moves to the left. The player who reaches home first is awarded 3 extra points. After all players are home, their scores are tabulated and the person with the highest total is the winner.

Variation. Use the same track with "E" and "M" cards using other units of measurement.

Sample activity 3 (Metric trains)*

Materials

1. A set of Cuisenaire rods for each player.
2. A centimeter ruler.
3. 3" x 5" equation card deck.

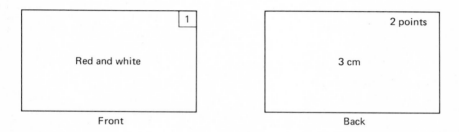

<table>
<tr><td>Front</td><td>Back</td></tr>
</table>

Procedure. The players roll dice to see who plays first. The first player takes the top card on the deck and builds the Cuisenaire rod train indicated by the card. Then the length of the train is measured and the answer checked on the back of the card. The player records the card number, his or her answer, and the points awarded if the answer is correct. The card is then placed on the bottom of the deck and play moves to the left.

Variation. Other types of objects and other units can be used.

Sample activity 4 (Spin-a-place)†

Materials

1. Place value charts like that shown (on the next page) for each player.
2. A die.

---

3. A spinner marked with metric prefixes.

4. Pointer tabs that show a basic metric measurement unit: *meter, liter,* or *gram.*

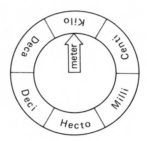

Thousands	Hundreds	Tens	Unit	Tenths	Hundredths	Thousandths

Procedure. The leader fastens a tab on the spinner and spins it. Each player should select the column in which a measurement will be recorded. Next the leader rolls the die. The number which comes up on the die is recorded by the student in the appropriate place value column of his chart. (For example, if the arrow stops in the region marked deci and the die shows a 5, the student would record a 5 in the tenths place on his chart.) Each player gets one point for writing the numeral in the correct column of the place-value chart.

Sample activity 5 (Punt, pass, and kick contest)

Materials

1. Trundle wheel designed to measure in some standard unit, such as a meter.

2. Marker flags.

3. Student word card.

Procedure. Students are given a football and three opportunities to pass, punt, and kick the ball. Students must release the ball behind a "release" line. A trundle wheel is used to measure the distance from the release line to the marker flags which are used to mark where the ball landed. The students' effort for each event is recorded on their record card. The best efforts are used to determine first, second, and third place.

Variation. Other athletic events such as a softball throw, shot put, javelin throw, soccer ball kick can be used and the results measured using a trundle wheel. Other units also can be used.

Sample activity 6 (Perimeter race)

Materials

1. A large card with drawings of geometric figures on it.
2. Paper and pencil for each player.
3. A deck of playing cards on which perimeter problems are written.

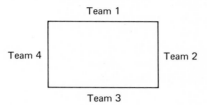

Procedure. Divide the class into small teams and give each team a deck of playing cards. Place the large card on a table with teams lined up by each side of the table. At a given signal, one team member gets a playing card and solves the perimeter problem indicated. He/she takes this answer to student leader who checks it. The process is repeated until each member of each team has a turn to try to solve a perimeter problem. One point is given for each correct solution. The team with the most points wins.

Variation. Use colored paper to indicate problem difficulty. Easy problems would be awarded one point; more difficult problems two or three points.

Sample activity 7 (Decimal match)

Materials

1. Sets of 3″ x 5″ student(S) cards with a linear measurement written on the front of each card:

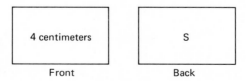

2. Corresponding sets of 3″ x 5″ cards with the decimal equivalents for each card in the first deck:

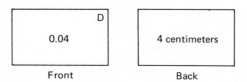

Procedure. Divide the class into pairs and give each pair two sets of cards. Place the set of S cards front side down on the table top. Place the other deck beside it front side up. The two players roll a die to see who goes first.

The first player turns an S card face up and declares whether or not it matches the card on the top of the other deck. The answer is checked by turning the latter card over. If it matches the front of the S card, the player gets one point. The next player takes his turn and so on. When time is called, the player with the most points is the winner. To assure the effectiveness of the activity, there should be at least 20 cards in each deck, and the decks should be stacked to guarantee a reasonable number of matches.

Variation. Use cards with other linear units.

ACTIVITIES FOR STUDENT INVOLVEMENT: COMPARISON OF AREAS OF REGIONS

The following examples will help you to design appropriate activities for the first phase of learning area concepts, namely, making direct comparisons of areas of regions.

Sample activity 1 (Metric regions)

Materials. One envelope for each student which contains twenty-four square regions all of the same size.

Procedures. On a table the teacher builds a plane region from a set of square regions. The teacher says, "Make a plane region that is *smaller than* mine." The students can check their construction by using a transparency to compare the sizes of the regions. The students get one point for each correct construction.

Variation. The teacher can ask the students to make plane regions larger than or the same size as a model region.

Sample activity 2 (Ordered regions)

Objective. To order plane regions from largest to smallest using a nonstandard unit of area.

Materials

1. Cardboard cutouts of various shapes and sizes.
2. Tracing paper and pencils.
3. One chart for each student.

Procedure. Have the students trace several of the cardboard cutouts on the tracing paper. Have them select one of the remaining shapes and check how many of the selected units it takes to cover the figure on the tracing paper. Have the students record their results in the following chart.

Type figure	Number of (unit name) counted
1	
2	
3	

Finally, have the students order the regions from largest to smallest based upon their measurements.

Variation. Have students order other regions on different bases—smallest to largest, same size as, and so on.

Sample activity 3 (Area claim)

Materials

1. Ditto sheet with dots arranged as indicated below.
2. A pencil for each player.
3. A die.

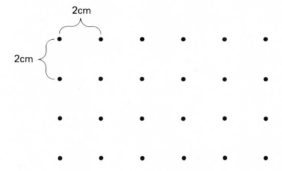

Procedure. Students sit around a table and roll a die to see who plays first. Play begins by the first player connecting any two dots with a straight line. Play proceeds to the left until someone completes a square. At this point the person completing the square lightly shades in the square and places his initial inside the region. The person claiming the most square regions is the winner. Therefore, each player should try to avoid giving the player following his play a chance to claim a region. A player may continue to play as long as he can complete a region.

Variation. Other types of figures can be drawn—triangles, parallelograms and so on.

**ACTIVITIES FOR STUDENT INVOLVEMENT:
AREA MEASUREMENT**

After students can conserve area, they should engage in activities where they use standard and nonstandard units to find the area of a variety of different regions.

Sample activity 1 (Geoboards)

Materials

1. Metric geoboard.
2. Rubber bands of various sizes and colors.

3. Twenty activity cards numbered 1–20.

Sample activity card

Make as many different figures as you can that have an area of 8 square centimeters.

Procedure. Have the students use different colored rubber bands and follow the directions on the activity cards. Have the students observe and discuss how the length and width of their regions differ yet have the same area.

Variations: Use other units.

Sample activity 2 (Scale drawings)

Materials

1. Several sheets of centimeter graph paper for each student.
2. A metric ruler for each student.

Procedure. Have students make a scale drawing of their bedroom on metric graph paper. Let 1 cm = 50 cm be the scale. Have the students decide how much carpet they would need to cover the floor and what space is covered by the furniture in their room.

Variation. Students could use graph paper and make a scale drawing to show the floor plan of their home.

Sample activity 3 (Comparing plane regions)

Materials. Paper cutouts of various shapes and sizes including a square region 1 dm x 1 dm.

Procedure. Have the students measure the area of their desk top using several of the paper cutouts. Have them complete the following chart and answer these questions:

1. Why do the measurements differ?
2. Which unit provides the most accurate measurement?

Shape	Size of desk top
1. circle	8
2. rectangle	6
3.	
4.	

ACTIVITIES FOR STUDENT INVOLVEMENT:
AREA MEASUREMENT BY USE OF FORMULAS

After the student has developed a good concept of area, and can measure areas of regions using direct methods, the use of formulas, where appropriate, should be developed.

Sample activity 1 (Card converter)

Materials

1. A 5″ x 8″ card for each student that displays rules for converting from one area unit to another.

2. Thirty 3″ x 5″ cards showing an area measurement on one side and its square decimeter equivalent on the other.

3. A die.

Procedure. Each player is assigned a number from 1 to 6. The dealer stacks the playing cards face up in front of him, and rolls the die. The player whose number comes up must convert the measurement on the top card to square decimeters. The player may use his card converter if he chooses. When the player completes his conversion he hands it to the dealer who checks the back of the card to see if the answer is correct. A correct answer means the player keeps the card and an incorrect answer means the dealer buries the card. In either event, the die is again rolled to determine who goes next. The player with the most cards at the end of play is the winner.

Variation. Card decks can be created that require conversion to other area units.

Sample activity 2 (Estimating and measuring)

Materials

1. 5″ x 8″ measurement and estimation cards like the one shown below.

2. A metric ruler.

3. A die.

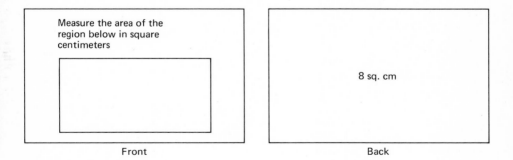

Measure the area of the region below in square centimeters

8 sq. cm

Front   Back

Procedure. Each player is assigned a number from 1 to 6. The dealer shuffles the cards and places the deck face up on the table. He rolls a die and the player whose number comes up must perform the task shown on the top card. When the player is finished, the dealer checks the answer with the one on the back of the card. If it's correct, the player keeps the card. If the answer is incorrect, the dealer places the card on the bottom of the deck. Play proceeds to the left. The player with the most cards at the end of play is the winner.

Variation. Use larger surfaces in the classroom and have students estimate and measure these areas.

Sample activity 3 (Area race)

Materials

1. 5″ x 8″ verbal problem cards involving the determination of the area of a region.
2. Metric ruler.
3. Two teams of 5–8 players each.

Procedure. At a signal one member of each team comes to the teacher who gives him a problem to solve. Each player solves the problem, brings his or her solution to the checker (teacher) and gets another problem for another member of the team to solve. This procedure is repeated until all team members have had a turn. The team gets 10 points for each correct answer and 5 points for an incorrect answer if the correct process was used.

Variation. Other units can be used.

ACTIVITIES FOR STUDENT INVOLVEMENT: COMPARISON OF VOLUMES

In the initial stages of the study of volume, students should engage in activities that involve the idea of comparing volumes of containers they can manipulate. The purpose of such activities should be use of the language of comparison as students solve problems for themselves in concrete situations.

Sample activity 1 (Glass comparison)

Materials

1. One tall, thin glass and one short, broad glass that have the same volume, three smaller glasses of unequal volume, and a metric measuring cup.
2. A jug of colored water and a funnel.

Procedure. Tell the students to look at the glasses and try to arrange them in a line from largest to smallest. Next have them check their work by using the metric measuring cup, funnel, and the jug of water. Ask them to explain the differences, if any, between predictions and the actual sizes of the containers. Keep the material available in the classroom for use during free play so that further experimentation can take place.

Variations. Vary the types of containers and directions.

Sample activity 2 (Tower match)*

Materials

1. A set of blocks for each group involved in the activity.
2. A table for each group.

---

* *Ibid.,* p. 37.

3. Sheets of graph paper marked to show how the foundation for a tower should be arranged.

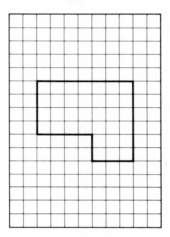

Procedure. One group selects a sheet like the one shown and builds a tower with the given base dimensions. The other groups are then asked to build a tower that has the same number of rooms (blocks). Have the groups check their towers against the model by matching (one-to-one) the number of blocks. Play continues by having the groups reverse their roles.

Variations. The directions can be varied to involve building towers having more or less rooms than the model tower.

Sample activity 3 (Dimensions)

Materials

1. A set of metric-sized blocks for each student.
2. Three decks of 3″ x 5″ cards which specify length, width, and height dimensions for a tower.
3. A die.

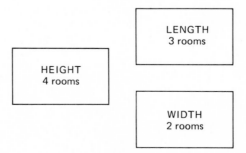

LENGTH
3 rooms

HEIGHT
4 rooms

WIDTH
2 rooms

Procedure. A student leader shuffles the dimension card decks and places them facedown on a table. Each player draws a card from each deck and must build a tower with the specified dimensions. Players get one point for each correct construction. Play continues as long as desired. The player with the most points at the end of play is the winner.

Variation. Change the directions to actual metric measurements; for example, 3 dm x 2 dm x 4 dm.

Sample activity 4 (Box sort)

Materials

1. Different-sized cardboard containers.
2. Centimeter and decimeter cubes.

Procedure. Have the students try to arrange the boxes from largest to smallest. Then have them check their predictions by placing appropriate-sized cubes inside the boxes to determine their actual size. Ask them to explain the differences, if any, between their predictions and the actual volumes. Keep these materials available in the classroom for further exploration during free time.

Variations. Change the shapes and sizes of the containers, and the size of the cubes.

**ACTIVITIES FOR STUDENT INVOLVEMENT:
VOLUME MEASUREMENT**

After students can conserve volume, activities are useful where students use nonstandard and standard units to find the volume of objects and containers. These activities should actively involve pupils in both estimation and measurement. Encourage the students to identify and use a set of personal reference measures for the most commonly used measures of volume.

Sample activity 1 (Estimating and measurement)*

Materials

1. Various sized bottles and commonly used containers numbered from smallest to largest.
2. Metric measuring cup.
3. Colored water.

Procedure. Have students estimate the amount of water a specified container holds. Then have them check their estimate with the metric measuring cup and record the results in a chart like the one shown below.

Container	Estimated volume	Actual volume	Number of units of error

---

* *Ibid.,* p. 35.

Sample activity 2 (Matching volume)

Materials

1. Set of cubic-centimeter blocks.
2. 3″ x 5″ cards with volumes specified.
3. A die.

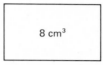

8 cm³

Procedure. The teacher shuffles the cards and places them face down on a table. The players roll the die to determine who goes first. The first player draws a card and constructs a tower that has the volume indicated on the card. The teacher checks the tower. Then the other players must build a tower with the same volume but different dimensions. A player who is successful receives one point. Play moves to the left and follows the same procedure. The player with the most points at the end of the game is the winner.

Variations. Use other cards with the volumes given in other dimensions.

Sample activity 3 (Prism volumes)

Materials

1. A set of centimeter cubes.
2. A metric ruler.
3. A die.

Procedure. Divide the class into small groups and assign each group member a number from one to six. Present each group with a rectangular prism constructed with the centimeter cubes. Roll the die and the person whose number comes up uses his metric rule to measure the length, width, and height of the prism, and then tells the volume of the prism. The teacher checks the answer, providing feedback as necessary. The teacher reconstructs the prism and play then moves to the left.

Exercise set

1. According to tradition, King Henry I of England decreed that a yard should be the distance from the tip of his nose to the end of his thumb. On the other hand, a meter was originally defined as one ten-millionth of the distance from the North Pole to the equator.

   Discuss the relative merits of these two procedures for defining a fundamental standard unit of measure.

2. Early in this chapter the statement was made that, ". . . linear measurements constitute the 'bedrock' upon which all other forms of measurement are ultimately based."

   Show how this statement can be defended in the case of the metric system. Specifically describe how the measurement of area, volume, and weight are related to linear measurement.

3. A simple procedure for determining if a child can conserve length is described on page 288. Study this procedure and then try it out with at least two children, one in the 6–7 age range and one in the 8–9 age range. Write down the exact questions you want to ask and the children's answers to them. Discuss the implications of your findings.

4. In the flowchart for teaching linear measurement, the first recommended learning activity involves having children directly compare the lengths of objects, and thereby acquire an understanding of the "longer than" and "shorter than" relations.

   Briefly describe why you would want a child to be able to conserve length before proceeding beyond this stage to more advanced concepts of linear measurement.

5. Make a list of as many reasons as you can why the use of nonstandard units of linear measure should precede the use of standard units.

6. List some convenient ideas for nonstandard units for linear measurement that individual children can use (e.g., handspan, foot length, etc.).

7. A simple procedure for determining if a child can conserve area is described on pages 288–290.

   Try this experiment with at least two children, one in the 6–7 age range and one in the 8–9 age range. Write down the questions you ask and the children's answers to them. Explain the implications of your findings.

8. As indicated by the flowcharts in Figs. 10.3 and 10.4, the teaching of the use of formulas for area and volume measurement is prescribed as a terminal learning activity. Describe the hazards that exist by doing otherwise.

9. The formula for the area of a rectangle is $A =$ base $\times$ height. Construct a teaching strategy that you think will enable a child to discover this fact.

10. The following diagram not only should help you see why the formula for the area of a parallelogram is $A =$ base $\times$ height, but it should also give you some ideas about how to design a teaching strategy for enabling a child to discover this fact. (It is assumed that the child already knows the formula for the area of a rectangle.)

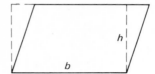

Explain.

11. The following diagram suggests that the formula for the area of a triangle is $A = \frac{1}{2}$ (base $\times$ height).

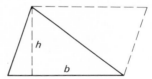

Explain why. Does your explanation suggest a teaching strategy suitable for use in the elementary grades?

12. Construct a set of one or more instructional objectives, together with mastery learning criteria and sample test items, for each component of the flowchart in

a) Fig. 10.1;   b) Fig. 10.2;   c) Fig. 10.3;   d) Fig. 10.4.

13. Develop a list of manipulative aids that you should have in your classroom for the purpose of teaching measurement.

14. Describe how measurement activities can be employed to teach the concepts of *approximation* and *rounding*.

15. Develop a game whose purpose is to help children develop the concepts of

a) linear measurement;

b) area measurement;

c) volume or capacity measurement;

d) weight (mass) measurement.

16. Make a list of reasons why the metric system of linear measurement is superior to the English system, and why it should be easier for children to learn and remember.

17. Complete each equivalence.
    a) 50 centimeters = ——— decimeters
    b) 170 centimeters = ——— meters
    c) 2 kilometers = ——— meters
    d) 4500 meters = ——— kilometers
    e) 50 millimeters = ——— centimeters
    f) 9 centimeters = ——— millimeters

18. Complete each equivalence.
    a) 1 square meter = ——— square decimeters
    b) 1 square meter = ——— square centimeters
    c) 1 square kilometer = ——— square meters
    d) 1000 square meters = ——— square kilometers

19. Complete each equivalence.
    a) 1 cubic meter = ——— cubic decimeters
    b) 1 cubic meter = ——— cubic centimeters
    c) 1 cubic centimeter = ——— cubic millimeters
    d) 1 liter = ——— cubic centimeters

20. Complete each equivalence.
    a) 2.5 kilograms = ——— grams
    b) 750 grams = ——— kilograms
    c) weight of one liter of water = ——— grams
    d) weight of three liters of water = ——— grams

21. Measure your
    a) height in centimeters.
    b) waist in centimeters.
    c) weight in kilograms.
    Then estimate and test the same measurements for one of your friends.

READINGS FOR ADDITIONAL STUDY

For each of the following topics, read one of the articles listed in the bibliography and write a one- or two-page report which consists of (1) a brief *summary* of the article, and (2) your *reaction* to the positions which have been taken.

22. Teaching concepts of linear measurement.
23. Teaching concepts of area measurement.
24. Teaching concepts of volume and capacity measurement.
25. Teaching concepts of the measurement of weight (mass).

Bibliography

1. Alexander, F. D. "The metric system—let's emphasize its use in mathematics." *The Arithmetic Teacher* **20** (May 1973): 395–96.

2. Bachrach, Beatrice. "No time on their hands." *The Arithmetic Teacher* **20** (February 1973): 102–108.

3. Blum, Hamilton S. "Introducing the metric system." *The Arithmetic Teacher* **22** (March 1975): 214–16.

4. Bourne, H. N. "The concept of area." *The Arithmetic Teacher* **15** (March 1968): 233–43.

5. Brougher, J. J. "Discovery activities with area and perimeter." *The Arithmetic Teacher* **20** (May 1973): 382–85.

6. Edson, L. "Metrication: new dimensions for practically everything." *American Education* **8** (April 1972): 10–14.

7. Hallerberg, A. E. "The metric system: past, present—future?" *The Arithmetic Teacher* **20** (April 1973): 247–55.

8. Hawkins, V. J. "Teaching the metric system as a part of compulsory conversion in the United States." *The Arithmetic Teacher* **20** (May 1973): 390–94.

9. Heard, Ida Mae. "Developing concepts of time and temperature." *The Arithmetic Teacher* **8** (March 1961): 124–26.

10. Higgins, Jon L. (ed.) *A Metric Handbook for Teachers.* Reston, Virginia: National Council of Teachers of Mathematics, 1975.

11. Knight, Carlton W., II, and James P. Schweitzer. "Using stream flow to develop measuring skills." *The Arithmetic Teacher* **19** (February 1972): 88–89.

12. May, Lola. "Introduce metrics . . . now." *Early Years* **2** (February 1971): 75–76.

13. National Council of Teachers of Mathematics. "Measurement." *Topics in Mathematics for Elementary School Teachers.* Washington, D. C.: The Council, 1968, Booklet 15.

14. Paige, D. D. and M. Jennings. "Measurement in the elementary school." *The Arithmetic Teacher* **14** (May 1967): 354–57.

15. Patterson, W., Jr. "A device for indirect measurements: an entertaining individual project." *The Arithmetic Teacher* **20** (February 1973): 124–27.

16. Steffe, L. P. "Thinking about measurement." *The Arithmetic Teacher* **18** (May 1971): 332–38.

17. Swart, William. "A laboratory plan for teaching measurement in Grades 1–8." *The Arithmetic Teacher* **14** (December 1967): 652–53.

18. Trueblood, Cecil R. *Metric measurement: activities and bulletin boards.* Dansville, N.Y.: Instructor Publications, Inc., 1973.

19. Walter, M. "A common misconception about area." *The Arithmetic Teacher* **17** (April 1970): 286–89.

Index

Abacus, 64
  use in addition, 105
  use in multiplication, 175
  use in subtraction, 135
Activity types (*see* Modes of representation)
Addend, 81
Addition
  of fractional numbers, 229
  of integers, 88
  of whole numbers, 79
Angle, 259
Array
  use in division, 208
  use in multiplication, 150
Associative property
  of addition, 82–83
  of multiplication, 155

Balance beam, 95, 128, 200
Balance scale, 295
Basic facts
  in addition, 81
  in division, 194
  in multiplication, 151
  in subtraction, 123
Binary operation, 79, 149
Bulletin board activities, 66, 69

Calculators, 171, 206
Cardinal numbers, 53, 65
Cartesian product of two sets, 149
Centimeter, 296
Circle
  related terminology, 260–261
Closure property, 75, 121, 191
Commutative property
  of addition, 82
  of multiplication, 152
Cone, 264
Conservation, 9
  of area, 288
  of length, 287
  of number, 55

of volume, 293
Constructions, geometric, 266
Coordinate plane, 255
Counting
  activities, 65–66
  concept of, 57
Counting frame, 212
Counting sticks, 95, 104, 129, 173
Cuisenaire rods, 59, 64, 74, 128, 166, 167, 202, 203, 243, 251, 301
Curve, 258
Cylinder, 264

Decameter, 296
Decimals, 239–242
Decimeter, 296
Denominator, of a fraction, 219
Developmental stages
  concrete operational, 3
  formal operations, 3
  preoperational, 3
  sensory motor, 3
Diagnostic teaching strategies, 27
Diagonals, of polygons, 261
Difference, in subtraction, 119
Discovery strategies of teaching, 23, 33
Dividend, 187
Divisibility rules, 214
Division
  as repeated subtraction, 193
  as set partitioning, 192
  as the inverse of multiplication, 191
Divisor, 191

Empty set, 51
Equivalent
  fractions, 219
  sets, 51
Euclidean geometry
  activities for, 273–276
  concepts, 258–259
Expanded notation, 138

Factor, 148

317

Factor rearrangement, 157
Flannel board, 242
Flash cards, 64
Flowcharts
    for teaching addition of whole num-
        bers, 89
    for teaching division, 195
    for teaching multiplication, 161
    for teaching subtraction, 124
    fractional number concepts, 223, 228,
        236
    measurement concepts, 285, 287, 289,
        294
Fractional numbers
    addition of, 230
    concept of, 223
    division of, 238
    multiplication of, 234
    subtraction of, 233
Fractions
    equivalent, 225
    improper, 228
    non-primitive, 226
    primitive, 226
    proper, 224

Gagné, 14
Games
    types of, 96–97, 109–110, 131, 163,
        165, 169, 170, 199, 201, 245, 273,
        276, 277, 298, 299, 301, 302, 303
    use in teaching, 22
Geoboards, 262, 273, 305
Geometric constructions, 266–268
Gram, 297
Graph paper activities, 174, 208, 211,
    246, 247, 248, 265

Hectometer, 296
Hexagon, 262
Hierarchies (see flowcharts)

Identity element
    for addition, 82
    for multiplication, 161
Improper fractions, 228
Integer, 62

Inverse elements
    in addition, 62
    in multiplication, 187

Kilogram, 297
Kilometer, 296

Laboratory approach
    use in teaching, 29
Lattice multiplication, 176
Learning hierarchy, 13
Least common denominator, 219
Liter, 297

Measurement
    basic considerations, 285
    of area, 288–291
    of length, 286–291
    of volume, 291–294
    of weight, 294–295
Metric system
    activities, 298
    prefixes, 296
    unit of area, 296
    unit of length, 295
    unit of mass, 297
    unit of volume, 296–297
Millimeter, 296
Minuend, 119
Missing addend, 119
Mixed numerals, 228
Modes of representation
    abstract, 91
    concrete, 91
    semiconcrete, 91
Multibase arithmetic blocks, 98, 131,
    172, 177
Multiplicand, 151
Multiplication
    as repeated addition, 150
    in terms of Cartesian products, 149
    of integers, 162
Multiplier, 151

Napier's rods, 180
Nomograph, 107, 137
Nonconserver (see Conservation)
Number line, 92, 126, 130, 204

Numeration systems
    decimal, 58
    nondecimal, 61–62
Numerator, 219

Objectives
    classification of, 9
    need for, 7
    preparation of, 8
Octagon, 262
One-to-one correspondence, 51
Order
    of fractional numbers, 226–227
    of whole numbers, 54–57
Ordinal numbers, 71

Paper folding
    teaching geometry concepts, 275
    techniques, 255
Parallel lines, 260
Pentagon
    hexagon, 262
    octagon, 262
    pentagon, 262
Periods chart, 68
Perpendicular lines, 260
Piaget, 3, 4, 54, 257
Place value charts, 108, 138, 179, 247
Pocket charts, 67, 101, 134, 210
Polygons, 261
Polyhedrons
    prisms, 264
    pyramids, 264
Prescriptive teaching strategies, 27
Prime number
    use in finding LCDs, 219
Principles, of teaching, 23–27
Problem solving
    related issues, 81
    teaching strategies, 31, 32
Problem types
    nonverbal, 126, 165, 201
    orally presented, 164, 201
    written, 30–33
Product, 145
Profile of achievement, 15
Protractor, 259

Quadrilateral, 261

Rational number (see Fractional numbers)
Ray, 255
Readiness
    as a factor in learning, 15
    for geometry, 257
Reading levels
    as a factor in learning, 26
    problems, 28
Rearrangement principle
    for addition, 84
    for multiplication, 157
Rectangle, 255
Regrouping
    in addition, 86
    in division, 198
    in multiplication, 154–160
    in subtraction, 125
Reversibility, 4

Segment, 255
Sets
    disjoint, 80
    empty, 56
    partitioning, 187
    subtraction, 122
    union, 79–81
Slide rule, 95, 129, 248
Space
    Euclidean notions of, 255
    topological notions of, 255
Square, 215
Stages of cognitive development
    concrete operational, 3
    formal operations, 3
    preoperational, 3
Structure, mathematical, 13
Subtraction
    as the inverse of addition, 121
    as "take away," 122
Subtrahend, 119
Symmetry
    about a line, 275
    about a point, 275

Task analysis, 14
Taxonomy, of educational objectives, 9–12
Term rearrangement, 84
Three-dimensional figures
  cone, 264
  cylinder, 264
  sphere, 263
Topology
  activities for, 271–273

Triangle
  as a polygon, 261
  equiangular, 261
  equilateral, 261
  isosceles, 261
  right, 261

Vertex, 259

Weight (*see* Measurement)